THE END OF IDEOLOGY
on the exhaustion of political ideas in the fifties
DANIEL BELL
LOLITA
VLADIMIR NABOKOV
INVISIBLE MAN
BY RALPH ELLISON
HOWL
AND OTHER POEMS
ALLEN GINSBERG
Introduction by William Carlos Williams
FLANNERY O'CONNOR
A Good Man Is Hard to Find
the CATCHER in the RYE
a novel by J. D. SALINGER
Bernard Malamud
The Magic Barrel

Beyond the
Gray Flannel Suit

BEYOND
the
GRAY FLANNEL
SUIT

Books from the 1950s
that Made American Culture

DAVID CASTRONOVO

continuum
NEW YORK • LONDON

2004

The Continuum International Publishing Group Inc
15 East 26 Street, New York, NY 10010

The Continuum International Publishing Group Ltd
The Tower Building, 11 York Road, London SE1 7NX

Previous portions of this work have appeared in slightly different form in *New England Review* under the titles "Holden Caulfield's Legacy," "Humbert's America," and "Norman Mailer as Midcentury Advertisement."

Printed in the United States of America

Library of Congress Cataloging-in-Publication Data

Castronovo, David.
    Beyond the gray flannel suit : books from the 1950s that made American culture / David Castronovo.
        p.   cm.
    Includes index.
    ISBN 0-8264-1626-8 (alk. paper)
    1. American literature—20th century—History and criticism.   2. Books and reading—United States—History—20th century.   3. United States—Intellectual life—20th century.   4. Nineteen fifties.   I. Title.
PS225.C37   2004
810.9'0054—dc22   2004006272

We gratefully acknowledge permission to reprint the following classic dust jackets on the front and endpapers of this book, as designed by Tosh Thomas Hall:

The Catcher in the Rye by J. D. Salinger, copyright © 1951 by Little, Brown & Co.
The End of Ideology by Daniel Bell, reproduced with the permission of The Free Press, a Division of Simon & Schuster Adult Publishing Group. All rights reserved.
A Good Man Is Hard to Find by Flannery O'Connor, copyright © 1953 by Harcourt Brace & World Inc.
Howl by Allen Ginsberg, reproduced by permission of City Lights Books
Invisible Man by Ralph Ellison, copyright © 1952 by Random House, Inc. Used by permission of Random House, Inc.
Lolita by Vladimir Nabokov, copyright © 1955 by Random House, Inc.
The Magic Barrel by Bernard Malamud, copyright. Used by permission of Bantam Books, a division of Random House, Inc.

In Memory of D.L.C.

Contents

Introduction

This book is about the remarkable literary explosion that took place between the late 1940s and the Kennedy years. It looks closely at the landmark works that are breakthroughs in American literature. There's no mistaking these books for the ones of the World War II years. They are charged with a new consciousness about everything from race and personal identity to the condition of the suburbs and the content of the American mind. The best books of the period are works of intellectual and imaginative activism: they have set off chains of thought and given us images and characters and scenes that are a permanent part of our heritage. The literary 1950s is a third flowering of American talent. Malcolm Cowley wrote memorably of a second flowering, the renaissance of the 1920s. The figures in his book—including Hemingway and Fitzgerald, Dos Passos and Wilder—were his candidates for a second great period in our letters: after the generation of Emerson and Thoreau, he wanted the 1920s and early 1930s to stand in high relief against the pale and problematic earlier period and the half-understood era after World War II.

The present book argues that American literature of the 1950s now asserts special claims to greatness. The books celebrated in this volume are the ones that have become part of the collective life of our civilization. They represent a mid-century awakening to new forms and new subjects and are brought together because they have long-range value for readers in the twenty-first century. They distill the modern American spirit—our ideas of beauty and justice, our love of fair chances and high aspirations, our self-questionings and sweeping evaluations of our national life, our intrepid pursuit of dark insights as well as our cathartic laughter, our mockery, and a desire to free ourselves of constraints.

After saying something about books from the 1950s that have had limited staying power—bread-and-butter naturalistic works like *The Man in the Gray Flannel Suit* and *From the Terrace* that appeared on the bestseller lists but that no longer seem to speak to our condition—I move directly to books that I think have more durable themes, styles, and visions. The works of imagination present us with characters who are very much of their time, but by no means strange amid the pressures of ours. These people are not so much relevant as essential. They may use language a bit differently from the way that we do, but they speak about things of permanent concern and their heads are filled with ideas and obsessions that we share. The essays and cultural critiques are not dead-end discussions of faded issues but intense arguments about vital controversies. Some of them contain ideas that are more active in our culture than their authors' reputations. We need not talk about Lionel Trilling or Clement Greenberg to be confronting the issues about literature and art that they helped to frame half a century ago. I believe that reading and rereading these books will help us to understand America's twentieth century cultural legacy.

That legacy contains the sea change of postwar America, leaving behind the immediacies of the Great Depression and World War II and taking up a new collection of conflicts. Our changing image of ourselves can be seen quite clearly by placing a signature movie, *The Best Years of Our Lives*, and a great speech, JFK's inaugural address, side by side. William Wyler's 1946 picture is an earnest melodrama about three men coming home to a small city after the war: one is a prosperous middle-aged banker who faces the strangeness of grown children, the thorny problem of loans for G.I.s—not to mention the matter of his own heavy drinking; another is a young man who would like to find a decent job, something better than his pre-war position at a drugstore soda fountain, and resume his married life—despite his wife's cheap infidelity; the third man is a young sailor whose hands have been blown off and who is seized by the terrible fear that he may be forever an outsider. The three are uncomfortable and anxious and made to face a series of trials involving self and family; yet for all the pathos and turmoil, none seems to want a glimpse of the things that loom ahead for America. Each hopes for the good life—and (so we are made to suppose) is living the best years of his life—but each lacks the faintest intimation of what that life means or what shape it will assume. Caught in their problems, they're also caught in a social drama that is charged with emotion while being rather static. The movie is meant to be reflective about twentieth century American life, and yet it is without any reflection. The best years of their lives—since they were to come into their full powers in the 1950s—were down the road, and the men themselves and their women seemed to have little curiosity about that road.

By the time JFK gave his inaugural in 1961, America was a different country—with new conflicts, a social and cultural landscape that bore little resemblance to what Wyler and his screenwriter Robert Sherwood put before us. During the 1950s the nation took on its late modern character—a country "tempered by war, disciplined by a hard and bitter peace." That hard and bitter peace included the Korean Conflict in which 54,000 Americans were killed between 1950 and 1953; it sounds like our condition at the beginning of the twenty-first century: war by another name, peacetime with mounting casualties. And Kennedy's themes of world poverty and American prosperity, fear of enemies and anxious solidarity with friends, seem like those of our world. When Kennedy took office, our problems and pleasures had essentially taken on the forms that we are now familiar with; we were no longer worried about adjustment; we were in search of new things. We were not content to be settled; we wanted what JFK offered: a New Frontier. But that frontier was an idea lodged in the heart—if not the politics—of the 1950s, not invented on a cold day in 1961. The decade embraced everything new, from highways to music to morality to art and ideas and storytelling. The 1950s were no return to normalcy, and the best books gave us the literary surprises that paralleled the surprises in science, technology, and domestic life. They became the books of our lives, artistic records of all that Americans were going through as they changed their environment, their expectations, and their sense of self.

The surprises of the postwar period often had the character of nightmare. Tom Rath, the protagonist of Sloan Wilson's *The Man in the Gray Flannel Suit*, wondered why he should get scared in peacetime. The answer is that the late 1940s and 1950s produced a remarkable number of new things to worry about. The HUAC investigation of the movie industry, which began in 1947, dredged up dirt about writers and actors—and ferreted out some Communists and Communist sympathizers here and there. It also wrecked the lives of people who were hardly menaces to American civilization. The Hiss spy case—protracted from 1949 into 1950—finally brought in a verdict confirming that the highest level of government could be penetrated by a Soviet agent—and that Whittaker Chambers, a rather wild character out of Dostoyevsky, was more trustworthy than Alger Hiss, a fine gentleman and stable public servant. After their arrest in 1950 on espionage charges, Julius and Ethel Rosenberg—an unlikely, lackluster

New York couple—entered the American consciousness as grand-scale betrayers or victims (as you cared to see it); they were executed in 1953 amid pious and false rhetoric about their decency and patriotism, and rabid calls for their death. In 1950, Senator Joseph McCarthy swung into action with his notorious campaign to expose traitors in the State Department. His was one of the longest running acts of accusation and innuendo in our history. Waving "evidence" before a TV audience of millions in 1954, he accused the United States Army of harboring Communists—and then proceeded to drop his poisonous remarks in the most unlikely places. But when he accused the Army defense lawyer Joseph Welch's young colleague Fred Fisher of Communist sympathies, Mr. Welch could take it no more: "Have you no decency?" was his stirring response. As we look at this Soviet-style intimidation of witnesses, we wonder how it could have happened to us. How could Eisenhower have remained silent? John Patrick Diggins has noted the President's private remark: he refused to "get into a pissing contest with a skunk."

But meanwhile McCarthy had pressed the buttons of a nation: Diggins writes that "the majority of Americans saw communism as an internal conspiracy as well as an external reality." They were scared in peacetime, and the legendary movie *The Invasion of the Body Snatchers*—with alien forces taking over the minds of nice Californians, making them lose their humanity and their ideals—came out in 1956, well after McCarthy had been disgraced in the media and censured by his colleagues. The mind snatcher had done his work. Many average guys, like Richard Yates's main character in the short story "The B.A.R. Man," considered truculent Communist baiting and sneering anti-intellectualism part of manly Americanism. Intellectuals like Diana Trilling were disgusted with the persistence of Stalinism in America, but also revolted by McCarthy's low-down dishonesty. The atmosphere was toxic—with charge and countercharge, suspicion, bullying patriotism, hypocritical Communist defense. Critic Leslie Fiedler hoped we would lose our innocence about the depredations of the left, but it turned out that we lost a great deal of honor and trust as well.

All this was enacted against arguably the worst new nightmare of all—atomic weaponry. The bomb of 1945 was a prelude to the hydrogen bomb, the fifties' own contribution to the history of fear and dread. This "superbomb" developed by Edward Teller was yet another gruesome fact that gnawed at the consciousness of Americans. Teller had broken with the skeptical and guilt-ridden J. Robert Oppenheimer, the great figure in the development of the atomic bomb; he wanted to go all the way with nuclear power while Oppenheimer saw the horror—and eventually was discredited by Teller and his allies and branded as a security risk. Accusations, innuendoes: Norman Mailer's remark—quoted by Douglas Miller in *The Fifties: The Way We Really Were*—that the 1950s was "one of the worst decades in the history of man" begins to make a kind of sense. But he and other writers had their material at hand—irrationality seeping into national life, a country with brand-new anxieties and moral vacuities. Paul Boyer, author of *By the Bomb's Early Light*, asked what the "appropriate aesthetic for the bomb" was. The even larger question is what the aesthetic realm did with the nightmares and the promises of the age. The answers are not equations of issues and art forms, slick or sententious polemics and topical works that evaporate like last year's headlines. The books from 1950s used the indirection of the artist—the symbolic and dramatic representation of dread and hate, hope and love—to embody what we were going through as a country. They made a break with conventional style and revivified language.

I begin with four books that played an important part in moving American literature beyond the borders of naturalism without abandoning the exactitude and vividness of the naturalists. Ralph Ellison's *Invisible Man* (1952), Saul Bellow's *The Adventures of Augie March* (1953), Bernard Malamud's *The Magic Barrel* (1958), and Flannery O'Connor's *A Good Man Is Hard to Find* (1955) share a combination of elements: each deals with hard naturalistic struggles—people trying to outmaneuver the world—yet each infuses these struggles with a lyricism and a yearning for transcendence. The books show people dodging poverty and bigotry and smallness of spirit; they take their characters beyond the sad confines and resignations of an older tradition and allow us to see moral and spiritual expansion and an overcoming of hard facts and grim circumstances. These books turn small American destinies into richly textured, image-filled adventures of the intellect and heart.

The second kind of book that has shaped our lives is about the consciousness of youth. This sort of book is not to be confused with the young-man-encounters-the-world books of an earlier age—everything from Hemingway's Nick Adams stories in *In Our Time* to *Look Homeward, Angel*, to *Young Lonigan*. Those books were about growth and change. The new youth books are closer to Fitzgerald's *This Side of Paradise*, which is to say they are about youth culture itself. These new books are about anti-pattern, the scattered impressions and impulses of young people in the post–World War II era. They are manifestos of immaturity, proud declarations of momentary feelings and responses. J. D. Salinger's *The Catcher in the Rye* (1951), Jack Kerouac's *On the Road* (1957), and Allen Ginsberg's *Howl* (1956) are about the blessedness of being unstable, impulsive, and immature. Each assaults middle-class respectability, champions irresponsibility, and offers a checklist of cool virtues.

Yet another kind of out-of-control book flourished in the postwar era: the thriller that explored the lives of unhinged people. In four important books—Cornell Woolrich's *I Married a Dead Man* (1948), Jim Thompson's *The Killer Inside Me* (1953), Patricia Highsmith's *The Talented Mr. Ripley* (1955), and David Goodis's *Down There* (1956)— the focus is on the labyrinthine mysteries within distorted people. The old concern of the mystery story—the who and why of a crime—gives way to a brooding treatment of consciousness itself. In these books criminals and misfits are shown flitting in and out of the broad daylight of life, leaving smiles and ordinary courtesies along with dead bodies. Such everydayness—the eerie mix of ordinary routines and monumental evil—is enough to make us distrust all that is familiar. These four novels brilliantly foreshadow our present taste for movies and books about the horror that may be just next door.

Nelson Algren's *The Man with the Golden Arm* (1949) and Norman Mailer's *Advertisements for Myself* (1959) are the next landmark works: they are the most arresting books from the postwar period about rebellion and the situation of the outsider. They celebrate transgression and resistance to our culture and our country, a not uncommon and an often unenlightening literary pursuit in their time or ours. But they go about their job of tearing down decent society with such spirit, authentic anger, and verbal inventiveness that they seem altogether different from the sententious protesting that comes in the 1960s and after.

The 1950s was also a period of satire and critical evaluation. While the lyrical naturalists, the champions of youth, the outsiders, and the explorers of the irrational made their marks, a contrary tendency reached full development: American writers produced major works of fiction and cultural criticism rooted in judgment, irony, and skepticism. The fictional anatomizing of culture and society at mid-century is at the top of the game in three books: Nabokov's *Lolita* (1958), Dawn Powell's *The Golden Spur* (1962), and Randall Jarrell's *Pictures from an Institution* (1954). These books pit the free, critical mind against consumerism and mass culture, academic and bourgeois pieties, trendiness, and chic. The major enterprise of the intellectuals—holding the actuality of American life up to standards of coherence and beauty—is carried further by these fiction writers: each offers a version of how America is dulling sensibility and killing vivacity and irony. These new observers analyze a new problem in American life: the coming of groupthink, the erosion of resistant mental habits and other forms of individualism. For all the plenitude and energy that these writers reveal in our society, there is also a sense that we are comically—and sometimes rather grimly—predictable in our tastes and folkways.

The new fictional observers work along parallel lines with a number of creative critics of literature, society, and art. Among the many significant books that attempt to form and reform our tastes we should hold these four in highest esteem: Lionel Trilling's *The Opposing Self* (1955), Clement Greenberg's *Art and Culture* (1961), Harold Rosenberg's essays on art and literature, and Dwight Macdonald's *Against the American Grain* (1962). Anyone interested in the state of American writing, the critical sensibilities of the 1950s, the sense and nonsense in modern ideas, the good and bad in modern taste, needs to know these works. They were written for a general literate audience, not for specialists or partisans of any sort. Their intention was to communicate, delight, and entertain by creating freestanding essays about our cultural life. Their authors were our first group of critics to feel the sustained pressure of Madison Avenue hype, TV, and mass marketing of images and ideas. They dealt with issues that have never faded: popular vs. high art, politics and the demands of literature, the media, quality (or lack of it) in popular fiction, the dumbing down of American life, conformity, kitsch threatening art, liberalism and conservatism in the cultural sphere.

And their message about intellectual honesty is conveyed with brilliant variations in four important books about race, religion, and ethnic identity: John Cheever's *The Housebreaker of Shady Hill* (1958), J. F. Powers's *Morte D'Urban* (1962), James Baldwin's *Notes of a Native Son* (1955), and Philip Roth's *Goodbye, Columbus* (1959), offer the group in America as a testing ground for ideas of integrity, a locale for stocktaking about what it means to be a mid-century person, an occasion for being critical about commonly held ideas of conformity and difference. Sometimes hilarious, sometimes mordant, these books take on the subject of being born to a different heritage than the average American. Cheever's world of WASP privilege, Powers's provincial Catholicism, Baldwin's Harlem world of storefront churches and poverty, Roth's struggle with status and Jewish identity: each situation is taut and conflict-ridden.

In 1960 John Updike brought out *Rabbit, Run,* his look at a Pennsylvania suburb in the age of the Mickey Mouse Club; in 1961 Richard Yates published *Revolutionary Road,* his version of the suburban situation, this time located in Connecticut. The two books are very different renderings of what had come to be a characteristic way of living. They are the late news about the 1950s, written by writers who were saturated in its idioms and reported the experience of what might be called American averageness—neither rich nor poor, neither privileged nor downtrodden, not conscious of ethnicity or religion. They round off a treatment of 1950s classics and make us aware of how complex the very familiar subject of suburban life can become when represented by a first-rate writer. Updike and Yates make suburbia the center of mid-century American spiritual crisis, and in so doing create permanent images of Americans struggling to make sense of their culture and themselves.

The third flowering that I have described was by no means immediately apparent to critics and commentators; while the important books came thick and fast in the 1950s, they didn't cause any immediate stir: change and genuine achievement—the pattern of real development in a national literature—has always been difficult to gauge. In the Preface to *Lyrical Ballads* Wordsworth was by no means enthusiastic about the atmosphere of the late eighteenth century. Edmund Wilson's initial reaction to the great writers of the 1920s was guarded and filled with reservations; but when he collected his reviews of the period in *The Shores of Light* (1952) he felt that he had after all been writing about great experiments and great achievements. In 1952, the editors of *Partisan Review* were doing their own stocktaking in a print symposium called "Our Country and Our Culture." The demurrals and backhanded appraisals of American writing hardly registered an awareness of the important postwar books that had been coming out. Nabokov's stories, his novel *Bend Sinister,* and Jean Stafford's *The Mountain Lion* appeared in 1947; Mailer's *The Naked and the Dead* in 1948; Algren's *The Man with the Golden Arm* in 1949—the same year that portions of Bellow's *The Adventures of Augie March* were printed in *Partisan Review*; Trilling's *The Liberal Imagination* in 1950; Salinger's *The Catcher in the Rye* in 1951 (not to mention Jones's *From Here to Eter-*

nity and Alfred Kazin's *A Walker in the City)*; Ellison's *Invisible Man* and Malamud's *The Natural* in 1952. The talent was conspicuous enough, yet the reaction was not especially enthusiastic. There was a steady set of demands issued by the majority of commentators, calls for something better in literature, even fearful claims that our best literary days were over. The participants were in the main heartened by America's receptive cultural climate, but few were willing to celebrate books. Although they were not quite in the middle of a third flowering, these writers and intellectuals hardly seemed aware of how good the late forties and early fifties were. Perhaps, as Arthur M. Schlesinger, Jr. wrote, political pluralism and tolerance were preconditions of cultural pluralism and all was going well. But the philosopher Sidney Hook added to that thought in his characteristically blunt manner: "All a free culture can do is provide opportunities for revolt: it cannot guarantee professional success." The poet Louise Bogan, a figure who started out in the 1920s, took a hatchet to the state of literature and the arts: the fifties were "an inter-geneation," a point of "stasis" in which there was no creative activity. A shallow, suburbanized public kept taste at a low level: this "petrified and nostalgic generation" liked the predictable, the recycled, the mechanized. Bogan—who was also a critic of standing—thought the gag was one of our favorite art forms.

Those standard setters of American intellectual life—Philip Rahv and William Phillips, editors of *Partisan Review*—were not exactly bowled over by the state of literary culture. Rahv, an immigrant who had struggled in his early days as an autodidact in Providence, Rhode Island, was not surprisingly a vigorous defender of the land of tolerance and free expression. But his spirits fell as he contemplated the *"embourgeoisement* of the American intelligentsia"; the fall in the barometer of protest and radical opposition in the late forties and early fifties necessarily indicated "a kind of detachment from principle and fragmentation of the literary life." What he described sounds like a national literature without the great themes, conflicts, and ambitions that lit up the era of the transcendentalists or gave excitement to the flowering of the 1920s. Phillips gave a clearer focus to this idea; what had happened for several years was a "dispersal of the avant-garde." American writers had turned away from the radicalism of the thirties and the experimentalism of the twenties; they were left with something even bleaker than thin traditionalism—a contemporary Americanism. Phillips thought at the time that Americanism was a matter of regional life and regional culture. As an old 1930s radical he feared the narrowness,

anti-intellectualism and open bigotry of the regional mind. He was less
concerned with the threat of mass culture than one of his star writers,
William Barrett. A philosopher and historian of ideas who had a taste
for controversy and a special distaste for the "embourgeoisement"
identified by Rahv, Barrett didn't mind taking several swipes at the
state of America culture. The art of the day was inferior, or put another
way, our great new art form was "streamlined mass journalism." With
a touch of Edmund Wilson's old cantankerousness, Barrett attacked
our interest in "speed, facts, know-how, our positivism, our extrovert
and technological mentality." Calling on his spiritual guide Kierkegaard, he proclaimed that journalism permeated everything—which is
to say everything was becoming strictly instrumental. Barrett topped
off his screed with a quotation from Hölderlin: "God is far off."

Such intense discontent—the well-focused interrogations of intellectuals who knew the terrain—was a sign of life, a reassurance that
the critical spirit was not comatose. Whether it was an adequate evaluation of what was around is another matter. Norman Mailer provided
the thunder for the symposium, diagnosing a society unaware of its
pallor and intellectual poverty. Artists no longer felt alienated or had
any sharp sense of what they should be alienated from. Once—
perhaps in the thirties—"the writer had a sense of his enemy and it
could nourish him." In 1952, our health and ease were making us obtuse and effete. Striking the chord of the Frankfurt School—that a ra-
tionalized social order repels all critical inquiry and dampens creative
thought—Mailer made America seem like a pleasant minimum security prison. And, despite their two cheers for free speech and demo-
cratic institutions, the other intellectuals described a country of
liberties and possibilities, but few high achievements in literature.

Now the very terms of their discontent are precisely what our culture presently lacks: their mission was not a matter of congratulating
their generation, bowing to the culture as it was, or scratching the
backs of their contemporaries. They frankly pitted bourgeois against
intellectual, honestly believed in the gap between high art and popular
culture, earnestly called for something that they believed hadn't materialized. As they hacked away at complacency—and exaggerated the
aridities of their time—they seem wrong-headed, yet very much alive
to what literature is and what it can do. In their search for the general,
they were ignoring particular significant writers—Salinger, the young
Bellow, Paul Bowles, Welty, Capote, Algren, Mailer. In the midst of
these talents they talked about standardization and stasis, the death of
the avant-garde.

Lionel Trilling made his contribution to the symposium in a different tone of voice: not one of the most dramatic statements, his short description of American cultural prospects in 1952 nevertheless has his peculiar subtlety, his elliptical way of making a crucial distinction. While others thundered or were ironical or dismissive, Trilling—almost like some English Whig transplanted from the nineteenth century to the age of the Bomb, TV, and Levittown—showed his fellow intellectuals the lines of development in contemporary civilization. Admittedly, "no cultural situation is ever really good"; but the mass culture emerging after World War II may, on balance, not be the problem that first stuck terror into the hearts of intelligent people. In an age with "increased power of mind in the nation"—by which Trilling was referring to the sum total of literacy and intellectual competence—one can expect that power to affect mass culture itself. Geniuses we will always have; and in the age of mass culture Trilling felt they would necessarily be attracted to that culture; with no roots or traditions to turn to, these superior talents would use mass culture as their raw material. Trilling further argued that mass culture may have interesting lines of development. As you stand back from this interpretation of our future, you can either mock or ponder. "Where?" or "Where not?" Trilling was responding to the ways ideas travel, cross-fertilize, and develop. Ultimately the collision of keen, raw intelligence and restless popular taste with new technology are going to produce an astounding variety of cultural goods. The high-quality books of the 1950s are such products, the splendid yield of a society where writers were influenced by new pressures and tempi, new confusions, discontents, and challenges. The very threats to literature that Rahv and Bogan and the others specified are the subject matter of literature.

The 1950s was an age of stocktaking; the previous two decades had addressed themselves to immediate problems of crisis and survival, to solutions for saving the country and the culture. By mid-century the great question was, "Where have we come?" Numbers of books appeared that viewed us in the context of American civilization and suggested what might be next. First there was Arthur M. Schlesinger, Jr.'s *The Vital Center* (1949), followed by David Riesman's *The Lonely Crowd* and Trilling's *The Liberal Imagination* in 1950; other cultural critics arrived with their interpretations of American complacency—notably Reinhold Niebuhr with *The Irony of American History* (1952) and Leslie Fiedler with *An End to Innocence* (1955); the social critics C. Wright Mills in *The Power Elite* (1956) and Vance Packard in *The*

Status Seekers (1959) attempted to explain changes in our views of class and entitlement. The decade was rounded off with Daniel Bell's *The End of Ideology* in 1960, a book that saw America as a nation emerged from the old conflicts of the 1930s. (Bell, like Fiedler, naturally referred to his era as a time of concluding and setting forth.) And finally Betty Friedan's *The Feminine Mystique*, appearing in 1963, offered dispiriting conclusions about women's false position in a country sailing under the colors of progress and opportunity. The book was also a wake-up call about what America needed to do in order to meet its social and ethical commitments. All of these writers were clear about one thing: America had reached the end of something and needed to begin a new cycle of development. In politics, the liberal answers of the past needed to be updated; in culture, our assumptions about the arts were likely to be lagging behind what artists and writers were actually doing; in society we were trying to compete in new ways—and needed to try harder. The period became a time for large explanatory narratives, books in which we explained ourselves to ourselves.

American experience was, within the span of a few years, the center of everything. Our dollars were propping up Europe; our mix of consumerism and social egalitarianism was enviable; our painters were getting the attention formerly accorded to European masters; our writers—Hemingway and Faulkner—were getting Nobel Prizes and exciting worldwide audiences as never before. What did we think of ourselves? The books mentioned above were surprisingly guarded, sober, and skeptical. Not one celebration among them. Contrary to the sloppy and confused notion that America after the war was smug and absorbed with its own splendors, the idea in widest circulation among critics and commentators was that America's grasp was subject to all the limits that history and human capacity had imposed. Morris Dickstein offers this summation: "Relentless self-criticism, not complacency, was the key to postwar culture." What was excessive in the contemporary American character? What was naive or innocent or simply foolish? While England after the war was forging a tradition of resentment and regret—including the old guard like Wyndham Lewis and Evelyn Waugh and the new Angry Young Men like Kingsley Amis and Alan Sillitoe—America was becoming the literary capital of reflection and analysis: our explanations of culture and society were cast in the form of doubts.

Lionel Trilling's *The Liberal Imagination* was an evaluation of the cultural state of the nation; it took the long view of our national habits and predicted what was likely to happen if we failed to refurbish the liberal program of the immediate past. America—the country of sound results in business and warfare, of happiness and prosperity as a goal—was the capital of world rationality and progress after World War II. But what about the dangers of such gifts? Our impulse toward freedom, our respect for variousness, our pursuit of possibility were marked by a prosaic, mechanical organizational power. Trilling drily noted our situation: "The paradox is that liberalism is concerned with the emotions above all else, as proof of which happiness stands at the very center of its thought, but in its effort to establish the emotions, or certain among them, in some sort of freedom, liberalism somehow tends to deny them in their full possibility." Our dominant national philosophy was political, which is to say "the organization of human life toward some end or other," in our case toward happiness. What concerned Trilling was that liberalism was losing its main force: "organization means delegation"—and ideas that can survive delegation are often lacking in "largeness and modulation and complexity."

The job that he proposed for the critical spirit was perhaps the most daunting cultural challenge of the new era: use literature and other works of the imagination to leaven the organizational powers of liberalism; use books and ideas to return the liberal energy of politics and social change to its first impulses. A quixotic project, but then again the kind of activity that humanists from Socrates to Matthew Arnold have been engaged in. Trilling was the man for his time in that the postwar period—triumphal, defensive, and hugely energetic—was all-too-worshipful of realism, results, and fact. His explanation of our literary situation in "Reality in America," the first essay in *The Liberal Imagination*, was as much about national character as it was about literary texts. It derived from a nineteenth century conflict that was more alive than ever in post–World War II America: the collision of hard facts with imagination, materialistic analysis with instinctual insight, utilitarian orderliness with romantic perception. Trilling—guided by J. S. Mill's proposition that romantic conservatism has something to teach practical reformism, that the poet Coleridge could enlighten the worldly philosopher Bentham—brought this Victorian precept into the world of contemporary American thought. He did so by adapting it to the terms of his first readers—a 1946 audience that he assumed had certain literary and cultural biases; the essay was still valid four years later. Basically, it divided American readers into Dreiserians and Jamesians, novel readers who loved plain facts and novel readers who loved finer perceptions. Dreiserians—with their taste for the naturalistic novel and its raw, clunky narratives—felt they were more in touch with the American spirit than Jamesians with their emphasis on the subtleties of consciousness. The larger question was clear enough to Trilling: should Americans continue to live in the world of Dreiserian social significance or should they venture into the more complex realms of Jamesian psychology?

His explanation of the American mind at mid-century began as an analysis of Vernon Parrington's *Main Currents in American Thought*, a book of the 1920s. Parrington's realistic bias in the study of American culture—his tendency to celebrate "the saving salt of the American mind, the lively sense of the practical, workaday world, of the welter of ordinary undistinguished things and people, of the tangible, quirky, unrefined elements of life"—is our liberal bias, the taste that dominated our cultural life in the 1920s and in 1950 (not to mention today). This stubborn, direct, no-frills call for realism and frankness, according to Trilling, is hopelessly naive. It lives under the illusion that the Dreisers are in touch and the Jamesians are the dreamers.

When we turn to the popular novels of the 1950s, Trilling's diagnosis seems entirely accurate: Americans liked predictable naturalistic fare—especially novels that had the flavor of Dreiser and the ingredients of the postwar years. My book, however, wants to direct readers in the new century to the great tradition of 1950s writing, those works that—to use Trilling's words—are various and complex rather than solidly real. Yet the baseline 1950s book of some quality but doubtful staying power was more Dreiserian in style and vision: books such as Hemingway's *The Old Man and the Sea* (1952), Sloan Wilson's *The Man in the Gray Flannel Suit* (1955), and John O'Hara's *From the Terrace* (1958) are about "the welter of undistinguished things and people." Even James Gould Cozzens's *By Love Possessed* (1957)—despite its involuted sentences and its high-toned protagonist—was enormously appealing to readers who wanted the staples of an older kind of novel—easily recognizable characters, clear story line, "life" as opposed to artifice. Sloan Wilson and O'Hara and Cozzens—astonishing as it may seem to us—once seemed daring and candid in their evaluation of sex, money, and class. Hemingway's enormously popular book once seemed to be offering a profound allegory of human suffering. And these writers' vivid command of concrete experience made them seem like naturalism's grandchildren; their melodramatic tone was geared to the sensibilities of the middle classes.

Herman Wouk's *Marjorie Morningstar*, an account of love and loss among prosperous Jewish New Yorkers, was another favorite in this real-life area—and not surprisingly it made a rather touching, solid movie with superstars Natalie Wood and Gene Kelly. For 1950s people, these experiences belonged to comfortable territory: they concerned resentment and regret that turn into resignation and endurance. Unlike satire, such novels take human frailty for granted and don't burden readers with uncomfortable alternatives; unlike literary experiment, there are no difficult fragmentations in these user-friendly fictions.

The 1950s had a large appetite for the naturalistic blockbuster, especially if it was served up with romance and guarded optimism. The reading public accepted a mature, upbeat understanding of life's limits, not of course to be confused with Camus's existential courage in the face of despair. Nora Sayre's *Previous Convictions* argues that this vague combination of maturity, balance, and objective facing of facts permeated the 1950s, killed off ideology, and led (at its worst) to Doris Day's "Whatever Will Be, Will Be." Although not quite capturing the anger of a hugely successful book like James Jones's *From Here to Eternity*, the generalization is close enough to capture the spirit of most bestsellers. These books steered clear of the edge of the modernist novel: they seemed to arrive without stretching anyone's imagination or challenging anyone's assumptions. And some of the most astute readers at the time, according to Sayre, were far from exciting—they may have read T. S. Eliot and Dylan Thomas in college, but they seemed as tame as the readers of the bestsellers: "In an age of lowered voices and pale cashmere, some of the young were humble romantics—humble because our parents' youth had been more adventurous than our own." That youth of the 1920s and 1930s—be it remembered—experienced bestsellers by Fitzgerald and Hemingway and James T. Farrell. The 1950s blockbusters cited above were of course a diverse bunch in terms of quality and subject matter. They suggest an audience with some amount of taste and curiosity about new things, but one with a none-too-demanding conception of storytelling. If truth be told, these readers were the likely devourers (even if in secret) of that other blockbuster of 1956 about manners and mores—Grace Metalious's *Peyton Place*.

Hemingway's *The Old Man and the Sea*, for all its attempts to preserve the stylistic mastery of his 1920s novels and stories, is the perfect thing for an audience in search of a "masterpiece" that has no challenges. Hemingway deals with the mystery of human loss and defeat without making the reader reach for insights: you are supplied with a neat and completely comprehensible account of failure—minus, of course, the agony, self-loathing, bitterness, and lashing out that accompany the real thing. Although working brilliantly with the details of the old man's days at sea, Hemingway seems to be at sea when it comes to basic human nature: he denies the horror of suffering, preferring to give a naturalistic account of material conditions overlaid with something like the affirmations of Rodgers and Hammerstein's *Carousel*.

This old man has, if not hope in his heart, peace and natural piety on his tongue. Impressive, grandiose, compelling in its way, the story is nevertheless rudimentary in its vision and self-parodying in its style. The emotional current running through it is like that of vintage Hemingway without quite being vintage Hemingway: "A man can be destroyed but not defeated." The line sounds like him, but the overall vision—once a question of living intensely and by so doing defying war and infirmity, social systems, and one's own demons—is now reduced to sententious and garrulous musings on fate itself. Having failed for six days to catch a fish, the Old Man decides to work "far out"; before leaving, he talks to the boy, a kind of straight man in his philosophical drama about losing. Sports are a good way of dealing with luck and skill and loss. "Have faith in the Yankees, my son, think of the great DiMaggio." To which the boy responds; "I fear the Tigers of Detroit." Which leaves the best line for the Old Man, a wisecrack worthy of Groucho Marx: "Be careful or you will fear even the Reds of Cincinnati and the White Sox of Chicago." Later on, after the struggle with the big fish, the old man loses his grip and abuses the sports allusions: "But I think the great DiMaggio would be proud of me today. I had no bone spurs. But the hands and the back hurt truly." This self-congratulatory, faux naif explanatory style is the worst of things; when Hemingway returns to naturalistic observation, he sometimes regains his old poise: "Why did they make birds so delicate and fine as these sea swallows when the ocean can be so cruel?" Another outburst is exceptionally eloquent, honest in a way that many of the talky passages are not: "Besides, he thought, everything kills everything else in some way. Fishing kills me exactly as it keeps me alive. The boy keeps me alive, he thought. I must not deceive myself too much." This "too much" is the old Hemingway—subtle, understated, tough on himself. The new 1950s Hemingway liked his raw naturalism cut with a strong measure of self-pity; the Old Man would like to buy some luck, if there were "any place they sell it." Not a bad line at all, but no sooner uttered than ruined by a begging qualification: what would he buy it with? A lost harpoon, a broken knife, two bad hands? We listen with regret as Hemingway betrays his modernism: he explains and unpacks his heart.

The Old Man and the Sea is a perfect fit for the part of 1950s taste that craved peace, closure, and clear answers. Trilling found the same limitations in Dreiser, especially in the latter part of his career; the old infelicities of style combined with a fake piety and resignation, something easy and factitious in its religiosity—a willed belief that it-all-means-something. Hemingway's Old Man is similarly thrust upon us at the end. He "lay for some time with the mast across his shoulder." The imagery of Christ's suffering is melodramatically tacked on to a story where there has been no credible belief in redemption. Readers evidently liked their endurance stories so spiked.

Another signature book of the period, *The Man in the Gray Flannel Suit*, charts its protagonist's endurance and resignation in terms that make the ordeal seem not at all bad. Whereas Hemingway overlays his protagonist's suffering with grandiose imagery and phony simplicity, Sloan Wilson extricates Tom Rath from snobbish family traits, small prospects, bad decisions, and wartime traumas by . . . giving him a better job and a better house in Westport, Connecticut. He gets these good things because of his basic integrity, just as Hemingway's Old Man finds peace back at his little house after an honest fight. Tom went to work for media tycoon Ralph Hopkins, but realized that his sense of unease ("Why the hell should I get scared in peacetime?") came from the false position he was in, both at home and on the job. For years he had been denying his wartime past: that he killed seventeen men and that he fathered a child by an Italian woman. For several months in the early 1950s he has pretended to be the right man for a great executive position; actually he is a basic nine-to-fiver of good ability and modest ambition. A mature contentment floods his life once he squares himself with his wife and boss. Tell your wife about the girl and the child; tell your boss what's wrong with his big campaign for mental health. (At one point Wilson has Tom speak about making "a major frontal attack" on mental illness—this in the era of frontal lobotomies.) By the end of the book, Tom recalls the inscription on a stone bench at his grandmother's fine country house: Robert Browning's "God's in his heaven."

The forced quality of this—like Hemingway's heavy imagery—should not make the reader ignore Wilson's ability to chronicle life in the 1950s: the bad war memories, stalled careers, and small destinies that were there for many. The book is more accurate than most melodramatic novels as it situates Tom not boldly climbing the corporate ladder, but matter-of-factly standing midway in a very ordinary career. In the novel's present time, Tom lives on the main thoroughfare in an unattractive house that has a heavily symbolic crack on the living room wall. If not the beaten-down character of Dreiser or some other naturalist, he's the variation in a nice suit; someone with debts, a dead-end job, dark secrets. Wilson makes him a type, the well-educated man with no special abilities or destiny, even at a time when economic myth and legend tell us that opportunity was bursting out of every office building. Tom's family connections—which have earned him his first job at a snobbish foundation—also seem like fateful circumstances: hopes of an inheritance keep him from going out and taking a chance. When he finally does go for better money in the media world, he finds out he wasn't made for the big time.

These rather dismal circumstances are rendered in a prose that is better and often clearer than the overall vision of the book: for while the novel is yet another American standard about enduring and surviving, the writing makes Tom's anxious state very real to us. Take, for example the war scenes that haunt him. The most memorable one is a scene of what happened to young paratroopers who had just landed in a field at night; they ran, as "big as snowmen," and were picked off by the German antiaircraft guns. In this horrific debacle Tom's unit is all but destroyed, and later he himself played a minor part in the slaughter by accidentally killing his best buddy Hank Mahoney with a misdirected hand grenade. Tom can't help "thinking of Mahoney running with the grenade in mid-air, poised there forever like Keats's lovers on a Grecian urn, Hank always young and alive, the grenade always outlined clearly against the sky, just a few feet above his shoulder." The single best stretch of prose in the book has Tom carrying Mahoney's body through swarms of medics and wounded, searching for "a real doctor." Close in quality is the recollection of a German boy whom Tom killed and stripped of his gear. He remembers going through pockets and looking at a letter written on tissue paper in a woman's hand.

What makes each of these scenes especially fine is Wilson's talent for placing them ironically in the midst of an upbeat American 1950s view of life. Consider this mixing of time frames in which Tom thinks of his Italian girlfriend and an Army buddy and his girl: "Tom and Caeser and Gina and Maria had sat drinking together on several evenings, and it had been almost like a suburban community, with the men all working for the same big corporation." Tom is being warned constantly by his wife Betsy that life's prizes go to the optimists, the cheerful, forward-looking go-getters who never sour a relationship or a deal with a cynical wisecrack. After thinking about the German boy and the delicate stationery, Tom—a slow learner of certain 1950s truths—wonders whether the boy was an optimist. In those passages where Tom's mind drifts from wartime extremes to suburban ordinariness, the book comes alive for the reader:

> They ought to begin with a course in basic training and end with a course in basic forgetting. The trick is to learn that it's a disconnected world, a lunatic world, where what is true now was not true then; where Thou Shalt Not Kill and the fact that one has killed a great many men mean nothing, absolutely nothing, for now is the time to raise legitimate children, and make money, and dress properly, and be kind to one's wife, and admire one's boss, and learn not to worry, and think of oneself as what? That makes no difference, he thought—I'm just a man in a gray flannel suit. I must keep my suit neatly pressed like anyone else, for I am a very respectable young man.

But *The Man in the Gray Flannel Suit* eventually detaches itself from Tom's isolation and collapses into a bundle of clichés about a brighter future and being at peace. The trouble is that Tom at peace is as far as you can get from intellectual honesty or historical consciousness. When he's most out of step with the complacencies of the fifties, he's a character worth remembering.

James Gould Cozzens's bestseller *By Love Possessed* was another work with a message about honesty, reason, and maturity. It too was rooted in old-fashioned naturalism—a vision of modern man caught in a web of biological destiny, economic necessity, and class. Like the other 1950s big sellers, it has a lot of answers and explanations: Cozzens, a skeptic and a rationalist, is greatly comforted by his own knowingness. A colossal social and intellectual snob, he looks down on just about everybody who is not professionally distinguished, WASP, and moneyed. A kind of Protestant, prejudiced version of John O'Hara, he observes everybody and everything in his little Eastern

Pennsylvania town; but unlike O'Hara his anthropological curiosity is not accompanied by heart and style. His prose—full of swirls and circumlocutions and odd diction—must have made him seem very adult and sophisticated to book-club audiences turned off by the adolescent bluntness of Mickey Spillane and other literary toughs. Although the early twenty-first century reader is turned off by many of these awkwardly written pages, he or she cannot help but be impressed by Cozzens's engulfing mind: there is something spectacular in his command of one town's opinions, prejudices, and class attitudes. His specialty is stripping away illusions about love, faith, and community and replacing them with truths about desire, doubt, and conflict. *By Love Possessed* is a lawyer's book, about lawyers and prosecutorial in style, with every character under fire from Cozzens's rather nasty imagination.

The plot consists of laying out a series of lies, illusions, and fantasies and thereafter displacing them with the facts. Arthur Winner, the protagonist and privileged consciousness, is a law partner in a local firm who over a weekend in the mid-1950s is confronted with every form of dishonesty a town can produce: an elderly partner is found to have been mingling funds; a local boy charged with rape is unmasked for the scoundrel he is; a retarded girl and her parents are trying to cover up infanticide; and Winner himself is trying to escape the truth about an affair he had with a partner's wife at the time of his own wife's death. Everybody is possessed by some truth-destroying passion: love of repute, lust, ambition, hatred of the class above. Cozzens reduces them all to their pathetic essentials: self-love and self-delusion. Over at the Union League Club there is a heroic painting that ironically distills his vision: the big, grandiloquent canvas of *The Battle of Chancellorsville* at the club's quarter railing is a spectacular lie; there really was no heroic charge of the Union side but rather "a brief blundering encounter in the dark with some lost Confederates." Yet the social fact of life that cannot be denied is "man's incurable willful rush to believe what he preferred to believe." When writing of love, Cozzens has the same reductive view. The following evaluation is vintage Cozzens: "in the manifold manifestations of the amative appetite one finds the one same urgent unreason, the one same eager let's pretend." Dwight Macdonald's analysis of Cozzens's bad prose neglected to cite the following tormented survey of "feelings' feasts" (i.e., the varieties of passion): everything from "lovings of the higher sort" to "glad gushings" to "coarser" fare is transformed and romanticized. "Before your eyes, the moment ago's plain piece of tail sea-changed, metamorphosed into something rich and strange." All this romantic transformation "to ennoble the bump of bellies." Love—even parental love—is delusory and tampered with in the interest of the lover's ego: it's often a form of "I love me." The vocabulary of love is handled with the rough dismissiveness of a logical positivist: "this assemblage of phrases that had no exact significance, of tauto-logical terms, of proofless postulations." Cozzens will admit that "the fervent saying of this kind of nothing did have meaning"—which is to say that the world is animated by nonsense.

Behind every grand concept or impassioned claim or high-flown sentiment is a cluster of misunderstandings and half-admitted desires. Arthur Winner's law partner is the most notable spokesman for this position in the book: a flinty, crippled man, Julius Penrose specializes in evaluating the childish spectacle of the society around him and loves to refer to the "Fool Killer"—a kind of nemesis—who hunts down self-deluders. A "club bore," according to Dwight Macdonald in his scathing review of the book, Penrose is nevertheless not wrong about what's going on around town—it's all evasion and lying and jobbery of one sort or another. Despite poor Helen Detweiler's decency, she winds up pathetically pleading for the innocence of her rapist brother; despite the cries for justice from the working-class people whose daughter has supposedly been wronged, the little people are essentially liars. Meanwhile, the DA is willing to drop a case in order to secure political support; and gentlemanly Winner, a model of judiciousness, has been in the grip of an unseemly passion. As Cozzens's raisonneur, Penrose preaches a doctrine of reason and moderation. He's so reasonable that, like Dr. Johnson, he knows reason won't work in this world: "To drive out a passion," he quotes, "reason is helpless; you need another passion." And he doesn't mind practicing his philosophy on himself. In the clinching scene about the old lawyer Noah Tuttle, a seemingly rock-ribbed man of integrity who had been mingling funds and therefore threatening the firm's reputation, we find out that Penrose kept his mouth shut at the time of the malfea-sance even though he wasn't a vested partner and had nothing to lose by the exposure of a colleague. His passion, it seems, was a sense of responsibility, a Conradian sense of the right thing in the face of other passions like aggression and envy and spite. This turning of stoicism into a passionate desire—being zealous about the recognition of life's limits, man's faultiness and delusions—is Cozzens's master theme.

His protagonist Winner does his best to align himself with the Penrose philosophy: he arrives home and declares, "I'm here"—I've endured the nonsense and dishonesty in others' natures and my own. The popularity of all this—bestsellerdom, a movie with Lana Turner—enraged Dwight Macdonald who saw nothing but middlebrow melodrama and resignation embalmed in bad sentences. He labeled the book "A Novel of Resignation," a specimen of a genre that involves small-time recognitions and accommodations to an awful social system. Not a tragic or even satiric coming to terms with life's limits, Cozzens's resignation is a supine acceptance of whatever is. Macdonald calls it the revolt of the middlebrows.

The last great 1950s study of resignation was John O'Hara's massive *From the Terrace*, published in 1958. The book is—as you care to see it—a monument to, or a mausoleum for, O'Hara's disillusionments. O'Hara was angry at the *New Yorker* during the 1950s and as a result stopped practicing the short-story form, arguably his strongest suit. He began to write resentful novels. The books he produced were phenomena: long, textured, discursive, loosely structured epics of disappointment in the twentieth century. The 1955 hit book *Ten North Frederick* was all about the unfulfilling life of Gibbsville, Pennsylvania's first gentleman, Joe Chapin, a patrician who falls afoul of the nouveaux riches and fails to realize his potential for leadership. In *From the Terrace* O'Hara allows his tale of frustration to swell to 900 pages, but the drift of the story is hardly different from that of *Ten North Frederick*: this time Alfred Eaton, a young prince of Port Johnson, Pennsylvania, doesn't quite meet a princely destiny. O'Hara packs the book with what went wrong—socially, psychologically, economically. The title—a mystery to the reader for many hundreds of pages—refers to what Alfred Eaton did after a somewhat distinguished career in business and public service: he came in from the terrace of his luxurious California residence, evidently a symbolic action that conveys Eaton's resignation to being a very rich failure.

Eaton's father, the owner of a great mill in town, lost his oldest son in World War I, and thereafter his bitterness made him inaccessible to young Alfred. Alfred's mother, meanwhile, had been carrying on an affair with a local big-spending landed gentleman. The effects of neglect and tawdriness—we are given to believe—produced a hardened and calloused Alfred. They also produced a young man who didn't quite know what to desire—his birthright in Port Johnson or a place in the great world. Striking out for the latter destiny, he gets involved in the aeronautics business with his former Princeton classmate Lex Porter; yet even though Lex's Uncle Fritz, a New York swell, provides plenty of capital, the two young men soon part company because they are unable to agree on where the business should go. Lex—imaginative and a chance taker—is totally unlike the grounded and rather ordinary Alfred. As a protagonist the latter is a rather colorless fellow; what vividness he possesses is a result of O'Hara's flair for social scene painting rather than for psychological delving. The excellent episodes in the Princeton Club or the Racquet Club or in a Wall Street banking house do little, however, to uncover his nature; actually we are more interested in the scenes than the character. At one point, after a preposterous act of heroism that gains the attention of the head of a great banking house, Alfred finds himself up to his neck in prestige on Wall Street. Rewarded like a character out of a folktale for saving a powerful man's grandson from drowning—O'Hara seems unashamed of this silly bit of fantasy—Alfred nevertheless fails to grasp the deepest satisfactions of money and power. Every prestigious setting seems to drag him down or lessen his sense of selfhood. Even becoming Assistant Secretary of the Navy under Roosevelt turns out to be a disappointment: he becomes a kind of golden loser; his connection with rich men who hold government contracts is a mark against him and compromises his integrity. Actually, he is yet another victim of the social system, not so different from the born loser of the naturalistic novel: all his ambitions are illusions; every step forward is actually a misstep. As he flies high in Manhattan and Washington, we get the queasy sense that he's losing ground.

These 1950s novels of resignation give us the sobering news of human limitation and defeat in very different forms; yet each hammers home a two-part message: don't lose sight of your own weaknesses; be mature enough to recognize what you can't control. Each of the immensely popular works has its peculiar vision of human suffering. Hemingway's book is streaked with tragic effects—some of which are inflated to the level of silly grandiosity. Sloan Wilson's story is matter-of-fact and cheerful in its resignation. Cozzens's novel is about vanity exposed and uses skepticism to cut people down to size. O'Hara's chronicle of frustration depicts America's proudest as they land in a limbo of disillusioned retirement. But the best books of the era offered assaults and surprises in place of the standard now-we-see-why formula of the novel of resignation. In the landmark books, nothing is meant to be, everything challenges.

chapter 1

Breaking Through

Four landmark books transformed the elements of the naturalistic novel and made them into something altogether new. Each soared above the tales of resignation. Each transcended the naturalistic mode while preserving its vigor and directness. Each experimented with language without losing contact with a readership hungry for vivid stories. These books that woke America up aesthetically and gave the modernist novel its second wind after Faulkner's and Hemingway's great period was over were art fiction in the tradition of *Ulysses*: ambitious works of experimentalism that left the familiar territory of Dreiser and James T. Farrell. They were not relentless reports on American failure told in the plain-as-paint language of the social chronicler. Ralph Ellison's *Invisible Man*, Saul Bellow's *The Adventures of Augie March*, Bernard Malamud's *The Magic Barrel*, and Flannery O'Connor's *A Good Man Is Hard to Find* were tremendous paradoxes in our literature: accessible modernist classics, fictions with thick symbolic and poetic texture that were nevertheless fun to read. American modernism of the 1950s blended the elite and the demotic, the poetic and the pedestrian, the recondite and the popular. The new books had the artistic boldness of the old modernist movement, but they were less obstacle-ridden and exasperating than *Finnegans Wake* or Samuel Beckett's novels or Faulkner's *Absalom, Absalom!* The four breakthrough books emerged against a general backdrop of dullish bestsellers—just as the work of Joyce, Woolf, and Conrad jostled with sturdy realistic works by Wells and Bennett. The backdrop works of the 1950s were very often respectable, and sometimes highly accomplished, but they were never original. They carried the baggage of an older tradition of chronicling, yet failed to adapt it in any new way.

Meanwhile, these four books defied expectations. If you were living in 1952 and heard that there was a new novel about race you might well have expected a second installment of Richard Wright's *Native Son*: this book—called by James Baldwin "everybody's protest novel"—was ruthlessly angry in tone, Dreiserian in its raw style, and reductive in its view of human motivation. In 1952, you would probably also have been aware of race as "the race problem"—which is to say a social issue explored in a book like Gunnar Myrdal's *An American Dilemma*. But Ellison's book would have been a shock. It wasn't an earnest exploration of injustice, a clenched fist, or a social study; instead it was a surreal conspectus of a black man's life—the rapidly altering course of a young man's moral and economic and intellectual career, complete with carnival and crucifixion, hilarity and deep depression.

The book went far beyond the bland expression "race problem": as a book about civilization, it focused on underlying ideas, rooted attitudes, and complex manifestations. While dealing with black/white antagonism on many levels, it was more involved with patterns than with panaceas. Like Charles Dickens in *Little Dorrit*, Ellison was a surveyor of civilization's discontents—and the irony and unintentional comedy that emerged from them. Dickens felt England was a prison house for most people—with humorous distortions of character abounding; Ellison felt America was a sustained drama of pretense with blacks and whites in their artificial roles.

Saul Bellow's *The Adventures of Augie March* is principally set in the Great Depression years. Bellow's protagonist, like Ellison's, is poor and struggling and lives a seat-of-the-pants existence. His list of occupations—from assistant to a wily old crippled man to dog groomer, eagle trainer, and international businessman-schemer—puts him in the league with the great picaros and sets him apart from victims. Buoyant and canny—if not always on the winning end of a deal—he is a South Side of Chicago Jewish survivor in the era of breadlines, relief, and agitprop. His story is too funny and filled with incongruity to bear any real comparison with tales of American victims. James Agee's *Let Us Now Praise Famous Men* looked with steady compassion at the suffering of the underclass during the late 1930s; Bellow's *Augie* has a dizzying array of responses to his wide-angle view of America. Strut and swagger alternate with pity and gentle humanity; the elderly and blind and retarded share the action of the plot with dressed up merchants' wives and wearers of Sulka ties; boxcar drifters are no more or less important than spoiled rich girls. Bellow makes them live in their Dickensian profusion of habits; he refuses to brand them: they are not victims, not oppressors, not deluded fools, not the playthings of fate. The book stands apart from the typical 1950s blockbuster about man's limits.

Bernard Malamud's *The Magic Barrel* was another crucial work of transformation and overturning. America after World War II was the country of hope, confidence, renewal: Holocaust survivors and other victims of the Old World's horrors and miseries could expect decent life chances and more. Yet Malamud's landmark book of stories seems to say something different. Jews in America suffer in a brand-new world: they somehow cannot help but possess the grim heirlooms of the ages—loneliness, poverty, bad luck. Malamud's collection of struggling shopkeepers, bad-humored retirees, brideless rabbinical students, and nowhere young people looks like nothing so much as the old crew of the naturalistic novel, the sitting ducks of circumstances. But in the course of a few pages they invariably burst into a fuller humanity. They are part of a mystery drama of the miraculous: spectacular things happen to them, as in a Chagall canvas, or quietly important things happen in head and heart. *The Magic Barrel* says plainly on every page that life cheats one of everything, but not of meaning and the ability to feel. The book is stunning antidote to the reductionism of *By Love Possessed*.

Malamud's Jewish book of miracles was preceded by Flannery O'Connor's Christian book of revelation, *A Good Man Is Hard to Find*. If readers were expecting uplift and reassurance and clear spiritual signposts—if they were expecting the good cheer and assurances of Bishop Fulton Sheen, the signature middlebrow preacher of the era who had his own TV show—they had made a bad mistake in selecting O'Connor. Her news of salvation was weirdly packaged, often streaked with blasphemy and sick humor, hard, austere, and Augustinian at a time when the popular taste favored common sense, reason, and maturity. Soft-core spirituality and feel-good preaching—nice words about love and responsibility—were widely available. But O'Connor gave heat and lightning and the complex language of the modernists as she fought her way out of the deterministic world of the naturalists. No, the world was not one big cheat, one going back and forth from O'Hara's terrace. But you would have to get used to purgatory to aspire to something better.

Ralph Ellison's *Invisible Man* is a big book about how we as Americans landed where we are—isolated, confused, angry, but not without hope. It does its explaining in flamboyant language—a mix of symbolism and slang. Claiming to riff like a jazz musician—go off on his theme with variations—Ellison describes the phase of modernism he is in: a sort of black American stream-of-consciousness punctuated with strong symbols representing moments of awareness for his protagonist. Ellison's critical intelligence keeps him clear of the rant and guff of most late twentieth century rappers. There's no rapping at all—only the riffing of a craftsmanly modernist.

As an explanatory narrative, *Invisible Man* cuts a wide swath. The struggle of a mind to account for the absurdity and injustice in American life, it has certain features of the epic. First of all the span of time employed in relating a personal struggle of large impersonal significance: Ellison uses some twenty years, including the narrator's youth and schooling in the 1920s, young manhood and starting out in the Depression, and leftist activity over the years in New York. The scenes in the South and Manhattan are done with phantasmagoric detail, suggesting Ulysses' adventures with monsters, weird, controlling antagonists, and various other impeders on the way to resolution and recognition. In Ellison's case the end point is not the Ithaca of wife and son and one's people: instead it's an intellectual position, a level of understanding achieved after experiencing the purgatorial career of an intelligent black man in the second quarter of the twentieth century. It's the basement in Harlem, lighted with innumerable bulbs powered for free because our protagonist has cheated the utility company. The scene is a surrealistic retreat from the brutality of capitalist America, the condescension of philanthropic America—or the duplicity of Communist America or Black Separatist America. The basement is a place to escape isms and ideologies—left, right, and complacent center.

The best way into the book and its complexities is the blunt question, "What does it say about us after fifty years? Is it still talking about an America we know?" There are two conflicts that live for the new century: they are both given the embodiment of the artist rather than the rhetorical treatment of the ideologue or the nosy literal-mindedness of the journalist. The first is the gap between comfortable people who control things and the bewildered mass of people who comply. Ellison is too intelligent to make the controllers one-track aggressors. His character Mr. Norton, the smug patron of a Southern Negro college, sleekly dispenses charity. He's no monster, but rather a sensible old gentleman who talks of responsibility, offers doses of watered-down Emerson, and straight-from-the-warehouse clichés about my fate and your fate. Norton is so mired in illusions that he needs shock therapy to awaken him to the life of Black America. He gets just that when our protagonist, the Invisible Man, lets him see the squalid cabins near the college and the local gambling joint and whorehouse, the Golden Dawn. Ellison, a moral realist to the last, knows that such complacent people don't rage or denounce; they merely sink further into a state of denial, escaping into their polite remoteness. The Invisible Man, for his part, can't understand the fall-out from this episode: don't the college authorities see that such a collision was an accident? How can they hold him responsible for basic ugly realities? Why is his good standing at the college dependent on a chance encounter? Why, in short, is he the serio-comic victim? The answer is that he has caused Norton to enter a world where he is not in control, where the chaos of real life threatens to overwhelm every convention and pious fiction.

Another major scene in the novel, the famous Battle Royal episode, conveys Ellison's ideas about control in a bizarre and a lurid way. Tossing aside the niceties of naturalistic plot logic, Ellison takes us once again into a nether world—this time not of the black underclass but of the solid business community. We see the underside of respectability as the prosperous local merchants decide to use blacks as playthings in a public demonstration of philanthropy. Our young protagonist, a smart high-school student worthy of a college scholarship, is asked to give a speech to the assembled locals: the occasion is made into an allegory of race degradation. The boy is forced through a three-part ritual, a raw, primitive way for the whites to assert superiority and establish hierarchy. When completely degraded, the boy is deemed worthy of his prize: a briefcase with a college scholarship inside. In order to win, he is first made to confront a naked white blond woman, then made to fight his fellow blacks with his fists to a point short of manslaughter, and finally made to grab at coins on an electrified rug. These images of sexual enslavement, aggression, and abasement have the flavor of Joyce's Nighttown, all the while avoiding Joyce's often inscrutable notation. Visceral and intellectual at the same time, the scene is topped off with a bit of degradation especially appropriate for a very good student—a nice-boy speech about neighborliness that he is made to deliver. As he uses his good vocabulary the audience alternately ignores and mocks him. Bruised and bloody from the prizefight he talks about "social responsibility"—and, above the din and cigar smoke, "equality." The mob balks at the lat-

ter—and the boy says it was a mistake; he misspoke himself while
swallowing blood. Thus Ellison on the subject of the controlled and
the controlling.

The second big theme in this book that is more alive than ever is
the conflict between selfhood and ideology, between the reasoning
person and the rhetoric of groups. The book is an intellectual's cri de
coeur, a defense of creative living and thinking as against the impor-
tuning and pressure of the collective. In our time, no conflict could
be more pertinent. *Invisible Man* is about the awakening consciousness in an era of illusions about power and race: the protagonist
comes to maturity as he matches wits with the Marxists and the Black
Separatists.

Ellison's depiction of American Communism remains a vivid and
exciting piece of writing, even at a time when Communism is so diminished. The core truth that endures is a picture of a controlling hierarchy with its rigidities and cruelties. A half century ago Ellison
recorded the cant of strategists who care more about master plans than
about actual people. As an artist and intellectual, Ellison refuses to denounce "the Brotherhood" as a godless plot against America. He prefers to offer a scathing portrait of intelligent people who refuse to
think. His Party members are on emotional and intellectual automatic
pilot, mouthing revolutionary rhetoric that is completely disconnected from the condition of the American suffering classes. Our narrator is a talented Southern boy recruited as a Brotherhood
spokesman, but he has the serious disadvantage of being unable to ignore direct experience, ordinary people, his own past, and his instincts. At the funeral of a black youth slain by the cops, he delivers a
speech that is totally lacking in Communist correctness: he speaks of
cruelty, of the value of one life, but he has no abstract lesson about the
working classes to lay on his audience. To the Brotherhood this is mere
sentimentality; direct human response is so much corny rhetoric and
futile appeal to mere emotion. Ellison, it should be noted, appears to
be delineating the mid-1930s phase of Stalinist activity, not the love
and solidarity phase of the Popular Front during the 1940s: this abstract approach to revolution—cynical, stripped of human consideration, focused on political ends and heedless of merciless means—is
very much alive in the contemporary pronouncements of our multi-
culturalists and cultural studies theorists. Seeing and denouncing the
power arrangements of America is a much more important task than
grasping the complexities of suffering individuals. Ellison's Commu-

nists are obsessed with "the all embracing idea of the Brotherhood"; such an idea had "given the world a new shape."

Our Invisible Man—never the ranter, always the ironic riffer on the absurdities of his time—decides to "yes" his superiors to death—or at least give that appearance; but he also has another idea in mind. Why not get some release from the rigidities of the bourgeois and proletarian worlds? Why not plunge into the anarchic world of King Rinehart, a bad dude in sunglasses and a white hat who does some gambling, some preaching, some shaking down, some thieving. To live in this world by night, while being a good Communist by day, might satisfy the whole man. The trouble is that Ellison's Invisible Man has little taste for the role of the outlaw: he makes us see that random dissing of society is futile and boring. Also futile—and terrifying—is the other form of radical disengagement—Black Separatism. Ellison's Ras The Exhorter is a Harlem fanatic who mocks our protagonist's humanism early on in the book and later tries to hunt him down during a midsummer race riot.

During the spectacular riot scene, the Invisible Man achieves a resoundingly negative recognition about his life that paradoxically lifts him above his surroundings: "I was one with the mass, moving down the littered street over the puddles of oil and muck, my personality blasted." It's the recovery of one's selfhood—the sense of being that has been overwhelmed by the promises of dialectics, revenge, and spite—that is the most urgent task. To begin it he first must see what has happened in Harlem: the Brotherhood has been using the separatist Ras to discredit and destroy our narrator and his sentimental ideas about humanity. But Ellison's spokesman for the human spirit blurts out the truth of it all before a crowd on one of the ravaged streets:

> "They want this to happen," I said. "They planned it. They want the mobs to come uptown with machine guns and rifles. They want the streets to flow with blood; your blood, black blood and white blood, so that they can turn your death and sorrow and defeat into propaganda. . . . Well, they used me to catch you and now they're using Ras to do away with me and prepare your sacrifice."

To win against this propaganda—as the protagonist does—it is necessary to have experienced the full course of political illusions, to have worked through the errors and recognized the nature of the confusion. Ellison uses the language of Thomas Carlyle's *Sartor Resartus*,

that great nineteenth century work about battling the mechanistic philosophy of utilitarianism. The Invisible Man, like Carlyle's Herr Teu-
felsdröckh, throws off the life-denying doctrines of his time. In 1952
Ellison was battling false enlightenment, demented romanticism, and
the dead hand of genteel racism. These states of mind are close to the
ones Carlyle described—cold rationalism, satanic Byronism, and complacent self-interest. And Ellison, like Carlyle, the teacher of the Vic-
torians, has taught us how to think about one of the besetting
problems of the modern era. In 1952 he found a common denominator
in the array of illusions—the drive toward uniformity. He urged a
flexibility of mind and a pluralistic social life that he called diversity,
miles away from our present appetite for dull correctness: "America is
woven of many strands. I would recognize them and let it so remain.
It's 'winner take nothing' that is the great truth of our country or any
country. Life is to be lived, not controlled." Ellison's book stands as
a protest against ideologies; in style and intellectual substance it blasts
the conventions of its time and ours. At the conclusion of the novel,
the Invisible Man is an autonomous man—living in hiding, it is true,
but exhilarated by his own insights and by the escape from what was
in store for men in gray flannel suits or members of the Brotherhood
or Harlem Separatists.

Saul Bellow's *The Adventures of Augie March* is another 1950s classic that breaks the naturalistic mold while maintaining close contact
with those naturalistic staples that win audiences over time—solid atmosphere, a character involved with more than his own psychological
conflicts, a style that is idiomatic yet not easily dated. Like Ellison's
book, Bellow's story bypasses the plodding, predictable journey
through the character's mistakes—and the inevitable collapse into resignation and maturity. One of the most buoyant stories in our literary
canon, the book is about the things a young man does in order to
avoid making peace with mediocrity. The Invisible Man battles the
mind-forged manacles that reduce his human stature; Augie battles the
usual life chances for a boy from the South Side of Chicago. While the
neighborhood boys sink or thrive during the Depression—stumble
into crime or misery, or grab one of a limited number of dull opportunities—Augie is unencumbered man, free of clear goals or desires of
any sort. His story belongs in the long tradition of the bildungsroman,
but it differs from many of the great tales of youthful aspiration and
growth in that its hero is not preparing to be an artist or a writer. Augie's gift is a more generalized ability to resist the usual options for an

American boy of his class; such an endowment makes him that most expansive of types—a free American. In order to reach this destiny he begins an apprenticeship with an influential old man in the neighborhood, William Einhorn, "the first superior man I knew." Confined to a wheelchair in the stronghold of his Chicago apartment, Einhorn conducts a fabulous array of small-time schemes and business ventures. Augie becomes his boy of all work, attendant, gofer. The old gent is an autodidact, worldly philosopher, tinkerer with inventions, and dispenser of advice and small jobs and handouts. He represents the spirit of enterprise, Emersonian self-help with a measure of tricksterism and just-inside-the-law shadiness. He lives by Francis Bacon's quotations—"ideas of what makes the man this and that"—and offers Augie the example of the practical intelligence in action. A Hephaestus forging his own tools of survival, he passes on his basic message to his protégé: the world gives a little in some places and resists in others; to learn those places is to live well. Augie becomes Einhorn's Alcibiades, neither a low-down product of his environment nor a laughable Luftmensch. His modus vivendi becomes Einhornian in the best sense: a life-availing, "world gypping" protest against determinism.

With the depressing elements of the 1930s at hand—including the dire poverty of the March family, visits from the city caseworker, grudging handouts from Grandma Lausch (an old Russian boarder who talks of her life among the Russian intellectuals and patronizes the poor Marches)—one would think that Bellow's tone would be fatalistic. In fact the book is Dickensian in its wit and its profusion of types—and like Dickens's novels complexly layered in its social vision. As it details the foreground of family poverty, the middle ground with its Chicago rascals, punks, nut jobs, swells, and rich bitches, its background with ideas of the self and allusions to philosophy and history, it has too much variegated life and too many conflicting thoughts to be a one-track study of entrapment or desperation in the city.

Augie moves easily from family alliances to neighborhood affairs to the larger world of ideas and abstractions—and then he moves back again. Never forgetting his ambition to be free, unspecialized, and open to experience, he avoids the ball and chain of his brother Simon's success and prosperity in the coal business; he also avoids—although he briefly tastes—the bottom-dog life of the crook. His list of roles and occupations from childhood to maturity is more picaresque than focused in the Horatio Alger style: "I didn't want to be . . . deter-

mined," he says. And so he wasn't. He started as the family's interme-
diary with the city welfare agencies, became an assistant newsdealer, a
dime-store clerk, a Santa's elf in a department store, Einhorn's assistant, assistant to a prizefight manager, assistant to thieves (in two
cases), shoe salesman, salesman in an elegant sporting-goods store,
smuggler of illegal aliens, book thief, coal dealer, labor organizer,
explorer and eagle-trainer, writer's collaborator, merchant seaman,
dealer in army surplus. Augie's rant against determinism says a great
deal about the Bellovian philosophy of life:

> And it's perfectly true, you have to be one of these spirits that get as if
> jumped into and driven far and powerfully by a social purpose. If some-
> body is needed to go and lie under the street, you be it. Or in a mine.
> Or work out joyrides in a carnival. Or invent names of new candy. Or
> electroplate babies' shoes. Or go around and put cardboard pictures of
> bims in barbershops and saloons. Or die in one subdivided role or an-
> other, with one or two thoughts, these narrow, persistent ideas of your
> function.

In place of these constraints Augie wants to awaken to the "axial lines"
in his life. Bellow has his protagonist lay claim to a heritage for the
self that has a Blakean grandeur:

> I must have had a feeling since I was a kid about these axial lines which
> made me want to have my experience on them, and so I have said "no"
> like a stubborn fellow to my persuaders . . . lately I have felt these thrill-
> ing lines again. When striving stops, there they are as a gift . . . they
> suddenly went quivering straight through me. Truth, love, peace,
> bounty, usefulness, harmony! . . . At any time life can come together
> again and man be regenerated, and doesn't have to be a god or public
> servant like Osiris who gets torn apart annually for the sake of the com-
> mon prosperity, but the man himself, finite and tapered as he is, can still
> come where the axial lines are. He will be brought into focus. He will
> live with true joy.

Augie's pal from the municipal college, Padilla, the math wiz and book
thief, puts this philosophy of instinctual understanding this way:
"Easy or not at all." Augie's own formulation is this: "The world is
held for you. So I don't want to be representative or exemplary or
head of my generation or any model of manhood." What he wants is
to "breathe the pointy, star-furnished air at its highest difficulty."

That difficulty is the complexity and wonder of life, the oddity and incongruity of human behavior—the mystery of things. It is not the taking on of ordinary burdens, allegiances, and obligations. I DON'T WANT TO BE DETERMINED is his motto.

Bellow's style—whether in the service of characterizing or creating atmosphere—is also detached from the determined world of the naturalistic recorders. His wild combinations—scholarly allusion and racy diction, high romanticism and aspiration alongside street smarts, poetic elaboration mixing with commonsensical directness—set him apart from the star players of the bestseller lists; the element of surprise—rather than the meticulous piling up of the predictable—is his hallmark. A Bellow sentence is an explosion of possibilities rather than a pursuit of something inevitable. Consider this group portrait of the students at the municipal college:

> they filled the factory-length corridors and giant classrooms with every human character and germ, to undergo consolidation and become, the idea was, American. In the mixture there was beauty—a good proportion—and pimple-insolence, and parricide faces, gum-chew innocence, labor fodder and secretarial forces, Danish stability, Dago inspiration, catarrah-hampered mathematical genius; there were wax-eared shovelers' children, sex-promising businessmen's daughters—an immense sampling of a tremendous host, the multitudes of holy writ, begotten by West-moving, factor-shoved parents. Or me, the by-blow of a traveling man.

The mix of high and low—the Miltonic ring of "tremendous host" occupying a sentence with "gum-chew innocence"—is only part of the effect. Harsh and idealistic also run together ("by-blow" and "factor-shoved" in the same stream as "genius" and "inspiration"). The blunt and the elegant—"pimple insolence" and "multitudes of holy writ"—are also here. What is not here is the piling up of a single effect—the hammering effect of the naturalist. Bellow's gift is a strange, almost seventeenth century blending of the idiomatic and the exquisitely literary: in an especially fine passage he paints in two modes—one like Poussin, the other like Reginald Marsh. Here Augie thinks about the idea of childhood, that time of "silken, unconscious, nature painted" pastoral before the "vice and shortcoming" of later life:

> But when there is no shepherd-Sicily, no free-hand nature-painting, but deep city vexation instead, and you are forced early into deep city aims,

not sent in your ephod before Eli to start service in the temple, nor set on a horse by your weeping sisters to go and study Greek in Bogota, but land in a poolroom—what can that lead to of the highest? And what happiness or misery-antidote can it offer instead of pipes and sheep or musical, milk-drinking innocence, or even merely nature walks with a pasty instructor in goggles, or fiddle lessons?

The curious wit and light touch have the effect of drawing us before a dismal aspect of life, but not dragging us down with plodding diction. This is Bellow's great gift in Augie: hard facts exposed with vivacity. Lionel Trilling felt that such facts were valued too highly by the liberal promoters of naturalism. Bellow—at once the frank speaker and the poet—knows how to make us feel something new about the old hard facts. Witness a little description of an industrial landscape during the Depression: "big, sad, comfortless." Soon the phrase is followed by a lapidary summation: "there is a darkness, it is for everyone."

But *The Adventures of Augie March* is also about adventures—in universities, whorehouses, lock-ups, and swell hotels. It makes 1953 a landmark year in American literary history.

Bernard Malamud's *The Magic Barrel* broke out of the predictable world of the naturalists in an entirely different way from *Augie March*: both books use the staples of Jewish-American poverty in an earlier era. Bellow is the delicate and elaborate stylist, deploying his erudition, his vast range of cultural allusions, and his fabulous command of incongruities. Malamud is a plain stylist, employing the direct diction of the teller of folktales. His barrel of tales is also quite different in notation and tone from Bellow's adventures. Augie confronts the contemporary, the hip and fashionable, the immediate, and the socially relevant; Malamud's characters live in American cities, but they seem to have transformed the cityscape into a New World shtetl, complete with old oppressions and terrors. The idiom is that of Eastern European Jews learning English or the plain language of the children of immigrants, not Bellow's wised-up, intellectually charged Chicagoese. And Malamud never lets his people forget their past. Augie March's "easy or not at all" should be rewritten as "difficult, or forget it" for a Malamud epigram. The characters inhabit dismal rooms, traverse oppressive streets, climb endless flights of stairs, and work in graveyard businesses. Yet the book mixes miracles with miseries; the typical protagonist lives in a folktale atmosphere where blessings and devastations appear without any of the logic associated with the realistic short story.

Take the elements of a Malamud plot: implausibilities, the actions of off-beat characters who commune with the supernatural and the fantastic, surreal sequences and dreams mixed with the smells of food and references to money. The title story melds fantasy and hard fact. In some twenty pages we watch a young rabbinical student named Leo Finkel go through the dizzying process of finding a suitable bride. The most striking feature of his search is that the matchmaker be employs, the elf-like Pinye Saltzman, is more than a commercial middleman. Malamud lifts us above the world described by Freud in his treatment of matchmaker jokes, a section in *Jokes and Their Relationship to the Unconscious*: the traditional arranger of romance was the conventional worldling with an answer for everything; shameless and endlessly re-sourceful, he could pursue a deal in the face of any obstacle. Mala-mud's Saltzman is all this and a supernatural manipulator of destinies as well. Whereas most matchmakers deal in the here and now—and in every cliché about compatibility—Saltzman deals in the irrational. He realizes that Finkel—a loveless student in desolate Manhattan—doesn't need specifications but the wild card of high romance—a girl who is absolutely not for him on any level of compatibility, but who is a perfect, contradictory, mysterious blend of qualities. Saltzman's barrel of usual eligible women includes one who is highly inappropri-ate, namely his own all-too-experienced daughter. Oddly enough this girl comes across as a "true personality," even in a photograph. The picture "gave him the impression of youth—spring flowers, yet age—a sense of having been used to the bone, wasted." Why is she different from the wasted and life-starved girls he has been shown? "Life," he thinks, "despite their frantic yoohooing had passed them by." The tenement humor and glumness is quintessential Malamud. The mirac-ulous answer to Leo's problem is also a Malamud specialty, a paradox rather than a logical outcome. When Leo first lays eyes on her, there's nothing that fits the pattern of his life. With her red dress and white shoes—not to mention her cigarette and her street-corner pose at a lamppost—she appears to be a hooker rather than a rabbi's wife. Gen-uine passion and attraction emerge from shock and discordance, not from laborious matching of requirements.

Who is Saltzman? An absurd mix of dignity and rascality, a good fairy and an old fox, renewer of lives with a desolate life of his own. Where is his office? Malamud has the old man's wife tell us: "In his socks." That's where miraculous things originate—in the no-place-special of daily life.

The other stories in the volume are by no means all as life-availing as "The Magic Barrel." They tend to fall into two broad categories— tales of romance and tales of loss; the first group, however, is often informed by the same bleakness as the second. "The Lady of the Lake," despite its dreamy title, is a jarring, bitter story about erotic catastrophe. Structurally it resembles "The Magic Barrel," but its emotional impact is worlds apart. A young man who works in Macy's book department decides to go to Italy to find the right woman. Like Finkel, he seems to be emotionally empty, the kind of person who changes his name from Levin to Freeman and wants to change his life accordingly. He has no convictions, and mere good looks and roman- tic ambitions are his only distinguishing marks. At Lake Maggiore he decides to explore the islands, hoping for exotic scenes and perhaps more. Sure enough he runs into a queenly dream girl, apparently the daughter of an aristocratic family living in a splendid villa. Malamud again employs the lynchpin character of the foxy old man, this time a tour guide who wants Freeman to stay with the other tourists and keep away from the villa. But like Leo Finkel, Freeman knows what he wants. The young woman asks him during their first meeting if he is Jewish; because of his phony role as cosmopolitan adventurer, he answers in the negative. In doing so he betrays himself and to his as- tonishment disappoints the girl. She turns out to be the caretaker's daughter and a former inmate of Buchenwald. With deceit in his heart, Freeman has nothing to embrace at the end of the tale but "moonlit stone." He's a loser who missed out on a miracle.

When Malamud depicts a winner, as he does in "The First Seven Years," he puts his man through a grim trial. Poor Sobel, a shoemak- er's helper for five long years, courts the boss's daughter with biblical patience. An old and rather unattractive suitor for a young girl, he uses books to win the girl's affections. We infer his success when we ob- serve her brushing off a rather conventional boy, one of the father's favorite customers. After a date with this cipher, the girl comes home and opens a book. The action nicely foreshadows the symbolic and highly stylized ending: Sobel pounding leather in the shop for another two years to prove his devotion. This miraculous resolution comes right out of the Old Testament.

Sobel's trials have a more hopeful cast than the romantic ordeals of the protagonists in "Take Pity" and "The Girl of My Dreams." Here, each character has allowed his expectations about a woman to drag him from ordinary unhappiness to abject misery. "Take Pity" deals with a coffee salesman named Rosen who wants to help a desperate widow, the inheritor of her husband's failing grocery store. The more he takes pity and offers his money and good advice, the more she rebuffs him. "Rosen, this woman don't like you," a census taker tells him. But he wrecks his life anyway and—in a terrifying scene—sees her apparition staring hostilely at him outside his window. "Happened what happens" is Rosen's devastating summation. In "The Girl of My Dreams," Mitka, a desolate, rejected writer who has burned his manuscript, contacts a woman whose situation seems similar to his. Both of them have written little stories for a paper called the *Globe* and the woman, under the alias Madeleine Thorn—by sheer Malamudian coincidence—has written a clever piece about the destruction of her own manuscript. The real Madeleine turns out to be a sad-sack mama who has lost her twenty-year-old daughter: her stories are all about this tragedy. Mitka, expecting some romance with a kindred spirit, has found one of Malamud's ineligibles, the antithesis of possibility. Mitka's hyperbolic way of dismissing Madeleine is wild and grimly funny and pathetic all at once: "For Madeleine he had this night come out of his burrow, to hold her against his lonely heart, but she had burst into fragments, a meteor in reverse, scattered in the far-flung sky, as he stood below, a man mourning." After hearing the poor woman pleading for companionship (and after he has eaten all the food in her shopping bag), he rejects her in a none-too-gallant way. His punishment is a return to his burrow where he will wind up romancing his pushy, plump landlady rather than the soulful Madeleine.

Yet Malamud's non-romantic tales of desolation are not without their miracles and sea changes. In the midst of terrible loss, there is often an arresting example of reclaiming hope. "The Mourners" deals with a quarrelsome retired egg candler—Malamud likes folkish occupations—who is holed up in his decrepit tenement apartment. Having abandoned his family decades before, Kessler is quite alone and the victim of an impatient landlord who will take no more of his dirty habits and constant complaints. Kessler is soon on the pavement with his pathetic possessions. In a fabulous redemptive scene, he is reinstalled in his room by the sons of an old Italian woman. The landlord Gruber is exasperated to the point of apoplexy, and then suddenly, after having contemplated the situation of his tenant, he "was frightened at the extent of Kessler's suffering." The mystery of pain and wretchedness, of neediness without any charm or grace or excuse, is Malamud's theme. When Gruber finally recognizes what he's confronting—a man mourning for a badly lived life—he falls down and mourns as well.

The Job-like sufferings of a poor tailor named Manishevitz and his sick wife in "Angel Levine" are relieved by an outlandish angel. Not a pitying and contrite ordinary man like Gruber, the Angel Levine is a tango-dancing Harlem character who hangs out in honky-tonks and is in the angel business on the side. "You are Jewish maybe?" asks Manishevitz. This wacky tale of compassion is not only about the healing of the tailor's poor wife, but also about a community of feeling that heals us all.

Malamud's other tales of loss are not as exuberant as "Angel Levine." "The Last Mohican" is about Fidelman, a scholar working in Rome who cannot open his heart to a street character and poor fellow Jew named Susskind. The story of a have and a have-not, a "faithful man" encountering a "sweet child," an all-too-sensible man and a schnorrer, "The Last Mohican" is also about emptiness. Fidelman cannot feel the emotions that are necessary in order to be a brother to Susskind; he sees little connection between this pesty, pushy, needy scamp and himself. He also does his research on Giotto without the necessary feeling for his subject or the understanding of one of the master's most famous frescoes. Only in a dream sequence can he recognize Giotto's theme of charity. Malamud concocts a spectacular blend of Christianity and Judaism, complete with the Dantesque Susskind appearing not as an absurd street character but as "this long nosed brown shade, Virgilio Susskind." In a synagogue, of all places, Fidelman is directed to a fresco by Giotto: "San Francesco don le vesti al cavaliere povero." But by this time all is lost for Fidelman: his briefcase is empty; his manuscript has been burned by Susskind ("The words were there but the spirit was missing"); his chance to be charitable by giving Susskind an old suit has vanished.

There's some hope for the young boy in "A Summer's Reading," but even here Malamud follows the deep currents of frustration, self-deception, and despair. George Stoyonovich is a neighborhood boy who quit high school but nevertheless managed to fool people into thinking he was a big reader. This brilliant, edgy tale of living a lie takes us back to the lie of "The Magic Barrel"—bluffing about the inner life. George wakes up to himself one day and opens a book. Things are grimmer for the storekeeper in "The Prison." At first glance Tommy Castelli's situation would seem to be that of the trapped loser of naturalistic fiction. Yet he has a curious psychological kink in his makeup: a desire to scheme vicariously. A local girl of ten steals candy from him every time she makes a small purchase; and each time this little theft occurs he experiences a thrill that shakes up his otherwise stultifying existence. The life of stealing is in itself a protest against the life-denying, penny-pinching world of his Prince Street store. In the end the child is caught by Tommy's ruthless wife, Rosa. The horrible resolution has the young thief depicted as a "grotesque dancer." With no feeling at all for her sympathetic, basically decent enabler, the child "thrust out at him her red tongue."

Malamud's book is about the collision of the harsh and the gentle; it is a strange mix of raw suffering and tender feeling that protests against the terms of ordinary life. Malamud creates characters who struggle against the brute facts of the naturalistic world—and who are capable of changing and achieving complex recognition; he forces us to see beyond the losses and deprivations. And even when his characters do not achieve a level of decency and compassion and intelligent understanding, we feel that these qualities are credible ideals.

In *A Good Man Is Hard to Find*, Flannery O'Connor's social notation is taken largely from the poverty, ignorance, and fanaticism of the rural South. Out of these she fashioned terrifying accounts of contemporary man's spiritual condition. Stylistically, she belongs with our preceding breakthough writers in that she loves the outlandish, refuses to be confined within the realistic mode, exercises a startling gift for imagery, and commands a formidable moral imagination. She is perhaps closest to Malamud in that they both produce small fables of empty and desperate people who often collide with redemption: down indicators are everywhere in both writers' stories, but promises also abound. It is the rare character who, like Augie March or the Invisible Man, is going places in this world. But that doesn't mean that the author can't lift the reader—and sometimes even the characters—out of despair.

The ten stories in the book have a shock value that is only equaled by their spiritual and ethical resonance. O'Connor's strategy is to terrify the audience into recognition. Her acid wit adds to the total unsettling effect. It goes to work not on folkways and manners—the usual objects of satire—but on character deficiencies and other kinds of smallness and dullness. Along with the shocks and the jabs, the reader gets the revelations—the stories of how people are lost or saved in this world.

The title story is about an inharmonious family taking a trip to Florida. A bored, irritated father, a mother with a face "as broad and innocent as a cabbage," a grandmother gabbing about her genteel past, and two sassy kids proceed on their comic route to death. It seems that the "misfit," a pathological killer, is "aloose"—and for the reader it's just a question of time before he appears. Meantime, we meet ordinary folk who are poorly equipped to see or feel or understand much—spiritual misfits of the non-pathological variety. Bailey, the father, just ignores his family; the grandmother and children provide the ironic and often unintentionally hilarious chatter and quarreling that reveals their shallowness. The old woman is dressed in her best: "In case of an accident, anyone seeing her dead on the highway would know at once that she was a lady." Of a country scene the woman comments: "Oh look at that cute little pickaninny . . . Wouldn't that make a scene now." At a barbecue joint called Red Sammy's she and the proprietor make their own. " 'These days you don't know who to trust,' he said." " 'People are certainly not nice like they used to be,' said the grandmother." Elsewhere she tells a witless tale about an old beau, one Mr. Atkins Teagarden, who brought a watermelon every Saturday to his lady love and also bought Coca-Cola stock when it first came out. The children are nightmarishly rude and disrespectful (hardly the good people the old woman is looking for) and their behavior forms an eerie contrast with the very respectful Misfit, a character met by chance when they are lost. The Misfit's country courtesy and deference are a prelude to horror. The grandmother, in begging for her life, salutes the Misfit's social quality: "You don't look a bit like you have common blood. I know you must come from nice people!"

After hearing more of this—including "you shouldn't call yourself the Misfit because I know you're a good man at heart"—the Misfit gives a chilling account of himself. O'Connor makes him an epigrammist of the demonic, one of her most memorable portraits of contemporary evil. His demented logic shows us how post–World War II terrorists and killers-for-kicks look at the world. Lacking mercy, grace, or faith, he thinks of Jesus as a misfit, someone who upset the balance of the world by raising the dead and performing miracles. Since the Misfit could not make the leap of faith, he chose the anti-faith of nihilism: not knowing for certain that Jesus raised the dead, he chose everything that goes with unbelief. "No pleasure but meanness," as he puts it. The killer's idea is that if faith is not easy and immediately available, unbelief is the natural choice. He is energized by sin. Mindless destruction is his form of creativity: according to his formula, the old lady would have been a good woman "if it had been somebody there to shoot her every minute of her life." O'Connor's madman of course has inadvertently revealed the terms of salvation; he's dimly aware that Jesus' mission was to set an evil world out of balance.

The best of O'Connor's work spooks us with such warped people and bizarre situations: the spiritual charge of the stories comes from the distorted consciousness as it faces sin and guilt. The Christian message—which is a universal message of personal redemption and renewal—is as oddly packaged as a Donne poem: images of violence and degradation are the medium through which we are allowed to perceive salvation. The progress of a Christian soul is painful and terrifying—and filled with bad jokes and wicked ironies at the expense of ordinary, complacent humanity. In "Good Country People," yet another story in which smug ideas of goodness lead to meanness—and meanness awakens the soul to a truer kind of goodness—O'Connor makes sport of several everyday moral idiots and uses them to spring a surprise about belief and faith. Mrs. Hopewell, a great believer in expressions like "Nothing is perfect" and "that is life!" lives with her one-legged daughter, a nasty-natured girl with a PhD, and a hired helper, Mrs. Freeman. The two women drive the daughter crazy with their provincial jabbering. The girl, a philosophy student, is so self-destructive and embittered that she has changed her name from Joy to Hulga. "When Mrs. Hopewell thought the name, Hulga, she thought of the broad blank hull of a battleship." Hulga is given to pronouncing on others' stupidity: to her mother she says, "Woman! do you ever look inside? do you ever look inside and see what you are *not*? God! . . . Malebranche was right: we are not our own light." This outburst serves as an unintentional remark directed at her own condition and destiny. She herself is a spiritual loss, no source of light: a young woman "whose constant outrage had obliterated every expression from her face, who would stare just a little to the side of her, her eyes icy blue, with the look of someone who has achieved blindness by an act of will and means to keep it." Her philosophy of life seems to be some grim reductive version of Existentialism, distilled by a marked passage in one of her books: "Nothing—how can it be for science anything but a horror and a phantasm? If science is right, then one thing stands firm: science wishes to know nothing of nothing." The abyss, the void, the emptiness gave spirit, energy, and courage to Albert Camus. For Hulga nothing produces testiness and spite. When an apparently naive Bible salesman comes to the house and tries to bring his "Chrustian" values to the Hopewells, Hulga sees a chance for an experiment in nothingness. Why not awaken him to the futility of his faith by seducing him, by making him abandon his Christian illusions for "a deeper understanding of life"? The trouble with this nihilistic lesson is that it backfires; the salesman gets the better of Hulga by stealing her artificial leg—and her philosopher's pride as well. In the process he manages to trick Hulga into saying that she believes in love. After first saying we are all damned, she winds up agreeing to prove her love, by of all things revealing her vulnerability. "Show me where your wooden leg joins on," he asks: and once she does, their roles are reversed and he becomes the tricky philosopher. Pathetically begging for decency from a common con artist, begging for good country values from a lowlife, she loses all dignity. His reply to the vanquished intellectual is plain enough: "You ain't so smart. I been believing in nothing ever since I was born!"

O'Connor's other stories also let us see that there is only confusion and meanness in nothing and that we yearn for something. In working out her plots, she manages to terrify and instruct. Her God, like Donne's, batters and ravishes and makes the earth a proving ground, a curious purgatorial place where common sense and complacency and well-being are destroyed. Anthony Burgess's *A Clockwork Orange* depicts characters whose relish for violence and cruelty at first seems like the disorder in the O'Connor world: young Alex and his gang use violence as an antidote to the deadened modern society that surrounds them. On first reading, O'Connor would seem to have the same strategy—only a dose of meanness will wake us up to the fallen world. Gentleness—or any kind of nice reasoning—will produce nothing but further moral confusion. Such a mad cure for what ails modern civilization is of course at the heart of literary modernism: immerse yourself in the destructive element. But unlike Burgess or for that matter Conrad, O'Connor has a Christian mission. She points us—if not her own characters—in the direction of renewal.

O'Connor loves to break down the walls of Southern niceness and find the down-and-dirty emotions behind them. If you hear that someone is decent folks, beware. In "A Circle of Fire" Mrs. Cope is a self-satisfied woman who thanks God for her property; she lives with a housekeeper, Mrs. Pritchett, who is also pleased with herself and

only grateful she's not like the folks you read about—iron lung pa-
tients who won't leave off sex and the like. Meanwhile, Mrs. Cope is
confronted with a menacing group of inner-city boys who come to
her farm to get some sinister kicks and get back at the social system.
These kids are as desperate as Burgess's gang, yet they are regarded
with disgusting condescension and indifference; children of the housing projects, they feel entitled to some fresh air, fun, and happiness—or if nothing else, some revenge. Mrs. Cope offers them a few
crackers and tells them to get off her land. O'Connor gives us Cope's
point of view, but somehow we are uneasy with bland sense and
selfishness. We're also not quite sure whether their laughter is "full of
calculated meanness." As they burn down Mrs. Cope's woods,
O'Connor likens them to "prophets . . . dancing in the fiery furnace."
No matter how we recoil from this tale of destruction—told with
phantasmagoric energy—we can't help but be struck by the truth of
its outcome: a sense of injustice doesn't express itself in attractive
ways, nor does it respond to an offer of crackers. Mrs. Cope couldn't
be further from insight, Christian charity, or any idea of community;
she tells her sensitive young daughter how much they have to be
thankful for, and in so doing, reveals the causes of the violence and
meanness: "they might have had to live in a development themselves
or they might have been Negroes or they might have been in iron lungs
or they might have been Europeans ridden in boxcars like cattle."
(This last reference is an appallingly ignorant woman's way of process-
ing the fact of the Holocaust.) At the end of the story, Mrs. Cope has
to confront her moral obtuseness; she assumes an expression that
"might have belonged to anyone, a Negro or a European" or her main
tormentor among the boys.

Another smug landowner, Mrs. McIntyre in "The Displaced Person," must learn about her own warped moral nature and about
Christ's message through a hideous "accident" involving an employee
on her farm: a poor Polish refugee whom she hires and exploits dies
in "an accident"—and it takes the gruesome death to awaken Mrs. Mc-
Intyre to the fact that the unfortunate man, a displaced person, was
betrayed and killed like Christ himself. Other characters also learn or
are redeemed only in extremis: a grim Christian comedy is played out
as people lose everything worldly and gain spiritual insight. The little
boy in "The River" has to drown himself in order to be baptized. In
"The Life You Save May Be Your Own," Mr. Shiftlet—the name is
heavy with allegorical significance—is a drifter who has abandoned his

brand-new deaf-mute bride. He has left the poor girl in a roadside res-
taurant, only to encounter a reminder of his callousness in the person
of a horrible hitchhiker. He picks up a boy who goes into a brutal
denunciation of his own mother, the kind of total moral letdown that
makes the world itself seem desolate. Shiftlet, as it were, sees another
side of his own meanness. He "felt that the rottenness of the world
was about to engulf him." He asks forgiveness and in doing so makes
the title of the story resonate with a significance that transcends
mere irony. He wants to take leave of his hateful self, all the while
of course knowing that he has ruined his life. "Oh Lord! . . . Break
forth and wash the slime from this earth!" The heavens produce "a
gaffawing peal of thunder from behind and fantastic raindrops, like
tin-can tops."

Moral idiots also abound: the reader does the learning as they stay
locked in their hate and bigotry. Consider the small-souled, pathetic
Sally Poker Sash in "A Late Encounter with the Enemy," a middle-
aged woman who wants her fellow normal-school graduates at com-
mencement to see that she's a descendant of a Civil War general. The
old man—rendered hilariously in all his senility and lecherousness—
imagines he's on his last campaign as he watches the black robes pass
by him. Sally imagines she's making a hit: "She wanted the general at
her graduation because she wanted to show what she stood for, or, as
she said, 'what was behind her,' and was not behind them. This *them*
was not anyone in particular. It was just all the upstarts who turned
the world on its head and unsettled the ways of decent living." Often
the morally obtuse are more menacing. Mr. Head, the nasty old man
in "The Artificial Nigger," has reluctantly gone on a trip with his
grandson because the boy wanted to see his birthplace. During a night
journey through a forbidding city, the grandfather has occasion to
deny knowing the child. "This is not my boy." Can anyone or anything awaken any decency in this old life-denying betrayer? In
O'Connor's world the sight of a Negro lawn jockey made of plaster,
just about the boy's size, does the job:

> They stood gazing at the artificial Negro as if they were faced with
> some great mystery, some monument to another's victory that brought
> them together in their common defeat. They could both feel it dissolv-
> ing their differences like an action of mercy. Mr. Head had never known
> before what mercy felt like because he had been too good to deserve
> any, but he felt he knew now. He looked at Nelson and understood that

he must say something to the child to show that he was still wise and in
the look the boy returned he saw a hungry need for that assurance. Nelson's eyes seemed to implore him to explain once and for all the mystery of existence.

Mr. Head, of course, is incapable of putting his sense of his awakening
into words: he can only tell the boy, "They ain't got enough real ones
here. They got to have an artificial one." The narrator, however, drops
the revelation in a phrase: mercy "grew out of agony." One of our
great image makers and wits, a poetic moralist with a gift for savage
mockery, O'Connor describes the agony of the modern condition in
totally outlandish terms that nevertheless amuse and awaken us to the
goodness that is beyond meanness.

O'Connor's world—like the worlds of Bellow, Ellison, and Malamud—is rich with mystery, unpredictability, and untamable poetic vision. It belongs to a start-up American tradition, a heritage made from
naturalism transformed by phantasmagoria and linguistic gymnastics.
Bellow, the urban poet and flaneur, is immersed in picaresque play,
street smarts, and philosophical questions of identity; Ellison, the
black novelist, is also fascinated by the variousness of his own nature
and determined to move beyond determinism; Malamud is the Jewish
fabulist looking for mercy and redemption; O'Connor is the scarify-
ing Christian poet set on dragging her readers to conversion.

chapter 2

Holden, Dean, and Allen

Another kind of book turned away from the older American story of struggle and hard knocks, from the well-established figures of the victim and the underdog. While Bellow and the other anti-naturalists used demotic language, symbols, and bizarre situations, three other writers found ways to make spontaneity and impulse the center of their art: breathless tones and jagged rhythms are their specialty. J. D. Salinger, Jack Kerouac, and Allen Ginsberg made the energies and moods of youth their master theme, and they each wrote a book that assaulted the reading public with an entirely new version of what it was to be young, besieged by messages from the heart and libido, and overwhelmed by the sounds and spectacles of postwar America. Each writer created an idiom for registering personal experience and for reporting the facts of our national life. The three reeling, dizzying psycho-social classics—*The Catcher in the Rye, On the Road,* and *Howl*—have revolutionized our ideas about the inner life and about social types, popular art, advertising, entertainment, drugs, sex, and relationships. Awakening us to instinct and passion and intense reaction, these three books play the role in modern American culture that great Romantic works such as *Lyrical Ballads* and *Childe Harold's Pilgrimage* played at the beginning of the nineteenth century. They offer a language of their own—purged of the old naturalistic obligation to prove a point, supercharged with invigorating frankness.

The Catcher in the Rye is of course more than a novel. A lightning rod for a new sensibility, a wisdom book for postwar students, a behavior manual for the age of impulse, it has had a life apart from the literary world and cultural worth and staying power beyond its literary value. Inferior in quality to the greatest consciousness-shaping works of American modernism—*The Great Gatsby, The Sun Also Rises, Invisible Man*—it nevertheless has the power to distill states of mind, spark identification, and live beyond its covers. Like certain songs or movie characters, it has become a part of the shared experience of a vast number of people in the second half of the century. People know the book who haven't read it with any care; others—like nineteenth century people who had heard about Mr. Pickwick or Anna Karenina—have heard the news of Holden Caulfield just by being alive. There are Web sites devoted to it; people live by it and, although we live in an un-Arnoldian age, it is probably one of our last remaining literary touchstones—youth and resentment and joy and angst, in book not CD, TV, or net form.

It came out in 1951, not exactly an annus mirabilis for American literature, but not a bad year either. *From Here to Eternity* was also published and became a best seller. The gap between the two books is the gap between an older world of naturalism—with its careful chronicling of injustices and hard luck and hard living—and an entirely new rendering of the American situation: but the distance between Jones's war in the Pacific and Salinger's peace and prosperity is hardly the crucial point; *Catcher* has a language, texture, and view of what counts that places it firmly in America's future; *From Here to Eternity* belongs with the classics of the past. Nineteen fifty-one was not a notable year for cultural change in America, either. Rock 'n' Roll, Brando's motorcycle in *The Wild One*, Dean's red jacket in *Rebel without a Cause*—the spring blossoms of the age of antinomianism—were nowhere in sight. What was plentifully available? Endless anticommunist screeds, anxieties about conformity, books about Social Problems, music that was sentimental and kitschy or part of the wit and heart of old Tin Pan Alley (the obnoxious kid Stradlater in *Catcher* whistles themes from "Song of India" and "Slaughter on Tenth Avenue"), liberal arts students who wanted jobs not ideologies. Salinger's book was the first embraceable book since the war: the first book with an idiom and an attitude of its own that made young people aware of something new about themselves. The novels that were coming out about the war would not quite do the job for these new readers. They needed their own book, something about the younger brothers who were kids at the time of the war. They also needed a book that didn't employ the locutions of the Great Depression, the rhetoric of the left and right, or the language of the war years, whether the staunchly patriotic slogans of the majority or the disaffected idioms of the isolationists among the intellectuals and the America Firsters.

At first blush Salinger's novel—a younger brother's account of himself—seems like a reinvention of a familiar story in earlier twentieth century literature: like *Winesburg, Ohio,* or *Look Homeward,*

Angel, or even Hemingway's Nick Adams stories, it's about a lonely young boy who thinks there is something wrong with the world, something essentially dead and phony and disgusting about the arrangement of things. But once linked with these books, *Catcher* detaches itself, for the most part since it is not a story about development. Holden Caulfield has no unfolding destiny, no mission—not even the dramatic moments of Nick in battle or Eugene Gant overcoming his mother's influence. Holden is a drifter whose life story is a muddle, a series of pathetic, comic, poignant incidents that are altogether unlike the destiny-building of the earlier books. Salinger turns against "that David Copperfield kind of crap"—and most other patterns as well. The book is antiliterary in a new way. Its pages are filled with babbling rather than talk that builds to a climax, impressions that are overtaken by afterthoughts, comic contradictions, half recognitions, and canceled insights. While sharing the basic subject of Hemingway and Anderson—lonely youth—Salinger invents a mode of his own: a managed incoherence, an attractive breakdown of logic that appeals to the confused adolescent in all of us. Sweeping denunciations are followed by abject apologies—only to be followed by other ridiculous pronouncements. Holden the muttering self fires off Holdenism after Holdenism. Try one of these: "I'm quite illiterate, but I read a lot." Or, "I hate the movies like poison, but I get a bang out of imitating them." Or, "A horse is at least human, for God's sake." Or, "The show wasn't as bad as some I've seen. It was on the crappy side, though." Or, "Listen. What's the routine on joining a monastery?"

Holden's idiom is the novel's glory, the property that has appealed to audiences for fifty years. A blend of explosive denunciation and heart-on-sleeve sentiment, it maintains a high tension for a little over two hundred pages. Since Salinger employs only the thinnest of plots—a linking of loosely connected incidents in Holden's downward journey—the rambling, ranting, and rhapsodizing are the main events. The idiom takes over as Holden's speech becomes the central conflict. How will he react next? We lurch from aperçu to aperçu, epigram to epigram—all of them drawing on carefully chosen contrasts: the boy's rendering of his world employs popular culture and classic literature, upper middle class taste and a thorough knowledge of urban tackiness, refinement and grossness, tender solicitude and harsh condemnation. The book is charged and energetic to the end because it never quite settles into a consistent point of view. As exasperating as this may be for readers who want character logic and clear motivation, the scattered remarks and volatility of the prose have taken hold. Its unreasoned judgments have also dug deep into our consciousness and connected with the unexplainable part of our lives. Can we account for irritation, repulsion, contempt? Are there clearly drawn correlatives for Holden's disgust, anger, and disillusionment? Do we have any evidence that the people he mocks are quite as pathetic as he would have it? Ackley with his pimples and bragging about sex, Stradlater with his dapper appearance and swagger, Sally Hayes with her hard-edged practicality and her little ice-skating skirt, the out-of-towners Marty and Laverne at the Lavender Lounge with their grammar errors and their gawking at celebrities? Are they enough to warrant Holden's *contemptu mundi*? If you have followed the crazy reasoning, listened to Holden's standards—sincerity, kindness, dignity—you will follow such judgments. These people are pathetic, either phonies or flops.

Holden's discontents and diatribes are infectious because we all have our irascibility and fastidiousness, and Salinger has managed to play on us by summoning up the perfect, grating details. Like Browning or Dickens, he has an extensive inventory of annoyances and human weaknesses, stupid locutions, and exasperating habits. The book is a treasury of the ludicrous, and its absurdities remain fresh a half-century later. Take Pencey's headmaster with his forced jokes and his toadying to rich parents; or the man at Radio City who says of the Rockettes "that's precision"; or Sally Hayes conspicuously embracing a gray-flanneled acquaintance as if they were "old buddyroos." Recall some Dickens characters—despite Holden's impatience with *David Copperfield*—and you will be in the same literary territory: Pecksniff with his "moral throat," Fagin's "my dear," Pumblechook with his hectoring. Like Dickens, Salinger has a masterful command of pretensions. At the Wicker Bar, Holden observes the singer, "Old Janine": "And now we like to geeve you our impression of Vooly Voo Fransay. Eet ess the story of a leetle Fransh girl who comes to a beeg ceety, just like New York, and falls in love wees a leetle boy from Brookleen." He captures the manner of Carl Luce, a blasé intellectual, with dead-on accuracy: "He never said hello or anything when he met you. The first thing he said when he sat down was that he could only stay a couple of minutes." There's no place quite like *Catcher* for savoring the cant and swill of contemporary life: "Newsreels. Christ almighty. There's always a dumb horse race, and some dame breaking a bottle over a ship, and some chimpanzee riding a goddam bicycle with pants on."

But once you have had your fill of Holden denouncing anything and everything, you naturally wonder what it all amounts to. Does Salinger deliver any real insight, any recognition? Is it all clever shtick or carefully managed nastiness? Are the *mots* a kind of superior talk radio? Pure spleen hasn't much staying power—negativism, as Cyril Connolly once remarked, dates quickly. But *Catcher* mixes its cynicism and irascibility with a rich brew of sentiment and idealism, a childlike faith that life contains more than pretensions and phoniness. In some ways it is more a wisdom book than a novel, a collection of pronouncements about living well and discovering useable truths. After thundering at the world, it offers compact packages of insight. Holden, the comic instructor incapable of running his own life, proposes exempla for his listeners: he's the half-cracked adviser who gets our attention by the strange slant of his doctrines. The most affecting doctrine of course is that of the Catcher in the Rye: this teaching—which twists Robert Burns's line from "meet" to "catch" is a typical Holdenism; half-informed, but totally emphatic, it produces meaning in the midst of confusion. It takes a highly recognized poem, mixes childish naivete with the poetry and mangles the original sense. The result is a curious restatement of the New Testament doctrine of thy brother's keeper: your mission in life is to catch little children before they fall off the cliff. No sooner do you see the odd simplicity and innocence of the doctrine's packaging than you recognize its powerful connection with other such statements in world literature. Salinger, by redesigning a sentiment about love and mercy and the innocence of children, takes a modest but quite definite place in the romantic movement; his imagery—either the figure of the child (Phoebe Caulfield or the little boy who sings a snatch from "Comin' through the Rye") or crowds of children endangered—is strongly reminiscent of Blake's language in *Songs of Innocence and Experience*. His moment of pure joy at first reminds us of Blakean joy. Looked at from a Blakean point of view, it's the all-but-incoherent utterance of the innocent, for example the voice in "Infant Joy": "I happy am / Joy is my name.—/ Sweet joy befall thee!" But the more specific insight of *Catcher* is a lesson out of Wordsworth.

The doctrine of *Catcher* is presented in Salinger's characteristic spatterdash, free-associational way. In a scene with Phoebe, he enunciates his position, but does so by raking through the past and stumbling on truth: the emotional truth of the Catcher "comes" to Holden—as it has to Romantic poets, to the Wordsworth of "Resolution and Independence"—after he has reviewed the spectacle of himself, rejected that self and the world that made it, and by chance discovered truth embodied in the quotidian, in the unproclaimed and unproclaiming world of everydayness; that truth is distilled in the actions of the nuns collecting for their order at the station, in the schoolteacher who mercifully covered the body of a young suicide—and in the sacred actions of Holden's dead brother Allie. Like Wordsworth, Salinger favors the didactic colloquy as a prelude to emotional awakening. A teacher—without a schoolroom of course—prepares the pupil for the recognition. The leech gatherer in Wordsworth, an old man who endures despite poverty and the harshness of the environment, has a few direct simple words—"apt admonishment" for a narrator who is depressed and caught in a web of self-absorption; he has his message, his example, his acceptance of life. Salinger's Phoebe Caulfield has her childish insights to offer an older brother caught in a similar emotional crisis.

Salinger, like Wordsworth, prefers a symbolic action or a dramatic scene to reasoning or mere words. Holden listening to Phoebe's childish jabbering and the narrator of "Resolution and Independence" listening to the old man's sparse advice: each character is more influenced by action than words. And each work is carried by spectacle and scene rather than by doctrine. Talk is important, but reasoned explanation will not yield insight. The last dramatic scene of *Catcher* shows Phoebe riding the carousel in Central Park, reaching for the gold ring. The depiction includes Holden's reaction—a joyous response, something that cannot be accounted for with logic or examination of motive: "I felt so happy all of a sudden, the way old Phoebe kept going around and around. I was so damn near bawling, I felt so happy, if you want to know the truth." In its way this is our literature's most memorable equivalent of Wordsworth's great awakening scenes: the discovery of joy and heightened understanding and the capacity to identify with others who are experiencing instinctual pleasure or fulfillment or satisfactory endurance. "By our spirits are we deified," Wordsworth put it. The awakening is like John Stuart Mill's famous recognition scene in the *Autobiography:* Mill's own depression lifted when he discovered the inner sense of Wordsworth's poetry. "What made Wordsworth's poems a medicine for my state of mind was that they expressed, not mere outward beauty, but states of feeling, and of thought coloured by feeling, under the excitement of beauty." Hard as it is to think of human feeling as a news item at the millennium—after nearly two hundred years of writers, poets, singers, and attitudinizers prying out the meaning of emotions—it seems new when Salinger is the investigator. Holden watching his sister has given contemporary American literature a moment like that of "Resolution and Independence" and that of Mill emerging from his despondency: the melancholy observer awakens to the joy of life by observing another's deep involvement in some form of release or reclamation. Mill calls the process of his awakening through poetry "the culture of the feelings." In reading the poems, "I seemed to draw from a source of inward joy, of sympathetic and imaginative pleasure, which could be shared in by all human beings." When Holden Caulfield was so happy he felt like "bawling," he wanted to pass on the elation—"God, I wish you could've been there." Be it said that the source of newfound joy— the culture of the feelings—is a child on a carousel, not a series of poems. Renewal in the twentieth century is the raw experience of being in the midst of life, colliding with joy and not wanting to account for why or wherefore; Mill's highly analytic account of renewal through the cultivation of feelings assumes a world where the individual moves easily among books and abstract ideas and ordinary experiences.

The mystery of emotional awakening is Salinger's main obsession in the book; his fear is that the discovery he has made—the connection between the innocent wise child and joyous renewal—will in some way be mocked or cheapened or otherwise devalued. Or generalized about or analyzed. He also fears himself and his all-too-human capacity to traduce his own vision. Afraid to publish, afraid of fame and publicity and critics and adapters and biographers, afraid of the sentiment that he himself has dispersed, he has become an elderly Holden, AWOL from the responsibility to give an account of himself; in Salinger's case he has bitterly resisted the responsibilities of authorship as we generally recognize it—including the obligation to be heard periodically. *Catcher*—since its publication—has been its author's holy book, never to be defiled by stage, screen, or other profane equivalencies. As any reader of Ian Hamilton's book on Salinger will easily recognize, the protectiveness of this author for his property is something well beyond author's rights. And the book itself is its own defense against cheapness and meanness; hardly a sentence passes without the narrator's making sure that he is not falling into the ways of the world.

Holden wants to immunize himself against corny rhetoric by employing every kind of hard-boiled phase and cynical dismissal that the publishers of 1951 would permit. The scenes of pure joy and transcendence come in the main near the end of a book that has taken devastating aim at the cheap emotionalism, histrionics, sappy effects, warm and fuzzy recognition scenes in movies, books, and life. The author has his own defensive tactics—whatever it takes to keep the sacred texts from being defiled.

Salinger's ideas of joy and renewal should be seen against the backdrop of Hollywood schlock: the awkward, hand-designed, and naive sentiment stands out against the formulaic and corny. Askew and spontaneous, the story line is far from the calculated mass product that Holden remembers from the movies. Contrast it, for example, with his favorite love-to-hate movie *Random Harvest* (1942), a tale of renewal about an Englishman who suffers from amnesia after the war. Holden tells us (with much distortion and invention) that the character "Alec" staggers around on a cane until he meets a "homey babe" who wants to rejuvenate him, share her love of Dickens—as well as get help in her floundering publishing business, badly needed since her cracked-up surgeon brother has been spending the profits. The complications—involving Alec's ducal status and his other girlfriend—are hilariously related (and embroidered) by Holden, whose own complications have none of the factitious neatness of this sort of plot. "Anyway it ends up with Alec and the homey babe getting married . . . All I can say is don't see it if you don't want to puke all over yourself." Hollywood in this case is the culprit, but elsewhere human feeling is mangled by the cant of prep-school teachers, New York sophisticates, phony intellectuals, doting upper middle class parents, even earlier writers. Dickens's David Copperfield crap is the best hint of all about Salinger's ambition to achieve his own breakthrough. True to the great project of Romanticism, *Catcher* throws off the meretricious past, purifies its spirit with a new diction, tone, and objects of attention. The decorum of earlier literature disappears, along with the dignity and seriousness and measured speech of modernist heroes like Jake Barnes or Jay Gatsby. In the carousel scene, the rain pours down and mixes with "Smoke Gets in Your Eyes" and "Oh Marie" and the spectacle of Holden in his hunting hat. No Frederic Henry here. The manic mode cannot and will not account for a hero, unpack clear causes, or offer careful delineations. The literary tradition is something to get a kick out of—the way Holden does from Hardy's Eustachia Vye—but not something to talk about much, or follow much. When Salinger taught writing at Columbia, he was disdainful of the whole notion of classroom analysis of works. Just read them. We murder to dissect. We even murder to account for or scrutinize.

This contempt for analysis and tracing of literary filaments from the past does not mean that the book fails to champion other disciplines. The central doctrine of the book—that each of us has a Catcher in the Rye lodged within—implies a strict code for living. In its ramshackle way, *Catcher* is a conduct book for the age of anxiety and conformity. No section of the book goes by without its precepts, prohibitions, and practical tips for cant-free living. It is one of the first manuals of cool, a how-to guide for those who would detach themselves from the all-American postwar pursuit of prosperity and bliss. Holden the dropout and outsider speaks like some crazed, half-literate Castiglione as he discourses on everything from clothing and bearing to the appropriate responses of a cool person. The following precepts are crucial:

- Ignore the messages of mass media ("The goddamn movies. They can ruin you.")
- Dream of a life in New England with a mute for your companion.
- Be "casual as hell."
- Avoid any air of superiority or trace of competitiveness.
- Value digressions more highly than logical arguments.
- Never use the word "grand."
- Scorn routine sociability.
- Observe the margins of life: the remarks of children, the conduct of nuns.
- Ignore the main acts. (The guy who plays the kettle drums at Radio City Music Hall is more important than the "Christmas thing" with "O Come All Ye Faithful.")

After fifty years these teachings remain a part of our culture. Young people—and their fearful elders—know that coolness is the only way. Formal discourse, sequential thinking, reverence for the dignified and the heroic: these acts closed by the 1960s. The voice of Holden played a part in shutting them down. Its tone—directed against prestige and knowingness—is as cutting today as it was in 1951: "I could see them all sitting around in some bar with their goddamn checkered vests, criticizing shows and books and women in those tired, snobby voices." Cancel the checkered vests and you're at the millennium.

But for all its durability, does *Catcher* continue to make sense to the mature mind? Is it infantile and simplistic, reductive and negative—the attitude of a kid who is soon to get the therapy he needs? One can only say that the scorn for conventions and the search for joy are a part of the ongoing Romantic project that started in the eighteenth century. Exasperating, irrational, and dangerous as these pursuits have sometimes proven, they show no signs of shutting down. Salinger's ardor and disdain have a bracing quality of their own, inferior to that of the great romantic artists but nevertheless still important at a time when we need to resist our own age of reason, its monoliths and abstract ideas of human progress. With its horror of groupthink of all kinds—be it remembered that, like George Orwell, the Salinger of *Catcher* has nothing good to say about politics, power blocks, commercial modernity, or any orthodoxy—the book is free of the worst tendencies of the late 1940s. Like Orwell, Salinger has profound respect for the decencies, pleasures, and truths that can be found anywhere. But unlike Orwell, Salinger is an anti-Enlightenment weaver of fantasies and denouncer of hard-headedness. If truth be told, his Blakean celebration of joy and wonder foreshadowed the wooliness of beatniks and hippies—and would become flabby and sententious in the Glass Family stories of the late 1950s. While Franny and Zooey's complaints about civilization are preachy and humorlessly tiresome, Holden's negativity remains wonderfully fresh in its inconsistency. He remains a bearer of a permanent truth: that you can't fake an affectional life; that you must live through absurdity, indignity, and pain in order to get a small return of happiness.

The other knockout post–World War II novel about the consciousness of youth is Jack Kerouac's *On the Road*. As a story about breaking out of the patterns of ordinary life—not being in school or working or married with a child—it seems to fulfill a central fantasy in *Catcher*: escaping to someplace, any place, where you can spontaneously savor America. Holden wanted Sally Hayes, the Park Avenue twit, to run off with him and start life in a cabin in the woods; Kerouac's young men and women get away continuously, turning Holden's idyll into a frantic joyride. A travel-cum-wisdom book about discovering pleasure and energy, it has several things in common with *Catcher*—an arresting narrative voice, a disregard for plot line, and a spatterdash way of delivering its recognitions. One of its central rec-

ognitions about the world of postwar America is very close to Holden
Caulfield's disillusionment with bored, blasé phonies: one must get
away from civilized pretensions. "Besides, all my New York friends
were in the negative, nightmare position of putting down society and
giving their tired bookish or political or psychoanalytical reasons, but
Dean just raced in society, eager for bread and love."

Once said, however, the qualities of the book contrast markedly
with those of *Catcher*. Sal Paradise, Kerouac's narrator and alter ego,
is our tour guide through a land of plenty, a late 1940s country where
almost everything is worth digging. Holden is our classic naysayer: a
specialist in frustration and a master of the put-down, he is as far as
one can get from Kerouac's cool connoisseur of the towns, the bars,
and the chicks. Pleasure flows off the pages in *On the Road*; everything—beautiful girls, delicious food, profound ideas—is there for the
taking. In *Catcher*, pleasure is on the margins, most sensations to be
rejected by fastidious Holden. Holden picks most people and popular
experiences apart; he actually has some of his best moments when he
goes the bored metropolitan cynics one better by delivering his own
cutting lines. What has he been for most of the book, after all, but
someone—to use Kerouac's terms—who puts society down? No
bread and love—in the Rabelaisian sense of joyous Epicureanism—for
him. But Kerouac's characters savor treasures and trash—midget auto
races and philosophy, the cheesiest kinds of popular culture and the
teachings of elitists. They are never standoffish—even about discours-
ing intellectuals, prosperous middle class types, tony Englishmen like
the jazz pianist George Shearing. They dig it all. And they are hardly
ever tired.

Kerouac's book is essentially about the discharging of energy—
automotive, sexual, and verbal. Going and coming and expressing are
much more important than any realization or recognition. It begins
when its narrator Sal Paradise reached an impasse in his life: "my life
hanging around the campus had reached the completion of its cycle
and was stultified . . . ." It soon proceeds to a kind of "franticness"
that makes Salinger's book seem like a holiday sightseeing tour for the
middle aged. Once wound up by Dean Moriarty, the only thing that
can dull Sal's appetite for movement and variety is a fever caught down
in Mexico. *Catcher* brings us to some resting place, some point of
higher understanding and joy. *On the Road* literally comes to an end
on its final page, but the reader leaves the book and feels that he is still
in motion. Every episode is swallowed up by the next thing, which in

turn is forgotten once Sal Paradise and his friend of the road Dean
Moriarty collide with the next experience. Nothing can quite be savored, because savoring involves reflection and comparison and memory—it's not the same as digging. Holden Caulfield—scattered as he
is—is capable of reflection; the characters in *On the Road* dig this or
that—Mexican girls, somebody's poetry, a city, or a sky—but the object that is dug evaporates a page later. And everything does seem to
blur into everything else. Kerouac's narrator is not a resistor, not a
creator of conflict between himself and friends, between himself and
his environment. With so much to say yes to, we forget the power of
no—or put another way, we lose the problems and obstacles that give
structure to a story. The book is an Odyssey of sorts—with some per-
ils, but few tears; strange sights, most of which are not malign; more
friends than enemies; Mexican thrills and drugs, but no Ithaca.

Sal and Dean are all exhilaration—and Kerouac's great gift is for
phrasing the terms of their energy. Nothing is recollected in tranquil-
ity, but a great deal is recorded with frantic exuberance. The book is
all highs, climaxes without any conflicts that accumulate or mean anything. There is not enough of the stultifying world to make us quite
appreciate the energy. But Kerouac succeeds on a page-here-a-page-
there level—in fits and starts—because of his extraordinary gift for
phrasing the terms of excitement and change and movement. The cu-
mulative effect is numbing, but the moment-to-moment effect of his
prose has made him a memorable narrative poet of sheer undigested
experience. His peaks are in every chapter of the five-part book—and
like the towns across America that he breathlessly characterizes, they
"unreel with dreamlike rapidity."

Some of the best sections are descriptions of riding or dashing
around, listening to music, or chasing women. His new pal-hero Dean,
a prison veteran with the physical presence of Gene Autry, has a kind
of "criminality" that is a "wild yea-saying outburst of American joy."
He calls himself a "hotrock capable of everything at the same time"
("and I have unlimited energy"). Elsewhere Sal puts the awesomeness
of Dean this way: "If you touched he would sway like a boulder sus-
pended on a pebble on a precipice of a cliff. He might come crashing
down or just sway rocklike. Then the boulder exploded into a flower
and his face lit up with a lovely smile." Comic grandeur is also part of
Dean's impact: "It was like the imminent arrival of Gargantua; prepa-
rations had to be made to widen the gutters of Denver and foreshorten
certain laws to fit his suffering bulk and bursting energies." Sal catches

the wave of Dean's "mad-to-live" personality and tells us what it's like
to be a disciple. Sal and he understand each other on "levels of madness," which is to say that the logic of ordinary relationships does not
apply. "Jailkid" Dean introduces college boy Sal to the thrills of a life-
time, introduces him to digging a world that he previously only tried
to understand. (He also abandons Sal—who has become sick inconve-
niently—in Mexico at the end of the book.) Dean has other followers,
and Sal tags along:

> But then they danced down the streets like dingledodies, and I sham-
> bled after as I've been doing all my life after people who interest me,
> because the only people for me are the mad ones, the ones who are mad
> to live, mad to talk, mad to be saved, desirous of everything at the same
> time, the ones who never yawn or say a commonplace thing, but burn,
> burn, burn like fabulous yellow roman candles exploding like spiders
> across the stars.

His characterization only really works for Dean: the other "dingledo-
dies"—Bull Lee (aka William Burroughs), Carlo Marx (aka Allen
Ginsberg)—are lost in the tornado of Dean's comings and goings.

His own life becomes a kind of running from one falling star to
another. Or taking a flatboard ride across the Plain States, arguably
one of the most successful passages in the book:

> The greatest ride in my life was about to come up, a truck, with a flat-
> board at the back, with about six or seven boys sprawled on it, and the
> drivers, two young blond farmers from Minnesota, were picking up
> every single soul they found on that road—the most smiling, cheerful
> couple of handsome bumpkins you could ever wish to see, both wearing
> cotton shirts and overalls, nothing else; both thick-wristed and earnest,
> with broad howareyou smiles for anybody and anything that came
> across their path.

The Minnesota farm boys who are driving are going to L.A. The rest
are along for the ride. "What are you going to do there?" "Hell, we
don't know. Who cares?" Under the stars Sal has one of his many
recognitions about the nature of energy: "I felt like an arrow that
could shoot out all the way." On the flatboard his fellow travelers include the hobo Mississippi Gene and a withdrawn kid—"so sad and
gone"—whom he's protecting, probably from the law. Their slow and
quiet manners contrast quite effectively with the velocity of the ride.

And Sal's nature itself is endearingly affected by the feelings of the moment: "They had no cigarettes. I squandered my pack on them, I loved them so." Once the student at loose ends, Sal becomes a connoisseur of the road, someone who likes boxcars more than fine wines.

Music and musicians are another source of the book's excitement. Kerouac's prose competes with the jazz rhythms and provides some of the best passages. Take the set piece on George Shearing at Birdland. It begins quietly as "a distinguished looking Englishman with a stiff white collar, slightly beefy, blond, with a delicate English-summer's night air about him" plays " a rippling sweet number." But soon Shearing began "to rock," and the passage rocks with him:

> slowly at first, then the beat went up, and he began rocking fast, his left foot jumped with every beat, his neck began to rock crookedly, he brought his face down to the keys, he pushed his hair back, his combed hair dissolved, he began to sweat. The music picked up. The bass-player hunched over and socked it in, faster and faster, it seemed faster and faster, that's all.

All this, we are told, took place in 1949 before Shearing became "cool and commercial." Intense energy, evidently, is the desired commodity. There's plenty available when Slim Galliard performs at a little club in Frisco. This sad-eyed black man plays piano, bongos, and guitar and specializes in igniting his audience by moving from all but imperceptible noises on the bongos to mad outbursts in which "he plays tremendous rapid Cubana beats and yells crazy things in Spanish, in Arabic, in Peruvian dialect, in Egyptian, in every language he knows." He also goes in for screaming out nonsense words—"hello-orooni . . . bourbon-orooni . . . all-orooni."

In the spring of 1949, Sal and Dean are in Denver in "the warm, mad night" of little Harlem where they hear a tenorman "blowing at the peak of a wonderfully satisfactory free idea." That tenorman "had it" and "blew down a hoarse, baughing blast, and drew breath, and raised the horn and blew high, wide, and screaming in the air." Kerouac pitches his descriptions of music at this level, making them among the most memorable bravura performances of the novel. Later on in Chicago it's Prez, a saxophonist with a tone like Lester Young himself, and his leader, a slender black tenorman, who blow solos in the "bop night." The latter performer is Prez's mentor and tries to make him forget clinkers and just "blow and blow" and care only about "the mere sound and serious exuberance of the music." Kerouac pauses—breathlessly—to give a one-paragraph history of the great bop innovators (everyone from Armstrong to Charlie Parker and Lester Young) only to rush back to the main action and the performance styles of the others in the group. The bass-player is "jabbing his hips at the fiddle with every driving slap": "Man there's a cat who can really *bend* his girl."

Speaking of which, Kerouac is a master of the romantic brief encounter—as charged and energetic as a night of bop. Some of his ardors last about two or three sentences—obsession or grand passion is hardly the idea. Digging "gone" waitresses is one of the major pleasures of being on the road. For Sal it's this way: "I went into a chili joint and the waitress was Mexican and beautiful. I ate and then I wrote her a little love note on the back of the bill." Or his reaction to the maker of "a rich thick milkshake": "Incidentally, a very beautiful Colorado gal shook me that cream; she was all smiles too; I was grateful." The "incidentally" says it all. Perhaps the most significant encounter for Sal is fifteen days with "the cutest little Mexican girl in slacks" who "cut across his sight" in an L. A. bus station. The idyll—which includes her child and even her family and even a lot of hard work picking cotton when they're living together in a tent—is a strange, accelerated, parodic version of family life. Sal becomes "a man of the earth, precisely as I had dreamed I would be." He sweats and nurtures and makes love, but soon it's time for a Kerouac leave-taking. "See you in New York, Terry." Just before that they had made love in a barn under a residing tarantula. Sal's romantic life is all set by the end of the book, again as a result of a chance encounter with "a pretty girl" who sticks her head out of a New York window and says, "Come on up . . . I'm making hot chocolate." "Sweet Laura," of course, is not the main act of *On the Road*. One of the babes that pass in the night, she's shadowy compared to Dean, Kerouac's jack-in-the-box as guide, philosopher, and friend.

All energy, all impulse, all possibility, all irresponsibility, Dean is a character for the postmodern season, someone who will attract readers well into the foreseeable future. If it's indeterminacy that you're after—the cool withdrawal from square abstractions and bourgeois social constructions—Dean is your man. But he also takes us back into the literary tradition, to a great early modern source of yea and nay. If it's play and liberation and release that you're looking for, Dean has roots in *Gargantua and Pantagruel*, a classic that combines nonsense, ribaldry, and revolt against the commonplace. All of the latter never quite become dated, and Kerouac, it must be said, gave them full expression in 1957. Like Rabelais, he lashed out in all directions against the conventions of his time. While many readers were concerned with the fates of men in gray flannel suits, Kerouac pioneered a new man in a new suit. Dean's "dirty workclothes clung to him so gracefully, as though you couldn't buy a better fit from a custom tailor but only earn it from the Natural Tailor of Natural Joy." The idea of newness, comfortableness, and pleasure takes us back to Rabelais. The Abbey of Thélème with its great proclamation—"Do What You Will"—bans poverty, chastity, and obedience and sets up riches, marriage, and liberty in their place. Sal and Dean and a large cast of pals and girls live by a late 1940s version of the Rabelais ethos. *On the Road* is the Abbey on wheels with the riches in the form of new experiences and tastes and people, the marriage in the form of serial encounters, and the liberty always there. "I haven't had time to work in weeks," Dean says. Bread and love and sensations are what they live for—with Dean enjoying "this gone Proust all the way across the country and digging a great number of things I'll never have time to tell you." Rabelais, let it be said, never wrote about "this gone Humanism," having throughout his book the scholar's high respect and seriousness and true understanding of his new literary tradition; and yet we cannot underestimate Kerouac as a bold proclaimer of newness and Rabelaisian appetite. Rabelais's Panurge is a lewd, poor, mischievous, kinetic, irrational fellow who likes nothing better than to play the trickster role and upset the applecart. Mercurial and sex-charged, he's Dean's literary ancestor. A scamp, seducer, and seat-of-the-pants survivor, he has a fabulous hold on other people, the same magnetism that makes Dean unforgettable.

   On the Road has these attractions, but it also has a certain aimlessness and perhaps even an emptiness for all its savored pleasures. In 1900, George Santayana published an influential essay called "The Poetry of Barbarism" that leads us to the heart of the Kerouac problem and the Kerouac appeal. Santayana analyzes the glories and letdowns in Browning and Whitman and manages to pinpoint the nature of barbarism: the barbarian is "the man who regards his passions as their own excuse for being; who does not domesticate them either by understanding their cause or by conceiving their ideal goal." What Santayana says of Browning's passions in his verse could equally well be said of Kerouac's enthusiasms in *On the Road*: they are "aimless in their vehemence and mere ebullitions of lustiness in adventurous and profoundly ungoverned souls." Dean Moriarty—like the barbarian "Myself" in Whitman—has tremendous receptivity to nature, city sights, "the movement and talk of common people." And Kerouac makes him very Whitmanesque in Santayana's sense in that he has the capacity to see things freshly, yet without the understanding and the commanding vision of a trained mind. This, to be sure, is digging, a vital means of perception that Santayana had no shorthand for in 1900. Digging also means moving from the vulgar to the sublime—from midget auto races to Proust. Dean, according to Sal, was also a compelling mass of confusions when he started down the literary and intellectual road. He was "all hung-up on the wonderful possibilities of becoming a real intellectual, and he liked to talk in the tone and using the words, but in a jumbled way, that he had heard from 'real intellectuals.'" Carlo Marx, we are told, got him "in there with all the terms and jargon" in "just a few months." It's difficult to be reassured by what the quality of thought would be after those months; yet it's easy to see that Santayana was describing such a mind when he wrote of Whitman's "sensuous sympathy" unaccompanied by real understanding of the human heart.

The real understanding would go beyond attraction and enthusiasm to some vision of what experience means. And if that counts, it surely leaves Kerouac's book as a classic of restlessness, a hymn to the turbulent and exciting self and to intense living, but also a book that confuses its readers. It promises revelations and insights into the infinite, and it ends with a sonorous and beautiful sentence. The narrator looks across the "raw land" of America and "all the people dreaming in the immensity of it," and thinks of "Old Dean Moriarty the father we never found." Now it's true that Dean settles down with his second wife Camille and "Amy and little Joanie." But it all takes place in a sentence or two. And the less said about the sense and coherence of Dean the father, the better. Kerouac's energy does not abate long enough to allow for any reflection whatsoever about the resolution he has just created. The very breathless ardor of it all makes Santayana's argument about barbarism an especially useful critical prism for looking at Kerouac's world. For in so clearly and cleverly indicating the limits and pleasures of Browning back at the turn of the twentieth century, Santayana gives us some of the right words to bring out the charms and intensities and exhilarations—as well as the shortcomings—of Dean and of *On the Road*: "And to the irrational man, to the boy, it is no unpleasant idea to have an infinite number of days to live through, an infinite number of dinners to eat, with an infinity of fresh fights and new love-affairs, and no end of last rides together." When you finish *On the Road*, you somehow do not think it's over. Things have stopped, but nothing is concluded.

This drive to act and talk and self-dramatize and move on is also a crucial feature of Allen Ginsberg's *Howl*, the great poetic testament of youth from the 1950s. The 1956 volume is a classic that stands beside Salinger's *Catcher* and Kerouac's *On the Road*: Ginsberg's book shares the spatterdash approach to creating stories and situations; agreeing with Kerouac that his kind of writer is inspired by the Holy Ghost—and believing in "First Thought, Best Thought"—he says no to everything mannered and mannerly, carefully thought through and highly wrought. This is the avowed aesthetic of *Howl*, a cry of agony unmediated by craftsmanship, traditionalism, regular metrics, Eliotic tightness and concision. It's the open poetic line—long, free, collo-quial, packed with images and phases that tumble out; it's the illogical connection, the bardic shout, and the bizarre juxtaposition. Lionel Trilling, Ginsberg's old teacher at Columbia, made Santayana-like comments about the rambling technique; he went so far as to say the work was all rhetoric and rant with no music or poetic beauty. But Trilling was wrong about at least one thing: Ginsberg's *Howl* was and is rhythmically alive—and its doctrines, far from being dismissible nonsense, are the heart and soul of postmodern rage against civiliza-tion, the money power and the destructive energy of a big and often heartless country. No madder than Edmund Wilson—the magisterial old critic who raged against the bomb and oppressive taxation and the death instinct in our culture in *The Cold War and the Income Tax*—Ginsberg was just a disheveled and crazy-as-a-daisy new version of the American radical who wasn't going to take it anymore. Salinger said no to phonies; Kerouac to a settled life; Ginsberg—without being a philosopher—stumbled into a wild critique of civilization and its discontents. The irrational was a protest against the repressive, and Ginsberg was out to champion all its forms.

At the heart of Salinger is the Romantic awakening—to the joy of life, to innocence, and to blessed people and scenes. Kerouac takes up the very same themes, yet his ramshackle narrative loses them in the welter of experience; the energy is so intense that it crowds out the recognitions. Ginsberg also all but loses the precise moment—the lucid awakening—in the fury and agony of his book. But what he brings to American literature is a remarkable lashing out, an inspired ranting, and a Rousseauistic yearning for peace and joy and innocence. He would like to claim some of Salinger's heart renewal, but his book is concentrated on the hellish process of learning rather than the moment of blessedness. *Hold back the edges of your gowns, Ladies, we are going through hell,* William Carlos Williams said in his pithy introduction to the volume. The basic subject of the poem is the hell of being young and aware in postwar America, of seeing the social suffering that is the accompaniment of a triumphant culture. Ginsberg—a supercharged storyteller in touch with society and the elemental—has not drifted off into his own hermetic world of sensations; despite his wild phrases and non sequiturs, he has a firm base to his work, the pain of American poverty, violence, and loneliness. Whether we, the readers, see it all his way—with his self-righteousness, embarrassing self-absorption, blatant indecency, and often dizzy social philosophy—is beside the point. He has a commanding way of facing us with his version of agony.

To unpack them one by one—poverty, violence, loneliness. Poverty is sometimes a tormenting condition, as in the title poem: "Moloch! Solitude! Filth! Ugliness! Ashcans and unobtainable dollars! Children screaming under the stairways! Boys sobbing in armies! Old men weeping in the parks!" Other times it's a settled sadness, as in "Sunflower Sutra": "Jack Kerouac sat beside me on a busted rusty iron pole, companion, we thought the same thoughts of the soul, bleak and blue and sad-eyed, surrounded by the gnarled steel roots of trees and machinery." Ginsberg's dirty mouth shouts at our national violence: "America when will we end the human war? Go fuck yourself with your atom bomb." Or at our violent imagination: "The Russia wants to eat us alive. The Russia's power mad. She wants to take our cars from out our garages." Or at the violence of our economic system against those "who were burned alive in their innocent flannel suits on Madison Avenue amid blasts of leaden verse." As for American loneliness—the estranged feeling of the individual consciousness hurried along in mass society—Ginsberg is a specialist, one who adds a gay twist and a dollop of wit to human suffering in "A Supermarket in California": "I saw you, Walt Whitman, childless, lonely old grubber, poking among the meats in the refrigerator and eyeing the grocery boys."

But poverty-violence-loneliness are subsumed under a more general heading, Ginsberg's unique form of dread. Part craziness, part drugginess, part gay angst, part hypersensitivity, this state of mind produces the horrible vision of the city that *Howl* offers, but it also produces moments of beauty, fellowship, and insight. Allen's torment is his world—and despite his disdain for Eliot, he has a wonderful ability to find physical correlatives for his state of mind; he succeeds brilliantly in gearing the image to the mood. Many of the lines are near-Eliotic in their urban seediness and despair: "who poverty and tatters and hollow-eyed and high sat up smoking in the supernatural darkness of cold-water flats floating across the tops of cities contemplating jazz." *Howl* is *The Waste Land* for the second half of the twentieth century, a wasteland out-of-control—not just the loneliness, the desperate city flats, the lust, the indifference, the bestial imagery and the grime—but vileness and madness thrown in. *Howl* is modernism over the top. Eliot controlled his urban hell, made sense of it, connected it with a coherent spiritual vision; Ginsberg splashes around in it, attempts to sermonize about it in the second section of the title poem, and finally ends with two sections of redemptive material—the first offers solidarity with his crazy fellow inmate in Rockland State and the final one offers a footnote-chant that declares everything holy. But the holiness—unlike the redemptive final lines of Eliot's *The Waste Land*—is an undifferentiated mass of images, a lesson that throws in anything and everything. "Holy the groaning saxophone! Holy the bop apocalypse! Holy the jazzbands marijuana hipsters peace & junk & drums." Not mysticism, but mixing it up. It's piety without discipline or decency, assorted bits of beat digging and Blake and Buddha and Jesus without any real commitment to anything but the shout-outs of Allen saluting his favorites and denouncing his enemies. In this gripping mix of elements the tone and the flavor override the sense. We are caught in the grip of enthusiasms and hatreds, not in the power of a vision. Intensity and interest of phrasing are everywhere in the beautifully compact, well-printed black-and-white City Lights edition of 1956, so different from the awkward, diffuse, indulgent version in the collected poems. The little book is a classic of celebration and offensiveness, a breviary for a new generation of devout, ecstatic, and angry readers. On the elated side there is Allen digging friends—Lucien Carr, Kerouac, Huncke, Burroughs, Cassady, Carl Solomon—body parts, cities, selected masters, old communists, and bums and madmen. There is Allen in a good mood, the playful wise guy as guru-patriot: "America I'm putting my queer shoulder to the wheel." Or, "My ambition is to be President despite the fact that I'm a Catholic."

Or there's humorously ticked-off Allen: "When can I go into the supermarket and buy what I need with my good looks?" Or "America
stop pushing I know what I'm doing." But the kvetching is always
near major agonizing: *Time* is "always telling me about responsibility.
Businessmen are serious. Movie producers are serious. Everybody's
serious but me." Or "America I still haven't told you what you did to
Uncle Max after he came over from Russia." Section II of the title
poem is all about what American civilization has done to Allen and
his friends and family: "What sphinx of cement and aluminum bashed
open their skulls and ate up their brains and imagination?" If Salinger's Holden set himself up as Castiglione for youth, Ginsberg's voice
echoes the themes of Freud in *Civilization and Its Discontents*. The
Reality Principle battles the Pleasure Principle, and always wins; its
victory, however, is a crushing defeat for aspiration and spiritual need
and bodily desire; unlike Freud the rationalist, Ginsberg paints a totally dark picture of the struggle. Suffering doesn't yield any higher
cultural result or any passionate human expression; it's a "soulless jail-
house and Congress of sorrows"; civilization simply "frightened me
out of my natural ecstasy!" Our outward existence is the mirror image
of our inner desolation: "Moloch! Moloch! Robot apartments! invisible suburbs! skeleton treasures! blind capitals! demonic industries!
spectral nations! invincible madhouses! granite cocks! monstrous
bombs!" That's the America of the Eisenhower years—lacking spirit,
insight, mercy, and fleshiness. Our sacrifices have yielded nothing; we
should have given way to every instinct, and we would have been better
off. Instead we "broke our backs lifting Moloch to heaven!" All our
higher and lower instincts—mind and genitals—had to give way so we
could have "robot apartments." All our aspirations have "gone down
the American river!" Ginsberg, in disgust, calls it "the whole boatload
of sensitive bullshit!"

So what's the way out? Evidently a kind of rededication to holiness,
a rather incoherent declaration of value. The dynamic of the poem is
totally without reason or logic. Here is a grand paradox of some sort:
you get holiness from the unholiness of reality. "Everything is holy!"
It doesn't matter much what Ginsberg has done to Buddhism; the
doctrine is manhandled, mixed with all kinds of Occidental ideas of
protest and rage and liberation. No self-respecting Buddhist would
ever accept Allen's message—his infantile tantrums and lack of discipline. But what does matter is the poetic effectiveness of the book. It
opens out the themes of Ginsberg's generation, makes the frustration

into more than a dry social problem. In *Howl* it all seems urgent in a new way. The poem carries you along, assaults your senses, amuses, excites. It's a marker in our literary culture because of its imagery and rhetoric and phrasing. In many ways it's the overture for the anarchic future of artistic expression—to hell with beauty and harmony and coherence and moral weight. Ginsberg's book made him the scout-master of countless transgressors against authority, the courage-giver that he called Whitman. Like D. H. Lawrence's call to blood conscious-ness, Ginsberg's howling counts in the making of the modern mind.

chapter 3

Angst, Inc.

Dread was the dark side of the literature of the youth culture, but it was the very lifeblood of noir fiction. Producing and publishing furiously after World War II, the noir novelists became central to the American 1950s literary picture for two reasons—their gripping, intense prose styles and their ability to convey a special brand of fear. In sentences that are brilliantly precise and often poetic in a hardedged way, their books emerge from the older detective fiction world of Dashiell Hammett and Raymond Chandler; yet they emerge without the elaborate business of detection or the vivid personalities of detectives. Stripped, usually, of the trappings and obsessions and clues of the whodunit, they concentrate on the metaphysics of anguish—the spectacle of distorted minds, the haywire behavior of outsiders and misfits, the mystery of despair.

The essence of a noir novel is never quite a matter of finding killers or even tracing mystery-story motivations like the old lady's money or the other guy's wife. As a sub-genre of crime fiction, the noir is actually weak in the staples of the basic type—plots are often screwy rather than clever and the whole figuring-it-out convention runs a very poor second to the scrutinizing of troubled souls. "Psychological probing" also seems an inadequate description of what these writers do. Their characters are not really psychological phenomena à la Jekyll and Hyde. What we get are characters who stumble into violence, collide with evil through some mischance. We are somewhere near the territory of modern tragedy: the books are about lost people who are part of the mystery of suffering—a nowhere urban employee with a yen to be somebody, an unwed mother-to-be with five dollars and a train ticket, a too-good-to-be true Texas sheriff with a twist, a piano player in a dive who wants to forget how he almost made it on the concert stage. Jim Thompson describes the characters this way: "All of us that started the game with a crooked cue, that wanted so much and got so little, that meant so good and did so bad." The characters are wide-open for more than psychological exploration: they make you think about why some people seem to be born to do horrible things. The settings of the noir stories, however, are not Poe's maelstrom or pit and pendulum or sealed wine cellar: the naturalistic imagination fleshes them out abundantly with their locales—the suburb, the small town, the lowdown bar or fancy resort. The reader gets his frisson from the contrast between the chaos of the people and the everydayness of the place.

Cornell Woolrich's *I Married a Dead Man*, Jim Thompson's *The Killer Inside Me*, Patricia Highsmith's *The Talented Mr. Ripley*, and David Goodis's *Down There* are the cream of this genre. They still read beautifully and seem fresh and alive even though we have had a half century worth of gruesome journalistic accounts of real crime and real killers, not to mention a blizzard of movies about killing-for-kicks. Their subjects are invariably sordid—incest, child molestation, sadism, dope, the joys of prostitution, warped and trapped humanity; in their time the books were lurid paperbacks, the underbelly of American fiction—lacking romantic sentiments, visions of a better world, even depictions of sustainable decency. The renewal in Salinger, Kerouac, or Ginsberg is nowhere in sight. What looms before the reader is the abyss, the emptiness of life: unrelieved angst. For all the depths of Ginsberg's *Howl*, there is redemption and blessedness. In Thompson's or Highsmith's books, people come up from the depths of criminal psychopathology only when they are playacting and pretending to be friends and citizens. Most of the time they are in an underground of crazed urges, disgust, and rage. And their light-of-day behavior—the routine courtesies and pleasantries, the helpfulness of killers—sets us more on edge than most accounts of crime. One of the commonplaces of real crime as reported in the papers is that the miscreant—apprehended, of course—turns out to be the kind of person who would help you dig your car out of a snowdrift or inquire about your sick aunt. That commonplace was once a new way to make edgy fiction.

Cornell Woolrich's *I Married a Dead Man* came out in 1948 and in certain ways set the noir program—jitters, metaphysical dread, murder, and the pleasant summer nights in a town named Caulfield. The voice that opens the narrative has a repetitive, desperate, incantatory quality. "The stars are warm and friendly here, not cold and distant, as where I came from; they seem to hang lower over us, be closer to us. . . . Oh, yes, the summer nights are pleasant in Caulfield. But not

for us." That voice is a woman's, and her account of "it" is the focus
of the opening. "It" is something between the printed lines of the
books that the character and her listener read and in the hand that
holds out the coffee cup to be filled; "it" is most obvious on the movie
screen and causes "us" to make our way up the aisle in the middle of
the picture. "It" is in the kiss of the two lovers, two lost ones. The
remainder of the book tells how the narrator fell into the lost world of
murder and cover-up. We follow a girl named Helen who has become
pregnant by a heel and is traveling west on a train with five dollars as
payoff. Woolrich plummets her into a preposterous mix-up with a
lovely new bride named Patrice and her handsome husband Hugh
Hazzard: poor Helen gets in a train wreck and at the moment of disaster happens to be wearing the ring that Patrice let her try on. Patrice
and Hugh are completely immolated. Now if you can accept this for
starters—and most people who have read *Oedipus the King* and know
of the murder at the crossroads should be able to—you are in for the
story of "Patrice" and what awaits her when she becomes the "daugh-
ter-in-law" of some rich people. The book is about trying to escape
the identity of Helen, the guilt and lying entailed, and the coming of
her nemesis in the person of the old seducer, Georgessen. The latter
shows up in Caulfield and threatens to tell the genteel Hazzards—a
plaster of Paris pair of kindly benefactors—that lovely "Patrice" has a
sordid past. "Patrice" meanwhile has won the heart of the Hazzards'
other son, Bill. The threat of Georgessen's truth—a melodramatic parody of the truth of great tragedy—is what brings Helen closer to Bill,
and closer to the anguish that will finally envelop her. It makes her
take a swig of brandy and kill her tormentor. And from that point on
Helen's real identity is not so much that of the girl with a scarred past
as that of the woman who will settle into Caulfield life as an unknown
murderess. Everything real and good and loyal is curdled and twisted
in Woolrich's world. Security for herself and her infant, a real home as
opposed to her horrid little room back home: these are the stakes that
have lost their value. Woolrich plays masterfully with her situation—
with the false life she's leading, which is decent and then turns horrible, with the grisly killing of Georgessen and the dumping of the
body, with every kind of instability of the self. Yet the richest quality
of the story is the moment-to-moment aspect of "Patrice's" life, rendered in jumpy sentence fragments or unsettling metaphors that fit her
secret world of doom.

Woolrich's specialty is a style that carries you through his highly contrived plot and lets you forget his synthetic supporting characters. "Patrice"—at the start a first person plural narrator, then the center of consciousness—is the occasion for effective musings and comparisons and little observations; all of these contribute to the thick and dark cloud that either hovers over every scene or seems to be moving in. Woolrich makes his readers nervous in very artful ways, through just the right turn of phrase and timing. By no means an elegant writer, he is nevertheless a master transformer of cheap phrases, well-worn images, and an array of disturbing effects. Take the whole business about getting rid of the body. Woolrich has perfect touches that blend everydayness and ghastliness. This is "Patrice" hearing the corpse being removed from the house: "She heard a slow, weighted tread of the gritty sidewalk—his—and accompanying it a softer sound, a sort of scrape, as when two shoes are turned over on their softer topsides, or simply on their sides, and trail along that way, without full weight to press them down." Soon Georgessen's body is propped in the front passenger seat of a car and makes "the same crunchy strain on the leather" that a live person does. In trying to dump the body on a freight car, Bill is connected with Patrice, not because she's assisting, but because she's his moral accessory: "He had a hard time getting him down the slope, he had to be a brake on the two of them at once, and the weight was double. Once the two of them went down momentarily, in a stumble, and her heart shot up into her throat, as though there were a pulley, a counterweight, working between them and it." The Woolrich simile is often ghastly and lurid at the same time, but the overkill has a mysterious way of working. In his degraded world the telephone receiver held by the pathetic abandoned Helen is an "ugly black orchid," the light in her room is a wilted tulip. "A carpet-strip ground to the semblance of decayed vegetable-matter, all pattern, all color, long erased, adhered to the middle of the stairs, like a form of pollen or fungus encrustation." Or take the Woolrich way of distorting a very ordinary thing—the phrasing on a five dollar bill which reads, "For all debts, public and *private*." "How could the engraver guess that that might break somebody's heart, some day, somewhere?" Objects in Woolrich's world are not charged and humanized as they are in Charles Dickens's world: they are not imaginatively alive, extensions of people's identities, but rather lonely, meaningless, hard, and ugly things that mock human beings. Human beings exist against a social backdrop that wants no part of them.

When it comes to Helen-Patrice's hellishly scrambled identity, Woolrich combines the cheesy and the clever to attain something all his own; in a telephone booth she is described this way: "She was like a doll propped upright in its gift-box, and with one side of the box left off, to allow the contents to be seen. A worn doll. A leftover, marked-down doll, with no bright ribbons on tissue wrappings. A doll with no donor and no recipient. A doll no one bothered to claim." Sometimes the style descends into pure cliché—"She climbed the rooming-house stairs like a puppet dangling from slack strings"—but most often Woolrich uses it to make his protagonist luridly alive. On her way to Caulfield after the train wreck and a long hospitalization, she is very much herself, which is to say someone whose identity lurches from dejection to terror. The hardware on her brand-new luggage, given by the Hazzards, has "'P H' trimly stenciled in vermilion on the rounded corners." She sits and remembers that last significant train ride, with the real Patrice. "There hadn't been this gnawing inside. There hadn't been this strain and counterstrain, this pulling one way and pulling the other." But the thing that is both unnerving and contradictory in this statement about the terror of the present is that Woolrich has just a few sentences before had "Patrice" observing all the commonplaces of a nice train ride. "The trees sailing peacefully by . . . belts of continuous motion. . . . Meadows and fields, and the little ripples that hillocks made off in the distance every once in a while. Going up a little, coming down again. The wavy line of the future." The present and the past are different kinds of anguish. And that very wavy line—in its context of calendar art scenery—leads eerily back to the stenciling on the luggage: "the fear wouldn't disappear. It wasn't just stenciled on a corner of her, it was all over her." And it soon leads to yet another line: "Sometimes there is a dividing-line running across life. . . . For her there was. It lay somewhere along those few yards of car-passage, between the compartment-window and the car steps, where for a moment or two she was out of sight of those standing waiting outside." You can be sure that Woolrich would mock literary theorists with their idea of "liminality," but what, after all, is this but that curious marginal state of consciousness in which sharp perception takes place? The girl is Patrice and not Patrice—the perfect noir enigma. And her new home will be a state of homelessness, every good value of which dissolves in the act of experiencing.

Besides his noir similes, his anxious sentence structure alternating with lulling passages of dull scene painting, his brilliant use of cheap

effects, there is Woolrich's marvelous timing and juxtaposing. He cuts
and manages the pace of a scene like a great film director. Hitchcock
took the basics of *Rear Window* from him—but he does it all on the
low budget of words, most often pretty tired everyday ones. Forget
the more conventional things like Mother Hazzard getting sick when
Patrice is about to flee her nerve-racking new home for honest destitu-
tion. Even forget the train wreck. What's most effective is Patrice—or
Patrice and Bill—and the screwy scenes in which Woolrich uses a
book or a movie or an inconsequential incident to heighten the tension
of their story. In the section in which Georgessen's corpse is sitting in
the passenger seat, Patrice is trying to get her mind off what's going
on by inventing a little story of her evening with Bill—something also
intended to serve as an alibi. "He's bringing me home from the movies"; she's in the back seat because "we had words." He then has to
recall the picture and details if they are to keep their story straight.
They saw "Mark Stevens in *I Wonder Who's Kissing Her Now*." Immediately Patrice is saying "When—when did the title-song come into
it? . . . Was that the opening number, they heard from the gallery?"
And Bill stumbles—wonderful because everything in the book is concerned with stumbling and accidents—and comes up with "That was
'Hello, Ma Baby.' Cakewalk number, don't you remember?" Readers
with a taste for the absurd, postmodern style, are likely to find *I Married a Dead Man* just the right combination of corn, kitsch, clichés,
and dread. But it's more than that—it's about what the brink of catastrophe feels like. When Patrice goes into the Hazzards' library to
read—and again, to escape a tense episode—she picks up the right ridiculous complement to her situation—the story of Marie Antoinette
trying to make her escape. She reads the following sentence: "Axel
Fersen drove swiftly through the dark streets." And Bill, at this point,
is coming home, probably aware that "Patrice" is not really "Patrice"
and therefore a menacing presence. Later, when they come together
for the dumping scene, they too will be taking a night journey out of
Caulfield. The Marie Antoinette book is also a wonderfully ironic text
to pick up by chance, especially since Patrice is trying to avoid identification with characters. She wants to forget herself, and for that reason has always disliked fiction: "Something about it made her slightly
uncomfortable, perhaps a reminder of the drama in her own life. She
liked things (her mind expressed it) *that had really happened*. Really
happened, but long ago and far away, to someone entirely else, someone that never could be confused with herself." Woolrich enjoys pun-

ning on escape: Patrice supposedly enjoys some escape from the
identification and from the fictional world that most people enjoy.
"She escaped from too much personal drama into a reality of the
past." But she then ran right into an escape story that is about a
woman who will be trapped.

"Patrice" goes scot free, but is caught in an awful conundrum—her
identity is a confusion that causes other confusions. Is "Patrice"
someone to be loved or a grifter and murderess? Bill says she is his
Patrice—and she didn't even exist until he met her and fell for her and
therefore created her; according to him, she has stolen nothing. His
point has a venerable heritage in European literature, calling to mind
Heinrich von Kleist's brilliant, tricky story "The Marquise of O" in
which a high-souled and innocent woman couldn't be pregnant because her seducer seemed like an angel. Kleist manipulates our ideas
of innocence and makes his tale anything but a sordid and hypocritical
denial of seduction. This tale of illusions and confusions points right
in the direction of Woolrich's novel—indeterminate uses of words and
slippery identities and entangled emotions. But such mental games
don't lead Woolrich to give up his hard-edged vision: on the final page
Patrice says it all, "It's in the very kiss we give each other. Somehow
we trap it right between our lips, each time. It's everywhere, it's all the
time, it's *us*."

Jim Thompson's famous novel *The Killer Inside Me*, the story of a
pathological character posing as Mr. Nice Guy in a Texas town, is another tale of evil told from the inside. It crisscrosses between the pretense of decency and the fact of monstrosity. Lou Ford is a murderer
whose sadism and sordid sexual past—he was abused by his father's
housekeeper—are not quite the main force of the story. Hannah
Arendt's book about Adolf Eichmann was several years in the future,
but we can certainly say that her theme of the banality of evil is on
every page of Thompson's novel. Lou's murders are methodical, matter-of-fact, and affectless. Most of the time Thompson's purpose is to
show him covering his tracks with blandness. His acts of murder take
up far less time than his platitudinous line: "my talk was a big part of
me," he says. And since we know the facts of modern horror, circa
1938–45, what remains to be told is their forms, the ways they are
entangled with everyday life.

In Lou's case, he is a career bore, the kind of guy who makes people
uncomfortable with clichés rather than with gothic creepiness. The

opening of the book shows him at the top of his form, finishing his pie in the diner and lecturing a waitress about basic decency: "We don't have many crooks in Central City, ma'am . . . Anyway, people are people, even when they're a little misguided. You don't hurt them, they won't hurt you. They'll listen to reason." Just as fine values and aspirations are curdled in *I Married a Dead Man*, the very terms of this insipid thesis are what Thompson goes to work on. Central City is full of crooks, and Lou is the homicidal maniac who pays them back. His half brother Mike was a building inspector from Conway Construction who met with a strange accidental death; Lou slaughters Elmer Conway, the wayward heir to the fortune, along with his mistress Joyce. In a sinuous plot that links up naturalistic elements about local corruption with the bizarre story of Lou's sickness, Thompson manages to show that Central City is a nightmarish place of double crosses and false appearances. Probably the most disturbing aspect of the book is Lou's role as big brother and kindly protector. The local diner owner Max Pappas feels secure because he knows that Lou has taken young Johnnie Pappas, a fairly wild kid, under his wing. "He's a different boy now, Lou. . . ." In one of the most chilling scenes, we find Johnnie in a jail cell, charged with a murder that Lou committed and capable of bringing forward a twenty dollar bill that would incriminate Lou. And Lou is up to his old game—carefully thought-through murder (made to look like a cell suicide) preceded by kindly talk and a bit of good sense about town life. He comforts before killing—and tells his young victim the moral of the story. We live in a screwed-up world, "The police are playing crooks in it, and the crooks are doing police duty." So much for the first proposition in Lou's speech to the waitress.

Secondly, people-are-people is an ironic misrepresentation of the characters in the Thompson world. They tend to be either victims or predators in a deterministic universe. They've been hurt and their object is to hurt you. Lou hates women because of childhood trauma, and any little irritation in his relationship with a woman can open the floodgates of the past. This of course is the stuff of the movies—more than a bit of *White Heat* with James Cagney. But it also becomes something more. The story of Lou facing his compulsions in the midst of being everybody's Rock of Gibraltar—not to mention in the midst of romancing a pretty schoolteacher and planning a honeymoon—is a tale of dread that deserves comparison with Flannery O'Connor's stories of polite killers and good reasoners who do hideous things. Recall that O'Connor's sinners usually begin by being sensible and polite in their hellish world. Lou is such a type and his final recognition is almost identical to that of O'Connor's criminal in "Good Country People." He recalls the story of a man who killed himself, his wife and kids, and mistress: "He had everything, and somehow nothing was better." O'Connor's con artist also finds "nothing" to be his value of choice—and he's surprised that the young woman he tricks doesn't know that this is what is in the heart of many a trickster. Lou Ford is the trickster and role player who also faces his own emptiness.

"They listen to reason," Lou says of people in general. Maybe this is the most disturbing statement of all, because the dynamic of the book is a matter of people being controlled and crushed in a world that seems perfectly sensible. Lou's girlfriend Amy is worried about the wedding plans while he's planning her death. Johnnie Pappas's father is thoroughly convinced by Lou's logical line. Lou is proud of himself, exults in his ability to chat reasonably on the edge of the abyss; after all, he has been a warped youth who found a perfectly plausible role for himself in Central City; he's played the rube for years, struggling against his demon. When the pressure mounts— when he can't help connecting a woman with the woman from the past—he overdoes the clichéd line: "but every now and then I'd catch myself in that dead-pan kidding, trying to ease the terrific pressure that was building up inside me." And, as he tells us, there's no law against his type of bullshit. As a doctor's son, Lou has access to clinical works about his kind of trauma: the afflicted one "appears to be entirely logical. He reasons soundly, even shrewdly. He is completely aware of what he does and why he does it." The sickness is "so seldom detected." In its way it is a sample of a diseased self that can explain itself, that thinks of itself as normal most of the time, and that has substituted chatting for raving. The book's power inheres in this calm explanation of evil. Like Woolrich working on good and evil, Thompson puts us in that terrible position of listening to the sense in madness. There's a terrific scene in which Lou—arrested and talking to his flamboyant country lawyer—learns the nature of his nature. Billy Boy Walker, complete with his own bizarre rationality, explains how he became a lawyer. A small quotation from an agronomy textbook changed his view of the world and of people: at one time in his life Billy Boy saw everything as black and white, good and bad. But then he read the definition that changed his life: "'A weed is a plant out of place.' Let me repeat that. 'A weed is a plant out of place.' I find hollyhock in my cornfield, and it's a weed. I find it in my yard, and it's a flower." "You're in my yard, Mr. Ford."

Thompson's book is a testament to what a gifted writer could do with 1950s appearances—the drone of everyday life, the small town sociability, the public manners and morals. He could turn them inside out and let his readers be set on edge by the most ordinary things. Even his seemingly innocuous passages have touches that upset the whole predictable world of the naturalistic novel; ordinary things don't come together with other ordinary things to produce a foreseeable reaction. Here's Lou Ford with a few remarks about how he's going to handle a "hustling lady" who's causing a stir in the town:

> Maybe we're kind of old-fashioned, but our standards of conduct aren't the same, say, as they are in the east or the middle-west. Out here you say yes ma'am and no ma'am to anything with skirts on; anything white, that is. Out here, if you catch a man with his pants down, you apologize . . . even if you have to arrest him afterward. Out here you're a man, a man and a gentleman, or you aren't anything. And God help you if you're not.

The last two lines—with their radical breakdown in logic, their plausible-sounding nonsense—have the perfect Thompson chill.

Patricia Highsmith published her classic noir novel *The Talented Mr. Ripley* in 1955, three years after *The Killer Inside Me* appeared. She had her own way of disturbing readers and defying expectations, largely accountable to her smooth style and studious avoidance of melodramatic speeches and monologues. But her protagonist slips right into place beside the other criminal nowhere people. He's also a nobody—not a rube in Texas, but a little mouse in a vibrant 1950s New York, the kind of fellow who is on the margin of all the fun and power, money and class. Tom Ripley knows a few people who are inside the loop, but he himself is living in a squalid East Side house and exploring the possibility of becoming a con artist. As the book opens, we learn that he's trying to get up the courage to extort money from strangers by writing them letters from the IRS. So far, he has scared a few people but hasn't had the courage to cash one of the checks.

The book is thereafter about Tom Ripley achieving personal autonomy and self-possession as he learns to be a murderer. Highsmith's narrative trajectory is the calm, plodding, effectual career of a killer without qualities, a non-self who is only able to fill in the blanks of his life by doing horrible things and turning the consequences—as a demented man would—into a parody of the good life. Highsmith uses the mingling of evil acts and pleasant results to hold her readers. And the basic vision of life—Tom's warped vision—is a 1950s fantasy of escaping the dreary terms of the workaday world by becoming a permanent vacationer on the Continent. Tom is not an expatriate in the classic 1920s sense of being disaffected with American values and culture; he is actually no more than a loser and an escapist with a twist in his nature; he wants to live well and tastefully, to acquire culture and refinement, to throw off all the tedium and humiliation of his early life. Highsmith arranges for him to be sent to Italy as a kind of ambassador to Dickie Greenleaf, a rich inheritor whose parents want him to come back to the States and work in the family shipbuilding business. Once abroad, Tom falls in love with Dickie's life—and his glamorous identity. Ease, leisure, a bit of painting, a lot of boating and desultory connoisseurship: these are Dickie's projects in a southern Italian village called Mongibello. Tom's own identity, a fragile thing at best, is soon overwhelmed by Dickie's: he ceases to want to live his own life and dreams of being a version of Dickie. The fantasy eventually causes him to murder his beau ideal and assume his identity. This, of course, is yet another noir story of a secret life—being someone other than yourself; and it also has the agonizing complications of the other stories we have examined—most notably the fact that Tom can never quite live fully in his new self. The book is a ferociously clever study of being a new self that cannot quite throw off the old self.

For a time, after killing Dickie, Tom lives and thinks and writes letters as Dickie. He takes pleasure in his possessions and masters everything from handwriting to mistakes in Italian grammar to producing a painting in Dickie's style. The horror of it all, however, comes across most vividly in Tom's creepy reactions. Highsmith drops the following line quite casually: it was "impossible to be lonely or bored, he [Tom] thought, so long as he was Dickie Greenleaf." He enjoys the high tension of being watched. "It gave his existence a peculiar, delicious atmosphere of purity, like that, Tom thought, which a fine actor probably feels." The constraints of acting give life a bizarre piquancy. And the metaphysical kick is thrilling, "He was himself and yet not himself." But the book has something else in store for Tom besides playing Dickie. Highsmith uses a twist in the plot to make it impossible for him to maintain the new identity. After killing Dickie's friend

Freddie—a brutal, absurd act only necessary as a cover-up—Tom must change back into his own skin and let the murder suspect be the vanished Dickie. The pattern is Tom the Nobody, then Tom assuming the identity of Dickie, then Tom transformed into Tom the Somebody. This last version of our protagonist is more vaporous, chilling, and problematic than the other two.

Highsmith spooks the reader by making Tom a self who's not a self. "Possession reminded him that he existed, and made him enjoy his existence," Highsmith comments from Tom's vantage point. She captures his pathological state of mind with dry precision: "not many people appreciated existence as he did." In an especially chilling scene that foreshadows his takeover of Dickie's identity, we see Tom—like some pre-adolescent—trying on Dickie's clothes and aping his gestures before a mirror. And, every step along the way, Highsmith makes Tom enjoy himself—this while we are unnerved. This murderer is childlike in his inability to connect acts with feelings, desires with meanings and consequences. The murders spring out of nowhere in that they are not carefully premeditated and preceded by illuminating interior monologue. And all Tom's reactions have a chilling infantile irresponsibility, an ability to ignore life's depths. As Tom says at the end, when he has escaped to Greece, "No use spoiling his trip worrying about imaginary policemen." By this point he thinks of himself as a man of the world, heroically setting for a new destiny like some Jason or Ulysses; we think he is a madman with superhuman defense mechanisms.

The experience of reading the book is made even more curious because Highsmith forces us—for whole stretches of the narrative—to block out judgment, outrage, and revulsion. Tom is made into a wimpy nothing of a man whom we find hard to hate. We watch his progress and don't quite register the appropriate anger. We're also constantly entertained by the color and texture of Mongibello, Naples, Rome, Sicily, and Venice. Highsmith makes it all seem like a 1950s vacation only occasionally punctuated by murder, a strategy that ultimate does the job of terrorizing us in a new way. Pervading the story is the atmosphere of a discover-life-and-yourself movie such as David Lean's *Summertime* or William Wyler's *Roman Holiday*. Like the Wyler film of 1953, *The Talented Mr. Ripley* is a tricky, clever story about someone who wants to escape a burdensome life and experience the freedom, release, and fun of Italy. Wyler's bittersweet story depicts a European princess, played by Audrey Hepburn, escaping her duties for only a day and touring the streets of Rome—with Gregory Peck. Highsmith's novel has Tom running the gamut of Italian scenes (fueled with espresso and martinis)—with his memory of Dickie always there for comfort. The delightful caprice of a Roman holiday— savoring Rome in all its excitement and majesty, being in love, having a secret, and not having to be yourself—is cleverly distorted by Highsmith: Tom is a gruesome Cinderella, excited by *la dolce vita*, changed by the power of his homoerotic feeling, and by the brutal murder of Dickie. Wyler's picture has the Hepburn princess achieving a kind of self-possession and independence as a result of her day of real living; Highsmith has Tom, no longer "a cringing little nobody from Boston," in demented possession of his destiny—not to mention Dickie Greenleaf's inheritance.

The Talented Mr. Ripley also has perfect command of nightmare, terrifying moments of recognition, and eerie glances backward. We're carried along by Tom's calm, affectless style of murder and sightseeing only to be interrupted by a wonderful tincture of fear. Take Tom's reaction to his palazzo in Venice with the narrow passageway—Viale San Spiridione, a mere "slit" between grand houses. He was able to go through the slit only when "a few cocktails had knocked out his fear." In the passage some "nameless, formless things haunted his brain like the furies." In another scene with a detective—the ultimate sleuth put on the case by Mr. Greenleaf, Dickie's father—Tom answers a question about Dickie's nature, and by doing so in his blank style, tells more about himself than could be accomplished in five pages: "I don't know what kind of people are apt to kill somebody." We're startled by the economical use of gruesome irony, as when Tom thinks that Freddie the corpse, being driven out of Rome to the Appian Way in order to be dumped, is getting the grand tour that he could not appreciate. Highsmith turns the scene—really the same one used by Woolrich, complete with corpse playing passenger—into a picture postcard series of panels—maybe Rome-at-Night. "Down the Hill to the Via Veneto, past the American Library, over to the Piazza Venezia, past the balcony on which Mussolini used to stand to make his speeches, past the gargantuan Victor Emmanuel Monument and through the Forum, past the Colosseum . . . . It was just as if Freddie were sleeping beside him, as sometimes people did sleep when you wanted to show them scenery." The sly, bland, clichéd comment on human nature is the essence of noir—a pleasant ride in Rome with a dead body. The narrator is as sinister as Jim Thomp-

son's Lou Ford. And study the book as you will, you won't find that
Highsmith gives you any relief from Tom's point of view: it's a holi-
day in hell in which Tom is going to buy a good art book about
Greece, his next destination.

David Goodis's *Shoot the Piano Player*, originally titled *Down There*
when it was published by Fawcett in 1956, is as far as you can get from
Tom Ripley's Italy. Most of the action takes place in Harriet's Hut, a
rough bar that offers some refuge from the desolate, windblown
streets of Port Richmond, Philadelphia. The characters are hardly in
search of the good life, and the plot is nothing extraordinary—just
a small tale of a loser who once won, then blew his life in a fit of
despair, almost grasped something good again, and returned—quite
calmly—to losing. Eddie Lynn, the piano player at Harriet's, shares
one thing with Tom Ripley: the noir dreaminess of someone who is
not quite himself. This form of metaphysical discomfort includes
knowing that everything you are doing and everything you are
amounts to a kind of hoax. Eddie is emotionally numb for most of the
book, in a daze because he can't bear to feel or remember. He is now
a shabby, hand-to-mouth entertainer in a place where he can forget
the two other selves he once occupied. A poor boy from South Jersey
who was taken up by the powers that be in the classical music business, he attended the Curtis Institute in Philadelphia and even made it
to Carnegie Hall. For a time he was Edward, the success. Goodis—
unashamed of the ricketiest of plots—has Edward marrying a devoted
Puerto Rican pupil who gives herself to a lecherous manager in exchange for her husband's big break on the concert stage. If you can
deal with this, you can also accept her suicide and the emergence of
another self, "Eddie" the wild, drunken skid-row brawler who'll do
anything to lash out at life. Most of the time, however, we are with
a third version of the self, numb Eddie—a smiling, compliant, no-
trouble nobody who plays the background music for the drunks at
Harriet's.

As the book opens, Eddie's zombie-like state is penetrated by his
crook of a brother and then—no surprises here—by another woman,
this time the tough, self-possessed waitress Lena. Eddie gets a second
chance to be Edward as he comes close to connecting romantically
with Lena; he also gets a second chance at being out-of-control
"Eddie" as he unsuccessfully protects Lena from a brutal bouncer and
two hoods who are after them—in true noir fashion—because of

money they never took. In a story like this—simple, stagy, more than a bit awkward—the only thing that can raise the material above the level of melodramatic entertainment is some curious combination of style and vision. Goodis has this combination—a droll, dry, fast-talking interior monologue for Eddie and a window into doom and dread for us.

Goodis's people and settings are described—unlike those in our other three writers—in-over-the-top language: none of Woolrich's vague physical descriptions or Thompson's and Highsmith's razor-sharp economy. The pictures are rich and textured. To begin with the types at the bar—Harriet and her bouncer boyfriend the Harleyville Hugger. Goodis has as much fun mocking such lowlifes as an essentially tragic story will permit. The tone is established by Eddie, for the most part the book's center of consciousness. Here's his take on the owner:

> She was a very fat woman in her middle forties. She had peroxide-blonde hair, a huge, jutting bosom and tremendous hips. Despite the excess weight, she had a somewhat narrow waistline. Her face was on the Slavic side, the nose broad-based and moderately pugged, the eyes gray-blue with a certain level look that said, You deal with me, you deal straight. I got no time for two-bit sharpies, fast-hand slicksters, or any kind of leeches, fakers, and freebee artists. Get cute or cagey and you'll wind up buying new teeth.

G. Wally Plyne, the bouncer's real name, is depicted as a sinister version of Curly in The Three Stooges. The barroom itself is an emblem for the state of things:

> It was at least thirty years behind the times. There was no juke box, no television set. In places the wallpaper was loose and some of it was ripped away. The chairs and tables had lost their varnish, and the brass on the bar-rail had no shine at all. Above the mirror behind the bar there was a faded and partially torn photograph of a very young aviator wearing his helmet and smiling up at the sky. The photograph was captioned 'Lucky Lindy.' Near it there was another photograph that showed Dempsey crouched and moving in on a calm and technical Tunney. On the wall adjacent to the left side of the bar there was a framed painting of Kendrick, who'd been major of Philadelphia during the Sesqui-Centennial.

The patrons are as out-of-it as Eddie—"booze-happy or booze-groggy."

Goodis is a master of capturing the idiom of small-time punks, thugs, and losers; their patter is his poetry, almost as it was for Ernest Hemingway in "The Killers." Feather and Morris, the two sharply dressed enforcers sent to get Eddie and take him for a ride, are cynical wiseguys trying to make him talk. Feather, a tiny fellow in a gray fedora, starts discussing "watermelons" in South Jersey—and Morris plays straight man. "How come I ain't seen the watermelons," Morris asks at one point. "These watermelon patches, I mean. They're sorta hidden back there—" Feather says. "It's nothing," Eddie says. But we know that watermelons are pretty important—the metonymy for some crime or scam Eddie's brother is involved in. The goofy exchange is a Goodis specialty, nicely on view in another scene in which some kids crossing the street annoy the gangsters and their captives, including Lena the waitress. "Just stay off my blue suede shoes," one of the kids says to Morris when he offers to break her neck. Morris says, "Goddam juvenile delinquents." Lena backs him up: "Yes, it's quite a problem." Specializing in the dry, the offbeat, and the bounced-off-the wall, Goodis offers a portrait of a former stunt dancer turned prostitute; Clarice is Eddie's confidante from his rooming house, a joker and wild card prone to doing handstands for no reason at all; in the role of another lover—someone trying to break through his apathy—she offers her daft self to a man who is incapable of involvement. When she confesses love, Eddie brushes her off, "Whatcha doing? Writing verses?" At the end she's the one who leads him back to his numbed existence as the piano player at Harriet's.

But Eddie's interior monologues and his disconnected conversations are the glory of the book: they let us see the emptiness of life and also offer something that isn't quite as predictable as the hardboiled talk in Hammett or Chandler. Whimsical and tough, distanced from the real world and all-too-aware of its horrors, Eddie the talker is an odd mix; his playing dumb routine brings a kind of philosophical distance to the immediacies of a crime book. He's the dreamer caught in a tangle of tough guys—and two tough girls who love him in their own way. His thoughts are always there to thicken the emotional atmosphere. The monologues, admittedly, are like lines from a good screenplay, largely because Goodis takes so much care in making Eddie's every word—despite his ennui—a bit of vital reality. Listen to him mutter about his "problem"—his attraction to Lena—and how to handle it: "Come off that, you know it ain't no problem, you just ain't geared for any problems, for any issues at all. With you it's everything for kicks, the cool-easy kicks that ask for no effort at all, the soft-easy style that has you smiling all the time with your tongue in your cheek." Or overhear him when he blocks out love: "All right, let's think about Oscar Levant. Is he really talented? Yes, he's really talented. Is Art Tatum talented? Art Tatum is very talented. And what about Walter Geiseking? Well, you never heard him play in person, so you can't say, you just don't know." One of the best scenes of emotional denial has Eddie and Lena "just standing here and gabbing." "What else could it be?" he comments. "I wouldn't know . . . I wouldn't know unless I was told." "I'll let that pass, he said to himself. I'd better let it pass."

The nihilism of Eddie's world and of the noir world generally is a nothingness that adds up to something: although we don't get values, fulfillment, or coherent selves, we do get pictures that are difficult to blot out. Related to the ironic and tragic mode, the noir novel is our equivalent of those ancient stories of ruination, blindness, and anguish. Is there any catharsis, any mile-high insight into life? Probably not. But the noirs make us think about warped human nature and scare us into some insights about ourselves. We never feel quite the same about pretending, living double lives, or having secrets.

chapter 4

Rough Customers

The noir novelists were not the only chroniclers of postwar dread, estrangement from decency, and immersion in underworlds of violence. Two writers with no reputation for producing criminal thrillers wrote signature books about what it's like to be totally cut off from the middle-class allegiances of the 1950s. Nelson Algren's *The Man with the Golden Arm* (1949) and Norman Mailer's *Advertisements for Myself* (1959) are separated by a decade, yet their depictions of the transgressor's life—drugs, rage, brutality, coolness, and contempt for authority—make them landmarks in American literature that belong together on a bookshelf. They are classic expressions of the rebellious mind lashing out at everything America fought for in the big war—security, country, honor, home, God, family. Demented and brilliant in their indictments of our civilization, they are at the same time part of our cultural heritage: they are blows struck at comfort and complacency and have their place in a long tradition of naysaying. At times clumsily written and mannered and full of their own rhetoric, they are never dull because they never lose sight of men struggling against the inexorable pressures of a proud culture. Algren and Mailer—one a naturalist who writes about drugs before the romanticizing of the drug culture, the other an expressionistic rhetorician who helped to glamorize getting high—represent the literary anger of the era at a pitch of excitement. The two books assault you with original language and try to overturn your comfortable notions about a stable life in a progressive society.

Algren's book was originally intended to be a war novel, but on the way to that familiar kind of story he found his real themes—poverty and the underclass, relentless commercialism and rapacity, the rise of the drug culture and the desperation of the addict. A reader of *The Man with the Golden Arm* in the new millennium will find the book painfully fresh in that there are agonizing alternatives for the junkie now, just as there were before drugs became part of the culture of

youth and affluence. Frankie Majcinek, our man whose arm is met-
onymic for defiance and pain, is not a hipster or recreational user. He's
no saint on two grains of morphine or sage with reefer. He's not William Burroughs with a fundamentalist junkie philosophy or Allen
Ginsberg toying with junk. He's no poet or proud junkie. He never
went past primary school and owns nothing but his Army clothes and
his illusions about being a drummer like Gene Krupa. Junk is shame-
ful, stuff forced on him when he was sick overseas in the Army. Junk
is what pretty girls like Molly-O want him to fight. Junk finishes you
as a card dealer and causes the men at a game to make way for you as
if you're a syphilitic. Frankie's pursuit of his fix is anything but glamorous. He's a recruit—if truth be told—from the old-time story about
the poor loser, the slum kid without a chance. Yet Algren manages to
do quite a lot with familiar materials of another era—the bottom-dog
schemes, prison scenes, sordid saloons, scurvy characters, back alleys,
and bad girls with heart. He manages to sweep through the Chicago
underworld and give a commanding account of how his characters are
destroyed in 1949 America. The book is actually a comprehensive social study rather than a story about addiction. Frankie, while the center of the action, is an occasion for letting us see everything that has
formed him: the manner of describing the other victims and victimizers—the low down of every variety and on both sides of the law—is
elaborate, richly textured, and dramatized at length. Every punk gets
his due, is given his memorable lines, is handled with Dickensian precision and wit. *The Man with the Golden Arm*—like greater books of
its era, like *The Adventures of Augie March* and *Invisible Man*—is a
world, an inferior, essentially deterministic world, but nevertheless a
place filled with credible human beings.

Algren's Chicago people are alive because they aren't manipulated
in a neat plot about evil, or good and evil, or salvation. Like the losers
up in Bronx court in Tom Wolfe's *Bonfire of the Vanities*, they seem to
have stumbled into their own lives. Their accounts of themselves are
pathetic, yet—in spite of their tragic fates—somehow hilarious. Dog-
nappers, dim-witted ice-house men, loafers, freelance hookers, con
artists are brilliantly transparent examples of how ruin in America is
achieved. And hardly a page goes by without Algren's mordant humor
brought to bear on the unbearable—"Always a pallbearer, 'n never a
corpse," says a son of his father. "You only make the same mistake
once"—a Berraism before Yogi Berra became a sage—is the controlling idea of the book. These people—held in the cage of the city, in-

deed often pictured in the lockup waiting for a hearing—are trapped in the mistake of their own existence, a life of confusion distilled by Algren's comic epigram. Each has his or her turn at expressing the sheer chaos of being a person. Each has a particular way of mirroring what's wrong with life. If at first you think these people are off-the-edge members of the underclass—not like us at all—then Algren is succeeding in his initial gambit. We are meant to be disgusted, only to become fascinated and gripped by the actual humanity of these distorted characters. Frankie has smashed up the life of his girl Sophie by driving drunk and putting her in a wheelchair. His awful guilt—and measure of decency—leads him to stick by her. But he is married to a woman who lives in a raging, manic dream of going dancing—and who wants to punish him for his sin. Unheroic and damaged from his Army days, he yearns for some release, some relationship that can make him forget his guilt, kick his habit, and start anew. We watch him find Molly-O, the discarded girl of a drunken brute, and we also watch him lose his chance for even a shred of happiness with her. He kills the drug dealer who calls Molly a whore and who has taunted him about his habit. In short, a revolt against his fate and a decent instinct on his part lead to murder and flight from the neighborhood and eventual suicide. What's wrong with Algren's Chicago is that it's an endless round of such pathetic ironies. Frankie's golden arm is a source of pride—he's a card dealer and the best; but his arm is also the symbol of his habit. His strength is a kind of brutal facing up to his own weakness—a kind of tough, nihilistic look at himself. He's no hero in the war with "the Krauts"—no hero on the back streets: "Ain't nobody scared of me my whole life." Algren the aphorist, whose lines distill the various characters' lives, puts Frankie situation's this way: "I was a big man awright—I was the man had to pick the fly crap out of the pepper with boxin' gloves."

The book itself is a storehouse of cynicism, alley wisdom, and well-phrased despair. In the same period as Albert Camus's *The Myth of Sisyphus*—a book about going on in the face of certain defeat—Algren gave us the American equivalent of Camus's battle with fate. The terms, of course, are totally street-wise, and the abstractions come out of the mouths of loser-philosophers. Consider Frankie's musings on honesty. Is there any such thing? Frankie thinks about his dim-witted pal Sparrow—4F because of "moral warpitude," mostly on the run for being "a lost-dog finder" and petty thief. (His goofy aphorisms—and his beer-drinking dog Rumdum—help lift the book from its re-

lentless darkness.) Eventually he will rat Frankie out to the police, but
not before he has played buddy and sidekick to a man in agony. "For
how does a man keep straight with himself if he has no one with
whom to be straight?" The answer—after all the betrayals—is the bare
possibility of one honest person. In Algren's world, however, such redemption is not an actuality. What we get instead is not the happy
ending, but the life-giving force that keeps Frankie going and keeps
him from descending to the animal level of pushers like the sleek Nifty
Louie and his slobbering henchman Piggy-O. Mixed in with the tough
guy resistance is an all-American sentimentality that Algren simply
can't avoid. Molly waits for him "listenin' to the Els go by, waitin' for
El cars." His reply: "I know how lonely it gets waitin' for Els." The
sadness of life in Polish Chicago—for Frankie, Sophie, and the others—is Algren's recurrent theme. Hilarity mixes with melancholy, but
melancholy wins out. There is nostalgia for the old town "when burlesque was burlesque"; there are fond memories of kids' street games,
even though the games had to do with being hit by garbage. But the
Algren summation is likely to be this: "The old days, the old ways,
before all the stoplights turned to red and there was still time between
deals for a laugh or two over a nickel beer."

Algren sets himself up as a kind of Chicago pessimist, ready to gen-
eralize about the downside of everything. One of his favorite locales
is the police station house, with officer Bednar evaluating the punks
who come his way. Bednar—aka "Record Head" because he knows
everyone's criminal past—is Algren's most reflective character, capable of seeing Chicago criminal life whole—yet, in the end, capable of
making mistakes that are no better than those of the punks. Someone
in a lineup had once told him—like a half-literate spokesman for an
organic community, a Charles Dickens of the underclass—"we are all
members of one another." Algren shows Bednar resisting the truth of
connectedness, fighting to the end for his cynical belief in solitude and
human worthlessness: "Somewhere along the line he had learned, too,
that not one was worth the saving. So he'd been right in saving none
but himself. And if that had left them all to be members of one another, then it had left him to be a member of no one at all. Had, in-
deed, left him feeling tonight like the most fallen of anybody." His
condition is ultimately more agonizing that Frankie's in that he lives
to know what he is incapable of atoning for. "Thieves, embezzlers and
coneroos, all might redeem themselves in time. But himself, who had
played the spiritual con game, there was no such redemption. There

was no redemption for such self-saviors." What Bednar is guilty of is a moral crime that no society can or wishes to punish—the crime of denying you're a member, of living to save your own skin. As he dramatizes Bednar's suffering, we begin to think of the fact-collecting officer as some latter-day Gradgrind from Dickens's *Hard Times*; he's completely impervious to the human feeling that swirls around him and totally immersed in detail. And like Gradgrind, in the final analysis, "He had been left to judge himself." Algren is, however, no nineteenth century man of religious sentiment, no romantic willing to cobble together a vision of redemption. He leaves us with the truth of Bednar's isolation: "Crocodile tears: he belonged to no man at all."

Algren is at his best when he collects the sins and wounds of society and arranges them in a gruesome, often bitterly humorous pattern. He's great at surveying collective misery, giving a bird's-eye view of what Chicago punks go through.

> But any one side of any jailhouse wall is never much different than any other side. There are only the same odd threadbare variations on the same age-old warnings against all the well-tried ancestral foes: whisky and women, sin and cigarettes, marijuana and morphine, marked cards and capped cocaine, dirty laughter and easy tears, engineered dice and casual disease, bad luck and adultery, old age and shyster lawyers, quack doctors and ambitious cops, crooked priests and ambitious burglers, lack of money and hard work.

Algren's lockup releases some of his most mordant, brilliant observations. At once a philosopher of despair and a comedian of the lower depths, he lets us in on the condition of the lost. He's our poet of hopelessness, which is to say the most unusual of American poets. To utter his truths, he has to renounce just about all the wisdom of transcendentalism, pragmatism, progressivism, socialism. He's left with a curious blend of hard naturalism—the Dreiser of *An American Tragedy*—and existentialism—a dogged, defiant attempt to face the terms of suffering and meaninglessness. How could such a writer have won the first National Book Award? He never mitigates his despair, has no avenue to transcendence, no ideology that gives his people a boost. It is also difficult to think of a writer in his time who retailed these kinds of observations about the underclass: "It wasn't so much lack of aptitude as it was simply the feeling that no work had any point to it. . . . They neither worried about the future, regretted the past nor felt con-

cern for the present. . . . They had never been given one good reason
for applying their strength. So now they disavowed their strength by
all sorts of self-deceptions." Algren's humorous nature also plays with
the stock phrases and ludicrousness of hitting bottom. Here is an instance of what being up against the wall means: "For these were the
very walls men meant when they said of another that he had his back
to the wall. Here it was that they put their stubborn necks hard up
against the naked brick, lied first to the right and then to the left, denying everything, explaining with scorn, swearing truth was truth and
all falsehood wicked: and every word, from the very first burning
oath, one long burning lie." Or reflect on Algren's look at criminals
and their loved ones:

> "Gracie came. Like she said she would. They wouldn't let her past the
> desk but she hollered down at me, 'Still wit' you, DeWitt!'"—all his
> worries solved because some dowdy old doll with a double chin and
> hair cascading down to her ears had hollered down to him through the
> concrete, the steel and the stone. He could face one to fourteen now
> with a splitting headache and a double-crossing lawyer because some
> Gracie or other had called some nonsense to him. Hope, tears and
> nonsense.
>   Born on the FM waves of the heart.

What will a new generation make of this, especially of Gracie? One
thing seems undeniable: in this book Algren triumphs over complacency, clichés, warm and fuzzy feelings, and all the verbal baggage—
the trendiness, propaganda, and piety—that have made us think of the
underclass as an abstraction. "We remember Frankie Machine / And
the Arm that always held up."

Norman Mailer's *Advertisements for Myself* is another act of defiance—filled with tantrums and inflated rhetoric—but nevertheless a
landmark in the literature of protest. After putting in some profitable
time as a naturalist with his war novel *The Naked and the Dead* and
with his Hollywood exposé *The Deer Park*, Mailer emerged as America's most outrageous rhetorician, someone who adapted the classic
idea of instruct-and-delight and turned it into insult-and-shock. His
famous essay on the hipster, "The White Negro," and the story "The
Man Who Studied Yoga" are the most valuable portions of the
book—if book we can call it. *Advertisements* is a classic in the form of

a great wreck—shards and fragments, junk and short-takes, polished
and brilliant prose in the midst of it all. A ragtag collection of juvenilia,
current writing, old and new fiction, the volume is an intermittently
inspired mix. But its conception is grand scale—a cultural history of
the 1950s and a story of artistic agony and growth. As a piece of writing it seems most akin to nineteenth century works about the painful
development of the soul. Mailer comes off like the Thomas Carlyle of
Sartor Resartus or of the early essays such as "Signs of the Times" and
"Characteristics"—the essential preacher of his time, the naysayer and
diagnostician, Jeremiah, prophet of consciousness, outlandish giver of
advice, definer of values, soul-barer, and breathtaking stylist. Like
Carlyle he is antiliberal, antiestablishment, wildly heterodox, sententious, offensive, self-absorbed, and frequently off-the-pier in his judgments. And like Carlyle—the virulent racist—he has acted out his
violent, indecent impulses. Out of control, he is nevertheless a writer
for many seasons because of his total commitment to upsetting his
readers, announcing the crises of his time, and taking his own direction in solving them. Scourge of the complacent—at times scourge of
the sane—he offers the wisdom and metaphysics of the outlaw, not
because he can ever quite claim to embody it, but because he thinks
we need it as a corrective to our distorted life. Like Carlyle he shows
us the spectacle of his own ardors, depressions, confusions.

The idea of *Advertisements* is to announce the exemplary drama of
his own consciousness brooding on the spirit of his age. Carlyle said
man had grown mechanical in head and heart, that the Enlightenment
and the dawning age of industrial progress had deadened the spiritual
capacity and awareness of the most intelligent. He offered himself as
an exhibit of what cold reasoning had done to one man. In like manner
Mailer offers himself as a victim of the postwar Zeitgeist, torn by the
conflict of Square and Hip, threatened by tranquillizing conformity,
bedeviled by his past success as a naturalistic novelist, set up by the
publishing industry to take a fall, pressured to deny the protean life
within himself. And on a level of conflict closer to home, Mailer's difficult, turgid, unreasoned, fragmented, uneven book is the tough-guy
writer's apologia for his literary life: why I did what I did, what I endured. *Advertisements*, in its way, is Mailer's golden arm held up
proudly, a transformation of Nelson Algren's deterministic story into
a story of artistic and spiritual development. Like Algren, he had the
courage to be brutal and uncompromisingly against mass-produced
ideas of the good life and the good middle-class conscience; but unlike

Algren, he was rebel and outsider as philosopher, someone with a message and a program of transgression rather than a stark picture of the transgressor's life.

Advertisements—like Carlyle's work—is so larded with self-indulgent and all-but-impenetrable prose that we might leave it behind in the new century. We might neglect the brilliant, incisive core passages of a very poorly edited work. We might lose patience with all the radical guff—the ranting passages about the beauty of rape and murder, the opaque and infantile philosophizing about the necessity of violence. We should be patient and listen to the diagnosis because no one was quite like Mailer in pinpointing the problems of the new age of American power and wealth and complacency. Grown older and having acquired new burdens and tragedies, Americans have not outgrown our post–World War II situation—that of a country on top of the heap, yet threatened from without and troubled within. Each of us could find the usable, readable parts of this miscellany—and there is something here for all but the most complacent. Anyone with the imagination to wonder about root social and spiritual problems will be engaged—and perhaps infuriated—by some part of Mailer's journey. The book is an anatomy of American inertia and social depredation and the anxiety and denial that attends our condition. It's the American 1950s, Mailer style. It's best read selectively—avoiding the feather-bedding, recycling, and other bulking up that makes Mailer tedious. Read these sections: "The Man Who Studied Yoga"; "The Fourth Advertisement for Myself"; all of section 4 titled "Hipsters." You will experience a symbolic tale of one tormented consciousness in its struggle to live.

Mailer's protagonist Sam Slovoda in "The Man Who Studied Yoga" is an honest portrait of what the liberal soul—godless, emptied of high purpose and courage—could be like in the 1950s. He's the exemplary spiritual failure that Mailer needs to portray before he can move us a notch higher. We need to know what despair is before we can appreciate Mailer's bootstraps-and-rhetoric approach to achieving power. We need to know what weak is before we can appreciate Mailer—a Rocky Balboa of American letters—getting stronger. The story unfolds on a long, dreary winter afternoon and evening in Queens. Sam has literary ambitions, and Sunday could be the time to get some work done on his novel. But instead he has invited friends over for a bit of excitement—a viewing of a pornographic movie. The gathering—uncannily like the awful party in James Joyce's "The Dead"—is an occasion for pretentious behavior, pettiness, warmed-over political resentments, and regrets about great things that never materialized. Sam, too, is like Joyce's unfulfilled protagonist Gabriel Conroy—troubled by unrealized literary ambitions, but locked in an uncreative job (in his case as a continuity writer for cartoon magazines). He's well meaning and has ideals, but like Gabriel he's envious, spiteful, gossipy, contentious—and yet, as Mailer grimly concludes after enumerating his faults, he's better than most. He's also hungry for sex and deep communion with his wife—the children are away—but will suffer disappointment, feelings of desolation—all the joylessness that came to Gabriel Conroy when he looked at himself in the mirror and saw an unheroic, spiritually impotent middle-aged man. "The Man Who Studied Yoga" is one Jerry O'Shaugnessy, this story's equivalent of a hero; he's not the delicate tubercular boy Michael Fury, the great romantic who captured the heart of Gretta in "The Dead" and, from beyond the grave, shamed Gabriel. But he's a parody of the romantic—an adventurer and later a Bowery bum—who took charge of his destiny. He has become a subject of conversation for the timorous souls who get their kicks by watching porn and discharging resentful platitudes about what's wrong with American society. Mailer has written the equivalent of Joyce's story about social paralysis—here the characters are leftovers from the radical 1930s and failed bohemians rather than fanatical Irish Nationalists and limited old folks.

The narrator who leads us through Sam's agonizing day is a kibitzer-cum-judge, commenting on every play and taking brutal stock of Sam's limitations. Sam is someone who thinks of himself as a rebel, but when given half a chance, he opts for disengagement. He's the type who wants to write on the condition of the American working man in the 1950s—the failure of nerve, the sellouts to commercialism—but hasn't the guts to argue his points. He believes in Marxist action, but writes an article that talks about the working man's anxiety. Mailer skewers him for his timorousness; without the courage to live, to defy—especially to defy his smug psychoanalyst—Sam will never quite be a man. He seems incapable of seizing manly pleasures—later in the evening he circles his wife like "a sad hound"—and expressing manly aggression. In the 1950s Sam cannot "recapture the pleasurable bitterness which resides in the notion that one has suffered for one's principles." Ironically, he accuses "kids" of living in the aimless world that he himself dismally inhabits; for them, he claims, "there's no revolt, there's no acceptance." That center of indifference—to borrow Carlyle's phrase—is what Mailer rails against in this story. The position of no position: the convictionless, gutless world that Sam lives in is all the worse because he knows plenty of radical chic vocabulary with which to describe it. He can talk a blue streak, but can neither act nor feel strongly about his beliefs. He knows about the depredations of the Communist Party, the Moscow Trials, the prison camps, but—in the damning words of Mailer the narrator—"he is straddled between the loss of a country he has never seen and his repudiation of the country in which he lives." Elsewhere in *Advertisements for Myself*, Mailer has a nasty, but telling, remark about the brilliant sociologist David Riesman, the crack seems to fit parlor radicals like Sam rather than incisive writers like Riesman: he "says so little in so many words and like so many sociologists gives little feel or sense of life itself."

"Life itself": the story before us is about nothing less. What should a man mired in opinions, anxieties, Sunday newspapers, and responsibilities make of his own life? Living in a time after the grand illusions about the classless society, Sam cannot find any comfort in the old Marxist resentments:

> ... Sam is thinking it might be better to live the life of a worker, a simple life, to be completely absorbed by such necessities as food and money. Then one could believe that to be happy it was necessary only to have more money, more goods, less worries. It would be nice, Sam thinks, wistfully, to believe that the source of one's unhappiness comes not from oneself, but from the fault of the boss, or the world, or bad luck.

The role of the artist is equally unconvincing when he tries to assume it. A novel that would "lift him in a bound from the impasse in which he stifles, whose dozens of characters would develop a vision of life in bountiful complexity, lies foundered, rotting on a beach of purposeless effort." A "formless wreck"—a mere collection of pages with no hero—is all that he has to show. Sam also must admit that no hero seizes his imagination. "One could not have a hero today, Sam thinks, a man of action and contemplation, capable of sin, large enough for good, a man immense." Jerry O'Shaugnessy, after all, has wound up on the Bowery. What hope is there for the Sams of this world or for any image that they could conjure up? And what hope has there been in the day's adventure, the porno movie? Hideous and dehumanizing, the picture exposed the suffering of a young woman whose violation brought back an old memory for Sam. Later, while trying to sleep, he reconstructs and makes connections, recalling that the degraded woman in the movie was a friend from the past. His afternoon of kicks had been someone else's tragedy. And the despair has no outlet—no book to be written or faith to be embraced or action to be taken. It's like Matthew Arnold's famous pronouncement about modern tragic situations that produce no release. "Everything to be endured, nothing to be done." Or so it would seem to Sam. Mailer, the brooding narrator, understands Sam's anxieties but is not doomed by them. He is no more Sam than Joyce is Gabriel Conroy. "The Man Who Studied Yoga" is a phase in the development of the artist as tough guy: Mailer follows a severely damaged version of himself, a 1950s victim of false consciousness, through a purgatorial Sunday in Queens.

The next significant step for that persona is a leap into the kind of real struggle that Sam has never undergone—putting one's soul and talent on the line in a win-or-lose situation. Sam never tested his talent, retreating instead into living-room philosophizing, big plans, and articles conceived in cynical disillusionment. "Mailer"—with all his braggadocio, complaining, drugs, and neurosis—nevertheless shows what it is like to be a writer, how even his inferior novel *The Deer Park* used bitter satire directed at Hollywood sleaze and failed creativity to defy the resigned side of the 1950s. By no means the best section in the book, "The Fourth Advertisement for Myself" is about the bruiser-as-writer, the creative man delivering his insightful punches and taking a terrific beating. If poor ineffectual Sam—with his fantasies of power and protest—had no book to offer as a challenge to a complacent society, Mailer had a book that the publishing people found dangerous, a potential court case, and a commercial disaster. "The Fourth Advertisement" is a powerful apologia, intended to explain and offend. The explanation concerns what a writer of Mailer's sort must do: move out of his accustomed mode—the success of *The Naked and the Dead*—and try an experiment in form, in this case a murky, scathing story about the decadence and emptiness of the movie business. Whether you like the book or not, the writing in defense of it is strong Mailer—better, if truth be told, than what it's defending—and prepares the reader for the most memorable sections of *Advertisements*—those on Hip, the White Negro, and Beat. The sad hound Sam—anxious even to his young daughters—is here replaced by a central figure determined to fight his way out of sadness. The prose is tough, sometimes awkward, but quite genuine and honest. Mailer concedes that *The Deer Park*, once finished, didn't seem to him like a masterpiece. But it was a station in his journey, and he did not want what his publisher wanted—a book picked apart by editors and scared into shape by the obscenity laws. His publisher—at first willing to take a hit on the advance and let the book go elsewhere—eventually didn't want to pay. At this point Mailer swung into action, defending his flawed product with some enduring protest.

Mailer's invective is rooted in his sense of the times: "If the years since the war had not been brave or noble in the history of the country, which I certainly thought and do think, why then did it come as a surprise that people in publishing were not as good as they used to be. . . ." Or put more wildly, Mailer was left with "the cliques, fashions, vogues, snobs, snots, and fools, not to mention a dozen bureaucracies of criticism." What's a novelist who's restless with old themes and styles to do? His talent had once been marketed very well, but something had gone wrong—he was unable to deliver the predictable goods. And the role of the novelist had changed: the writer was no longer "a figure in the landscape." If you want to talk about the death of the author—that commonplace of end-of-the-century literary theory—Mailer was probably the first major figure in our national letters to realize that writers could no longer be writers in that old, rocked-ribbed, self-confident sense. They were ghostly presences on a balance sheet—or, at best, personalities in the public relations game. "One had become a set of relations and equations, most flourishing when most incorporated, for then one's literary stock was ready for merger. The day was gone when people held on to your novels no matter what others might say." Mailer's one-man resistance act was a matter of refusing to let his novel be eviscerated and resisting the temptation to let a mediocre manuscript go into print. He started to rewrite the book in galleys, transforming it into a story of personal responsibility. This is no place to analyze *The Deer Park*: the point is that Mailer in *Advertisements* tells us how he rewrote a halfway decent book about the cruelty of the world and made it into a book about the weakness of his characters. In short, he avoided the naturalistic clichés about harsh reality and delved into the mysterious territory of damaged selves. He faced the central insights of "The Man Who Studied Yoga." The process of getting the manuscript to the publisher is filled with the agony of being Mailer—of Seconal, Benzedrine, marijuana, bouts of depressions and bursts of energy. For all the bluster, swagger, and romance

in this tale of creative transcendence, there is also a curious honesty in
the telling: the book was not all it could be, not what it might have
been with two years' more work. Nor had Mailer much hope of
achieving a grand plan for an eight-part work. Nor would he ever
write a projected book about a concentration camp. This "Fourth Advertisement for Myself" is a strange mix of elements: a glamorous tale
of resisting the mediocrity of his age, yet a rather depressing account
of failures. The aggression and determination of this section brace up
Advertisements for Myself, make all the pain and doubt and struggle
invigorating.

Mailer's mid-century self expands to its full size—bursting out of
the limits of Sam's Slovoda's life, moving beyond the muzzy tentative-
ness of "The Fourth Advertisement"—in the justly famous essay "The
White Negro." This is Mailer's Everlasting-Yea, his twentieth century
equivalent of Carlyle's cry of exhilaration, insight, and personal redemption. It shows Mailer facing the opposing temptations of his generation—the allure and slickness of Madison Avenue, the whining and
nostalgia of the Old Left. He cobbles together his homemade philosophy of Hipness. As he expounds, we get a book of directions for overcoming inertia, an owner's manual for a newly formed self. Now
whether we want to own such a self is another matter. And Mailer is
far from being a salesman here. This is a manifesto with a sense of its
own dangers, a how-to and persuasive essay that has its doubts about
its own doctrines. Unlike the broad tradition of American books
about how to improve yourself, "The White Negro" contains explicit
warnings. Those who want to knock Mailer's sincerity may even de-
tect a hint of caginess and detachment from the outrageous beliefs. At
one point hipsters are referred to as "them," with all their psychopathology, but with all their life. Squares are static; hipsters are vectors.
To try on the hipster self, you have to be prepared for risks, awful
side effects—going crazy, losing touch with others, becoming a fascist,
being a bit of an ignoramus. (Mailer the intellectual points out that
hipsters "swing" and seem to understand complex ideas, but are often
illiterate.) But one thing you won't have to worry about is the horror
of nonbeing, of floating wraithlike in the air of other people's values
and ideas. (The hipster, like Yeats's "worst" in "The Second Coming,"
is filled with passionate intensity—and Mailer forthrightly envisions
the coming era as a time of violence.) The essay is perhaps the last
great testimony of self-making in American literature—later books on
determination are all about success and happiness, being a woman or

an executive or a minority. This one is in direct line with Emerson: he who would be a man must be a hipster. Like Emerson, Mailer is prepared to take brilliant shots at the world as we know it: at every kind of square, conformist, and tradition-bound type in view; like Emerson, he enjoys being outside the city of sense and reason. And like Emerson, he is proudly rude and often grandly above it all.

Mailer's Emersonianism is a prescription for his generation: "to create a new nervous system for themselves," rejecting the "antiquated nervous circuits" of society, parents, and the past. And Mailer's version of life-giving power—sexual, aggressive, rhetorical—is everywhere at odds with the social wisdom of the past. He describes his ethic this way: "what makes it radically different from Socratic moderation with its stern conservative respect for the experience of the past is that the Hip ethic is immoderation, childlike in its adoration of the present . . ." The "lifemanship" of Mailer's essay is intuitive, not learned or inherited—it's about the discovery of inner energy and "the burning consciousness of the present." Emersonianism is at the root of this consciousness—of its urgency, impatience, and irrationality: "Great men . . . have always . . . confided themselves childlike to the genius of their age, betraying their perception that the absolutely trustworthy was seated at their heart, working through their hands, predominating in their being." It's a dangerous way to live. Emerson says it has "edge"; Mailer admits it's close to self-destructiveness—but both find that the alternative, some accommodation to past models, is a form of suicide. Emerson says so flat out; Mailer goes into lengthy descriptions of what it means to kill off the vital self.

Mailer's hipster—seizer of the moment, creature of impulse, disbeliever in "the socially monolithic ideas of the single mate, the solid family and the respectable love life"—is a kind of pychopath, which is to say an adventurer who refuses to sublimate his sexual and aggressive instincts. Now if Ralph Waldo Emerson sounds far from such experimentation, consider the passages in "Self-Reliance" that hold up the boy or the fractious child or the rude skeptic as a model. Emerson's "nonchalance of boys" disdains, refuses to conciliate, calculate consequences. "A boy is in the parlor what the pit is in the playhouse; independent, irresponsible. . . ." Infants also impress Emerson with their force and freedom from divided purpose. They have no sense of "the strength and means" opposed to their wills: "Infancy conforms to nobody; all conform to it; so that one babe commonly makes four or five out of the adults who prattle and play to it." And further compare

Emerson's put-down of maturity, "the man is as it were clapped into jail by his consciousness," with Mailer's look at the unhip compromiser in the age of conformity: "A man knew that when he dissented, he gave note upon his life which could be called in any year of overt crisis. No wonder then that these have been the years of conformity and depression. A stench of fear has come out of every pore of American life, and we suffer from a collective failure of nerve." The unmanning of the individual—Emerson's "Society everywhere is in conspiracy against the manhood of every one of its members"—is the focus of Mailer's screed. Listen to it in his cry for orgasm—a sometimes poignant, but more often ridiculous demand for improved selfhood through enhanced intercourse. Perverse, truculent, flying high above the superego—into some realm beyond manners, sense, artistic order, and decency—"The White Negro" is one of our most stubborn and unusual protests against being a mature adult. All you ever needed to know you learned not on an analyst's couch, in a family, at a school, on a committee, but listening to jazz, raging, or having sex. And what you don't need to know is the wisdom of 1950s intellectuals—Freudian ideas of renunciation, Lionel Trilling's ideas about moral complexity and maturity. "The White Negro" is a gateway to a kind of mad autonomy, a royal road to self-absorption. And like many important works of thought—Blake's *The Marriage of Heaven and Hell*, Marx's *The Communist Manifesto*—its life and breath is contained in its outbursts, its illogic, its offensiveness. A small essay that follows "White Negro" is meant to draw some distinctions between Hipsters and Beatniks and in so doing separate the mild-mannered coffeehouse Beat and his roots in old bohemia from the dangerous hipster "with that muted animal voice which shivered the national attention when first used by Marlon Brando." Mailer, in his own talky way, was attempting to produce similar shivers.

In a coda to part 4 of *Advertisements*, Mailer reproduces a 1958 interview with Richard Stern titled "Hip, Hell, and the Navigator." The piece—given Mailer's patchwork, ramshackle structure—is part of the kind of book he is writing. It stands as a summation of his ideas about Hip—and a refutation of those who say that *Advertisements* is all rant and doubletalk. Stern asked Mailer a provoking question: Is Hipness a pose of some sort, a kind of playacting and adventurism, or is it a serious aspect of a writer's life? This gave Mailer his chance to explain how hipsters' experiences—the drugs, music, sex—relate to expression. He argues that the hipster "lives in a state of extreme awareness," and, far from being the scattered, random, detached drug-head, he is actually a man with intense powers of concentration. Mailer says, "His page becomes more filled." He is the supercharged observer. What he observes is our civilization's descent into deadness, the steady erosion of our sensual life by our organizational life. And before long Mailer has made this decline into a cosmic struggle—with God and the hipster struggling to preserve lifemanship and civilization pointing the way to death.

The attack on powerful civilizations of course is nothing new in modern thought—its line runs from Jean-Jacques Rousseau (with his hatred of cities) to the young Marx (with capitalism drowning all values in "the icy water of egoistical calculation") to D. H. Lawrence (with his "vivid and fresh," small-is-better Etruscans as against his imposing, monument-building Romans). But Mailer had his say at a time when most Americans were dependent on the organizational powers of civilization and when most had the feeling that the life of the senses was a private business. Mailer insists that sense experience is damaged by the very logic and mental construction that has made us a powerful nation. And he has lasted longer with his message—the message of uninhibited hipster waging a "noble" (one his favorite words) battle with the civilized square—than others of his era. The anti-repression message was the master theme of Norman O. Brown's scholarly study *Life against Death:* man must find a way out of the life-denying forces that seem to constitute his reality. But Brown's discourse—fine as it is—does not have the urgency of Mailer's work. Mailer's *Advertisements* is the poetic expression of this argument—metaphoric, slangy, breathless, filled with memorable phrases. He warns us that we may destroy ourselves in "the cold insensate expression of due process of law and atomic radiation." He writes of the "teleological" drive of the senses; that drive is our "navigator" in a world where we are otherwise caught in the drift of technology. His core prose pieces in *Advertisements for Myself* are classics in a long tradition of literary discontent. And they are unusually bracing in that their rhetoric is a one-man performance, not the voice of a power block.

chapter 5

The New Observers

Mailer's coruscating critique of American civilization was essentially rhetoric and argument. The major fictional observers of American manners had their own ways of manhandling the conventions of the era and making them into scathing stories. Vladimir Nabokov, Dawn Powell, and Randall Jarrell went to work on a range of middle-class American pretensions. Each writer saw the postwar scene aslant—with an eccentric, ironic eye. Each found the anomalies in our lives, made us laugh at our trends and fads, refused to let us accept ourselves on the terms of the mass media—or on the precious terms of bohemia or academe. Mailer, the savage rhetorician, denounced the complacency of the age in the generalized way of the philosophical essayist. But these writers—dramatizers rather than polemicists—captured very specific American habits: our movie fantasies, extravagant expectations, social rigidities, bad tastes, and outrageous ways of being ourselves. They gave us a mid-century compendium of American ludicrousness. Not quite satiric because they had no definite corrective purpose, not quite sociological because of their exaggerations and curlicues and quirky asides, they were nevertheless inventors of permanently important images of America—pictures of folly and limitation, for sure, but also fabulous, absurd, loopy versions of the national condition that were, each in its own way, acts of love.

Nabokov's *Lolita* used extraordinary means to present his version of American civilization after World War II. His novel was a moral outrage, a nasty insult to the national character, a poke in the eye at progress, and a brain-herniating assault on the good old idea of a love story. The book was everything a postwar novel shouldn't have been—sexy in a creepy rather than farmer-boy salacious way; snide about American manners without offering some gauge of integrity in the form of a hero and some satiric ballast; and intricate, quirky, and intellectual when—as Trilling warned in *The Liberal Imagination* back in 1950—Americans like brute power, emotion, and raw fact in their social fiction. The book should have been a publishing disaster, given the moral literalness of the times and the books on the bestseller list. In fact it was spectacularly successful and has become a classic view of America and Americans. Nabokov's techniques were nowhere else to be found—the slyness, the social observation melting into mysterious musing, the sardonic European voice mimicking (and sometimes falling in love with) American idioms and clichés, the buffo and sophistication, the jostle of the morally outrageous and the all-too-human, the jocose survey of us—our expressions, foods, manners, living rooms, religious convictions, movies. At the time—the book came out in 1955 in Paris—there was no labyrinthine Pynchon or nutty Bartheleme, no playful Barth or mordant Heller to send up American pop culture and social habits with wit and brio. We had no Joyce of our own, no one who could manage compelling narrative, comic wordplay, social criticism, and pathos all at once. There was also no synoptic observer of the manners of the American people—no one who went cross-country depicting our general nature in a time of prosperity.

Nabokov did for the late forties and fifties what Dickens and Tocqueville had done for the mid-nineteenth century—brought an alien eye and a judgmental prose. Humbert Humbert's Old World taste, sophistication, wide reading—despite his sick obsession—are fascinating; New World vulgarity, naivete, and movie literacy are laughable. Nabokov's United States is a kitschy, culturally debased, infinitely comic source of entertainment; and we—Americans who find Humbert perverted and indecent—are nevertheless made to go along with his perceptions because they mine a permanent truth that Dickens and Tocqueville discovered about us: our noisy, self-celebratory side. After war and Depression and war in the twentieth century, Nabokov recrystallized an unflattering image of our civilization that came from the mid-nineteenth century, offering a comprehensive critical view of what is absurd about a new country. This is not about Main Street or the North Shore of Long Island or Brahmin Boston: it's a transcontinental look at our temperament, done on a scale of the great foreign evaluators. *Democracy in America*, an abstract work about a tyrannical majority culture—with its over-the-top political rhetoric, boosterism, and contempt for the individual—is the intellectual ancestor of *Lolita*, a work about the defeat of a subtle European elitist. Nabokov's book shows forbidden love, art, and high culture misunderstood and manhandled—as the movies and the theme motels and the ordinary loves live on. Dickens's *Martin Chuzzlewit* foreshadowed Nabokov's

America more concretely: it's a survey of the bragging, the crudity of manners, the loud humor and dead seriousness, the lack of skepticism and the self-celebration. Just compare Dickens's Elijah Pogram, a boasting politician, with Nabokov's bumptious headmistress Miss Pratt at Beardsley School—in each case the air thick with clichés, howlers, digs at the wisdom of the Old World and narcissistic gems. Each character is describing an ideal type, the first the rugged American of the 1840s, the second the well-adjusted teenager of the 1950s. Pogram proclaims,

> Our fellow countryman is a model of a man, quite fresh from Natur's mould. . . . He is a true-born child of this free hemisphere. Verdant as the mountains of our country; bright and flowing as our mineral Licks; unspiled by withering conventionalities as our air broad and boundless Perearers! Rough he may be. So air are Barrs. Wild he may be. So air our Buffalers. But he is a child of Natur', and a child of Freedom; and his boast to the Despot and the Tyrant is, that his bright home is in the Settin Sun.

Miss Pratt explains,

> We are not so much concerned, Mr. Humbird, with having our students become bookworms or be able to reel off all the capitals of Europe which nobody knows anyway, or learn by heart the dates of forgotten battles. What we are concerned with is the adjustment of the child to group life. This is why we stress the four D's: Dramatics, Dance, Debating and Dating. . . . Dr. Hummer, do you realize that for the modern pre-adolescent child, medieval dates are of less vital value than weekend ones [twinkle]? . . . What on earth can Dorothy Hummerson care for Greece and the Orient with their harems and slaves?"

Nabokov takes us on a national tour of inflation and distortion— linguistic ("Maffy On Say" for my fiancée), decorative ("the pictures above the beds were identical twins"), culinary ("they call those fries 'French,' *grand Dieu!*" or "cottage-cheese-crested salads"), romantic (the breakfast nook "simulating that Coffee Shoppe where in their college days Charlotte and Humbert used to coo together"). He shows off the swagger and silliness and hoopla, not for satiric purposes but out of sheer joy. No matter where Humbert is, he finds Americans promoting themselves, being as brassy and bombastic as he is reserved. The New World rhetoric and aesthetic is comically triumphant as the Old World of sensibility and subtlety tries to hide itself. And we become, as we read, minority partners with Humbert the trangressor-protagonist, accessories and savorers of his social and cultural observations. These latter are a combination of mischievous pleasure and intellectual repulsion. Susan Sontag's remark about Camp describes our bond with Humbert as he looks at the campy spectacle of America: we're fascinated and repelled, drawn in by the outrageous and ever conscious that, somehow, it's pretty awful. Nabokov teaches us to relish the silliness that we might otherwise take for granted. His American spectacles mirror Lolita herself—ethereal nymphet but "cheapest of cheap cuties," part sublimity, part vulgarity. They are infinitely seductive, intriguing—advertisements that lead you on and immerse you in delight and disdain. One of Nabokov's favorite literary techniques—metamorphosing things and people—is central to Lolita and to the nature of Camp: objects become other objects. Try these: "A winery in California with a church built in the shape of a wine barrel" or "A zoo in Indiana where a large troop of monkeys lived on a concrete replica of Christopher Columbus' flagship." "A natural cave in Arkansas converted to a cafe," "a replica of the Grotto of Lourdes in Louisiana," "Colonial" inns, roadside facilities called "Buck's-Doe's," just-like-home-raid-the icebox kitchens in hotels or the Frigid Queen milk bar. Don't forget about Charlotte Haze trying to be a cosmopolitan sophisticate and Clare Quilty, the ultimate protean man. And, finally, there is Humbert transformed by the American scene.

Everything and everyone frantically strives to be something else—bigger, more ideal, grander, cuter, more sophisticated. All drinks, as Humbert notices, are ice-cold. And many of the transformations are funny and ominous at the same time: Take "Big Frank," the guy in charge of the motel where Humbert is resting while Lo is in the hospital. He is a walking mirage, and at the same time a living amusement park of kitschy tricks:

> At twenty paces Frank used to look a mountain of health; at five, as now, he was a ruddy mosaic of scars—had been blown through a wall overseas; but despite nameless injuries he was able to man a tremendous truck, fish, hunt, drink, and buoyantly dally with roadside ladies. That day, either because it was such a great holiday, or simply because he wanted to divert a sick man, he had taken off the glove he usually wore on his left hand (the one pressing against the side of the door) and re-

vealed to the fascinated sufferer not only an entire lack of fourth and
fifth fingers, but also a naked girl, with cinnabar nipples and indigo
delta, charmingly tattooed on the back of his crippled hand, its index
and middle digit making her legs while her wrist bore her flower-
crowned head. Oh, delicious . . . reclining against the woodwork, like
some sly fairy.

Lolita is about the extremes of America. Nabokov soars as he discovers our totally original ways of twisting and unbalancing everything from food and lodgings to education and religion. To Humbert
America is a country of wonders and curiosities, awful and exquisitely
campy surprises. And where else, paradoxically, is Humbert to find a
way to sublimity but on the highway of vulgarity? And where would
he—or Nabokov—be without the demotic, the trashy, the kitschy, the
inanely inflated? Nabokov would have been left with his rather pathetic 1930s short story about an older man who got rid of his middle-
aged bride and seduced her daughter. Without his passion for American junk—which is his subject, his ambience, his characters' idiom,
his grand passion—he would be like Milton without Satan, a writer
stranded with his ideas of goodness and truth. No 1950s America, no
legendary novel.

The people in *Lolita* are Nabokov's complex tribute to Americanism—not to be taken entirely seriously, but not mere satiric punching
bags either. The characters straddle that territory between parody and
pathos. Begin with Humbert, a European trying to appeal to Americans, trying to pass as a suburban father. In *The Annotated Lolita,*
Alfred Appel makes reference in a note to the *New York Herald Trib-
une's Penny* cartoon, a strip done by Harry Haenigsen that started in
1943. The comic depicted a bobby-soxer whose pipe-smoking, news-
paper-reading dad was always around to put his dry or chortling two
cents into the infinitely amusing, fresh, and restless new world of teen
culture. What becomes apparent to the reader of *Lolita* is that Penny's
dad is the paradigm of Humbert: at one point Nabokov has his character awkwardly poised with his new pipe and bulky newspaper—
both suburban middle-class props inappropriate to Humbert the
Hound—as he observes the behavior of his teenager. Humbert
watches Lolita carefully as she admires the cartoon: "Her eyes would
follow the adventures of her favorite strip characters: there was one
well-drawn sloppy bobby-soxer, with high cheekbones and angular
gestures, that I was not above enjoying myself." *Lolita* is a kind of

perverse, sustained *Penny* cartoon with Humbert playing his uneasy part while enjoying his bobby-soxer. Nabokov delights in showing him learning to handle our native materials—be they locutions or manners or everyday things. His public persona has to be the American-dad persona, but he wears it hilariously. The solidity of Penny's dad is blended with the diction of the pedant, a whiff of the movie glamour boy, and the intentions of a dirty younger man—the combination of elements is what makes Humbert a splendid amalgam, a true melting pot of traits. Look at this one for the Nabokovian blend of elements: " 'Come and kiss your old man,' I would say, 'and drop that moody nonsense. In former times, when I was your dream male [the reader will notice what pains I took to speak Lo's tongue], you swooned to records of the number one throb-and-sob idols of your coevels [Lo: "Of my what? Speak English"]. That idol of your pals sounded like friend Humbert. But now, I am just your *old man*, a dream dad protecting his dream daughter.' " Humbert, unlike Dickens's protagonist Martin Chuzzlewit with his lectures about the faults of Americans, has a curious, sly way of exposing us to ourselves—and yet making the exposure pleasurable. A wonderful outburst here and there, a *mot* ("throb and sob idols"), a turn of phrase—never a sermon. Humbert's outbursts and cracks are wonderfully timed units of affectionate disdain. Without them, there is no *Lolita*. The lyricism, alternating with the tongue-in-cheek stiffness, alternating with real annoyance, alternating with genuine curiosity make the following passage the essence of Humbert; it is written of course in "Humbertish," a quirky hybridization of Old and New World speech, not in Lo's idiom:

> A combination of naivete and deception, of charm and vulgarity, of blue sulks and rosy mirth, Lolita, when she chose, could be a most exasperating brat. I was not really prepared for her fits of disorganized boredom, intense and vehement griping, her sprawling, droopy, dopey-eyed style, and what is called goofing off—a kind of diffused clowning which she thought was tough in a boyish hoodlum way. Mentally, I found her to be a disgustingly conventional little girl. Sweet hot jazz, square dancing, gooey fudge sundaes, musicals, movie magazines and so forth—these were the obvious items in her list of beloved things. The Lord knows how many nickels I fed to the gorgeous music boxes that came with every meal we had! I still hear the nasal voices of those invisibles serenading her, people with names like Sammy and Jo and Eddy and Tony and Peggy and Guy and Patty and Rex, and sentimental song

hits, all of them as familiar to my ear as her various candies were to my palate.

But to reach the heart and soul of Humbertian slyness, one must watch him evaluate Charlotte Haze, that quintessence of American camp and kitsch. Big Haze is a vehicle for Humbert's spleen, Schadenfreude, and general nastiness. She is the embodiment of pretentiousness, a wondrous example—an ideal type—of the person trying to be something other than herself. The mangled French ("Dolores Haze, ne montrez pas vos zhambes."), the attempt at Old World amenities (coffee on the piazza), the artiness (the Van Gogh print), the international flavor of her decor (the Mexican knickknacks), the aura of the good person (struggling with the truth of sexual need and social ambition), the kittenish manner (in conflict with the middle-aged reality), the parental integrity (masking the jealousy of her daughter): Nabokov unpacks the whole bag of bourgeois tricks and makes them central to the novel's meaning. Charlotte is decent, when compared to a pervert, but somehow not on the side of anything we as readers could possibly admire. She's the ludicrous side of the national character—given to self-serving and sententious speeches, outbursts of righteousness, displays of sentiment. She's a living, breathing kitsch artifact, down to the diction out of self-help books. Humbert lamely inquires whether Lo will be happy at Camp Q. Charlotte parrots the psychobabble of the 1950s, but cannot help lacing it with the deep-down resentments of a competitive woman: " 'She'd better,' said Haze. 'And it won't be all play either. The camp is run by Shirley Holmes—you know the woman who wrote *Campfire Girl*. Camp will teach Dolores Haze to grow in many things—health, knowledge, temper. And particularly in a responsibility toward other people. Shall we take these candles with us and sit for a while on the piazza, or do you want to go to bed and nurse that tooth?' 'Nurse that tooth.' " Who wouldn't prefer to nurse that tooth?

Nabokov has made us say to ourselves, like Milton's Satan, that "to do aught good never will be our task, / But ever to do ill our sole delight." We're on Humbert's side—which is to say we're against cant and hot air of all kinds; yet we're damned—tragic victims of our sensibilities, incapable of living in a normal world of Big Hazes. Lionel Trilling's observations about doomed love—Tristan and others—is wonderfully on target: *Lolita* is about that great Western battle between passionate sensibility and decency. Nabokov has also pioneered a new topic in American letters: the situation of the highly conscious individual—up to his neck in ideology, breathing in pop psychology, advertising slogans, the rhetoric of gung-ho 1950s America, but trying to find some space for his own desire. One thing Humbert and Lo can agree on is the oppressive rhetoric of the age. She's questioned by him about Camp Q: "'Well—I joined all the activities that were offered.' 'Ensuite?' 'Ansooit, I was taught to live happily and richly with others and to develop a wholesome personality. Be a cake, in fact.'" Neither Humbert nor Lo in her nymphet phase is in any danger of "being a cake"—they are cool, judgmental, ironic, sly, and rather cruel. To Humbert, Charlotte is "the old cat," "a weak solution of Marlene Dietrich," a spouter of book-club clichés who lacks a "soul." To Lolita, her friends are adversaries: little Ginny McCoo is lame and mean and nearly died of polio. If asked to choose "between a Hamburger and a Humburger, she would—invariably, with icy precision—plump for the former." Although Humbert is fastidious and Lo wallows in the junk culture, they both enjoy debunking and deflating the conventions of home, school, community. Humbert is a connoisseur of teen cynicism: "The Girl Scout motto," said Lo rhapsodically, "is also mine. I fill my life with worthwhile deeds such as—well, never mind what. My duty is—to be useful. I am a friend of male animals. I obey orders. I am cheerful. That was another police car. I am thrifty and absolutely filthy in thought, and word and deed." They share responses—tongue-in-cheekiness, mock earnestness, sneering evaluation, wisecracking (for Lo), and wit (for Humbert). The difference of course is that Humbert directs these attitudes toward the culture as a whole, toward parenting advice in books, Duncan Hines, and movie stars. Lo reserves her disdain for the decencies of home life and has plenty of ardor for the commercial trash of the highways and the magazines.

On the Road with Humbert and Lolita is totally different from being on Jack Kerouac's road—it's judgment on one side, with Humbert's voice dominating and making ironic poetry out of the ads and motels and social types; on the other, it's Lo's voice begging for more amusement, hype, and glitz. No Sal Paradise and Dean Moriarty digging the American scene, this couple looks out from the car window in a different mood. *Lolita* is not about digging America; it's about a peculiar, uneasy, humorous way of savoring the crude power of the country while knowing full well that you're in a tragic mess. A fabulous, overpowering landscape assaults two doomed people, but that landscape turns dismal just when it should be sublime. Humbert's European imagination conjured up a bold Appalachian Mountain region—"a gigantic Switzerland or even Tibet, all mountain, glorious diamond peak upon peak, giant conifers, *le montagnard emigré* in his bear skin glory, and *Felix tigris goldsmithi*, and Red Indians under the catalpas. That it all boiled down to a measly suburban lawn and a smoking garbage incinerator was appalling." And almost everything that is dismal and annoying is also ominous. Take this piece of artful sociology with its put-downs at the expense of several American types:

> Oh, I had to keep a very sharp eye on Lo, little Limp Lo! Owing perhaps to constant amorous exercise, she radiated, despite her childish appearance, some special languorous glow which threw garage fellows, hotel pages, vacationists, goons in luxurious cars, maroon morons near blued pools, into fits of concupiscence which might have tickled my pride, had it not incensed my jealousy. For little Lo was aware of that glow of hers, and I would often catch her *coulant un regard* in the direction of some amiable male, some grease monkey, with a sinewy golden-brown forearm and watch-braceleted wrist, and hardly had I turned my back to go and buy this Lo a lollipop, than I would hear her and the fair mechanic burst into a perfect love song of wisecracks.

The book is an unwholesome, uneasy buddy story about two people in such a situation: the one with his fixation and his high culture tastes, the other with her eye out for the next treat and thrill. Humbert the lover scorns the maroon morons; Lo the beloved—like a lady in a courtly romance who is oblivious of her lover—is enchanted by them. Yet where would Humbert be as a literary creation without a culture of goons in luxurious cars to exasperate him, lift him to poetic heights, and sharpen the pain of loving Lo?

The critical attitudes of the book—embedded in puns and every kind of humor—are a part of the ongoing American critique of "masscult and midcult." Nabokov—like Dwight Macdonald in his famous 1960 essay—is a pioneering observer of the effects of pop culture, middlebrowism, and the culture industry. *Lolita* is a brilliantly illustrated guide to cultural inanity—and builds up a vision of disdain in such a way as to make Nabokov one of the major evaluators of post-World War II culture. He shows us immersed in products, movie plots, song lyrics, and mass-produced wisdom. He has fun while skewering us. Macdonald delighted in showing the mishmash of cultural products that have no authentic identity: his famous one-liner about the Revised Standard Version of the Bible is a case in point—"like taking apart Westminster Abbey to make Disneyland out of the fragments." Humbert, refusing to do the standard globe-trotting with his "brand-new large-as-life wife," parodies the dazed tourist's version of Englishness and comes up with a similar travesty:

> I can well imagine the thrill that you, a healthy American gal, must experience at crossing the Atlantic on the same ocean liner as Lady Bumble—or Sam Bumble, the Frozen Meat King, or a Hollywood harlot. And I doubt not that you and I would make a pretty ad for the Traveling Agency when portrayed looking—you, frankly, starry-eyed, I, controlling my envious admiration—at the Palace Sentries, or Scarlet Guards, or Beaver Eaters, or whatever they are called.

Macdonald's point about masscult—whether in movies, songs, or magazines—is that it provides built-in response for the consumer and never offers anything that isn't already known—no new pleasure or stimulation or idea. The point is actually taken from Theodor W. Adorno's observation about popular music: "The composition hears for the listener." In *Lolita,* the movie going fits this description: Lo's favorite pictures—"musicals, underworlders, and westerners" (the last a sly mangling of westerns)—are generic, no-name affairs that provide us with our reactions. Each type has its own set of conventions, props, and formulae—quite like Liberace's candelabra as cited by Dwight Macdonald. Humbert is a master at detecting the building-in process, giving us just the right details, including the ways the genres read him—as proud father of Lolita on stage in *The Enchanted Hunter,* as criminal, and as desperate man in a showdown with his nemesis Quilty. The movies—in all their falsity—ironically provide just the right foreshadowing of his fate:

> In the first, real singers and dancers had unreal stage careers in an essentially grief-proof sphere of existence wherefrom death and truth were banned, and where, at the end, whitehaired, dewy-eyed, technically deathless, the initially reluctant father of a show-crazy girl always finished by applauding her apotheosis on fabulous Broadway. The underworld was a world apart: there heroic newspapermen were tortured, telephone bills ran to billions, and, in a robust atmosphere of incompetent marksmanship, villains were chased through sewers and storehouses by pathologically fearless cops (I was to give them less exercise).

Finally there was the mahogany landscape, the florid-faced, blue-eyed roughriders, the prim pretty schoolteacher arriving in Roaring Gulch, the rearing horse, the spectacular stampede, the pistol thrust through the shivered windowpane, the stupendous fist fight, the crashing mountain of dusty old-fashioned furniture, the table used as a weapon, the timely somersault, the pinned hand groping for the dropped bowie knife, the grunt, the sweet crash of fist against chin, the kick in the belly, the flying tackle; and immediately after a plethora of pain that would have hospitalized a Hercules (I should know by now), nothing to show but the rather becoming bruise on the bronzed cheek of the warmed-up hero embracing his gorgeous frontier bride.

Nabokov caricatures what Macdonald calls "a substitute for the unsettling and unpredictable (hence unsalable) joy, tragedy, wit, change, originality and beauty of real life." The vacuity, however, takes on an interest of its own because Nabokov's language galvanizes it into life. What's formulaic and insipid suddenly becomes original and funny. The worst of our culture emerges as art. Nabokov, like Joyce, can spring an epiphany out of dross. Through a turn of phrase ("grief-proof sphere of existence"), an unpredictable observation ("a robust atmosphere of incompetent marksmanship"), a startling alliteration ("would have hospitalized a Hercules"), or a devastating irony (a corny situation pointing to pathos) he effects his own transformation, makes an insight slither out of the old form of an inanity. He is our master of popular culture in the sense that he masters it for a greater purpose than mere irony or kidding or low-level satire. We cringe, but we also rise above the junk and laugh and cry because we see that passion shines forth from American kitsch.

One of the book's most notable examples of dross-into-poetry is Humbert's excursion into lyric verse writing. He calls it a psychopath's outpouring, but what it really amounts to is a weird parody of the new world he has lived in with Lolita. At once jocular and tender, slangy and artful, sly and wounded, it shows what Nabokov made of various kinds of American junk. Out of lurid notices in post offices—

> *Wanted, wanted: Dolores Haze.*
> *Hair: brown. Lips: scarlet*
> *Age: five thousand three hundred days.*
> *Profession: none, or "starlet."*

Out of American automobile obsession (without which there would be no *Lolita*)—

Where are you riding Dolores Haze?
What make is the magic carpet?
Is a Cream Cougar the present craze?
And where are you parked, my car pet?

Humbert becomes a country music lyricist, with his usual flair for a pun:

Oh Dolores, that jukebox hurts!
Are you still dancin', darlin'?
(Both in worn levis, both in torn T-shirts
And I, in my corner, snarlin').

And by the end of the poem—imagining himself chasing the runaway Lolita with a cop, using a movie climax to describe the scene ("Whip out your gun and follow that car")—he is still in the grip of popular culture:

My car is limping, Dolores Haze,
And the last long lap is the hardest,
And I shall be dumped where the weed decays
And the rest is rust and stardust.

Hoagy Carmichael's sentimental favorite "Stardust" is on Humbert's lips because he needs Hoagy to be perfectly himself and true to his Lolita.

Finding ludicrousness and pathos in culture—using mediocre art rather than kitsch to read metropolitan minds and to make characters come alive in the 1950s—was the specialty of Dawn Powell, one of the best novelists of manners of the postwar period. No Nabokov in her intellectual grasp and imaginative penetration, she nevertheless used the pretentious, the awful, the trendy, and the brassy as her primary material. Powell has lately become a much respected figure, praised by Gore Vidal as a major comic novelist and brought forward as a brilliant fictional stylist and letter writer by Tim Page. Her particular gift involved taking a comprehensive look at various social types, nailing down foibles, spotting the ludicrous. Yet the experience of reading her fine novel about 1950s Greenwich Village, *The Golden Spur*, is not quite like reading Sinclair Lewis's *Babbitt* or Mary McCarthy's *The*

Group. Powell's breakneck, dizzying narrative does not seem much
involved in flaying characters alive. The book is about a young man
named Jonathan Jamison from Silver City, Ohio, who comes to Manhattan to find out the truth of his paternity. His mother—once a bohemian of the 1920s with a pack of stories about artists and writers
and her great unnamed love—had returned to Ohio pregnant with
Jonathan, married a flour products salesman John Jamison ("all he
reads is sales letters, all he writes is orders") and led a conventional
life. Jonathan has pieced together her story of art and glamour and is
determined to seek out her old friends in hopes of learning what he
himself might be made of. He is soon caught up in the kind of ridiculous, absurd existences of people in the arts—both the old crowd and
the new crop of artists, writers, and hangers-on. Powell has a deft way
of showing us limited, often self-deluding, and more often silly bohemians—and falling in love with their faults. Like Nabokov, she
doesn't invent her version of 1950s America for strict satiric purposes:
the goal is pleasure and wit, not some sententious point. She takes a
look at the older phase of Greenwich Village, the writers who remember what life was like before rents rose and publicity ruled the arts.
They are a wonderful collection of strugglers and survivors. But she
is especially sharp in studying the starting point of the postmodern
condition, the stage at which the culture industry with its demand for
names and trendy goods has displaced the makeshift world of the artist and writer. The book is really about an American artistic community that has undergone a radical shift—no longer is it sufficient to
have something to say in print or to represent on canvas. The creator
in the new Village is now swept up by forces that determine the substance and nature of his creations—not to mention his survival. The
whirlwind of commercial demands, fashionable parties, in-and-out
groups, superfluous older people, and the in-touch young are
Powell's subjects. To adapt a line from Lionel Trilling's *The Liberal
Imagination*, Powell writes about the crossroads between art and
trendiness. In so doing, she enlightens and entertains readers without
making us draw conclusions.

Spectacle is Powell's specialty—the look and pace of heated-up
New York life in the era of the Abstract Expressionists. She goes from
scene to scene—from the epicenter of the story at a Village bar called
The Golden Spur to the margins in midtown and even to Connecticut—and shows us the way the creating classes (and their fellow travelers and parasites) lived then. The Spur is in many respects the book's

protagonist—more than any character it gives shape and meaning to the story. In settling into a neighborhood, Powell tells us, the most important thing is to have your bar—apartments and jobs come and go, but the hangout is the defining place. The Spur dates back to the speakeasy days and has a rather unspoiled, seedy charm: in the present action of the book it functions as a primitive Internet, a recovery center, a clubhouse for writers at loose ends. It touches all the lives and gives the characters a medium in which to be distinctly themselves: they can ramble, whine, cry, reminisce, feel better, hope. If Powell weren't so skillful a writer—able to make the Spur's habitués into living, quirky, unpredictable people—we might mistake this for a souped-up intellectual version of *Cheers*. But only listen to the talk—and follow the threads of relationships that extend around town—and you will discover Powell's complex vision of society.

Jonathan—Telemachus as a Midwestern rube—goes out to find stories of the past and in the process manages to meet everyone from the elderly lady of letters Claire Van Orphen (who goes to the Spur for the first time with Jonathan) to barflies like the pink-haired Lize Britten and her dizzy pal Darcy Trent. The plot—wherein Jonathan discovers his real father (a rich old philanderer who bankrolled a gallery), achieves social and professional standing in that same pretentious art gallery, and soon thereafter gives up on the world of glamour that he has just conquered—is very sinuous, quite amusing, but hardly equal to Powell's people.

These characters are profiled in deft, traditional-discursive passages and dramatic scenes. There is author Claire Van Orphen, once an employer of Jonathan's mother and a veteran from the 1920s. She comes complete with her thirty-year-old couturier clothes, illusions, corner cutting on meals, and small literary output. Powell knows the character down to the last detail—from the small travel articles for magazines to the beige silk cape to "cover any defect." She also informs Claire with a dignity and pathos that make her genuinely interesting. To her uptown sister who patronizes her writing and her pinched lifestyle—and to the new young people in jeans—Claire is a stranger in her own territory. Wouldn't it be great, Claire muses, to have someone to share a red-letter day with? The bitch sister—thanks to Powell's use of the omniscient point of view—also helps to complete the portrait of Claire: "it's as if she had to have a transfusion from the past every day in order to get through the present." Darcy Trent—two generations away—is handled with equal skill. Powell gets it right as she pinpoints the solidity of your basic harum-scarum of the period:

> She seemed womanly and practical too, and you thought Darcy must be like those small iron pioneer women in the Conestoga wagons, whipping men and children across the prairies, sewing, building, plowing, cooking, nursing, saving her menfolks from their natural folly and improvidence. The fact was that Darcy had never darned a sock, seldom made her own bed, thought coffee was born in delicatessen containers and all food grew in frozen packages. Her practicality exhibited itself in tender little cries of, "But you'll be sick, honey, if you don't eat something after all that bourbon! You must eat. Here, eat this pretzel."

The Powell approach to human nature is subtle, despite the ludic language and love of silliness: as a satirist of a kind, she studies foibles and real character defects, but she lets her people have their humanity. Claire's sister Bea—for all her 57th Street chic—is probably as lonely as Claire; of her deceased husband she thinks, "I don't know why on God's earth I missed him after he was dead, because I missed him more when he was alive."

The last line—a signature Powell epigram—gives the flavor of her comic vision, a view of people rooted in sadness, irony, and the need to brace oneself up with a clever answer to life's disappointments. The book is filled with characters who come back at the awfulness of ordinary experience—at the common run of dispiriting events and false people and depressing mischances that face us all. No wonder Edmund Wilson—that intrepid writer who disliked Kafka and refused to give way to disappointment—loved Powell: she shows up life for what it is and refuses to be bitter or to lie down. She actually takes a certain pleasure from the unpleasant, as in this line about "the heady New York air": "that delirious narcotic of ancient sewer dust, gasoline fumes, roasting coffee beans, and the harsh smell of sea that intoxicates inland nostrils." One of her best-drawn characters, the artist Hugow, says it perfectly; over the summer he's been kept by classy Cassie Bender, a big-time gallery owner; he spent time lounging around with "the cream of the Cape," received a lot of adulation, and saw a lot of dune grass. What he wants is to get back to "people who hated him for himself alone and not because he was doing all right." Hugow—fed up with being fed—wants to want, not to have. He's looking, on returning to the city, for that unnatural sickly green of bums' complexions. The idea is to "let God's own dirt back in." And the sheer fun of the book is Powell's account of how her people—all of whom have put in time at the Spur—gain a comic acceptance of whatever it is that they're stuck with.

Each character does his or her bit to build up the Powell attitude—a wry, whimsical, wised-up view of what the literary and artistic life is often like. Two of the best portraits are of old-timers who are still hanging in—the blocked and neurotic writer Earl Turner, a terrific talker and Spur loyalist, and his sometime super-successful friend Alvine Harshawe. Both had been "around the same places at the same time with the same ambition," the difference being that Earl's a loafer with a small talent and Alvine was once a dynamo with a small talent. Alvine says to Earl that together they would make a good author: one with a determination to write, the other with a determination not to. The two need each other in order to feel good and make sense of their own lives. Earl uses Alvine's flashy career to whine about his own hard luck and to get a little masochistic satisfaction out of the role of failure. Powell lets him splash around in one-liners: "how lovable of him to be a confirmed flop!" "If others were always sure you'd need the safety net, you usually ended up in it." Mixed in with his self-destructiveness is a good deal of grandiose fantasizing: he imagines himself taking the down-and-out Harshawe to lunch at 21. What he wants most out of the literary life is to be overestimated like his friend. Without Alvine to be patronized by and to kick around in his imagination, he's lost. When Alvine suffers a breakdown—losing his grip, his wife, and his dignity—Earl nearly goes to pieces: "I'm used to being jealous. That's my security. Alvine's my old North Star, I mean he's got to be up there in the sky." Powell, like top-notch satirists, makes toxicity seem quite funny.

Alvine is a different kind of a case. These days he too isn't writing, although he wished he were. "Damn it, you didn't have time to write if you wanted to keep your fame in good condition." Powell really knows the writer's excuses from the inside—and strikes off wonderful lines about inertia: "For the last five—no, ten—years he'd been holding his day like a live target for anyone to shoot full of holes." For all his cockiness and East Sider pretense and lap-of-luxury smugness, Alvine is also a loser. Powell's phrasing—very often quite homely metaphors given a sophisticated spin—captures his situation; his thoughts "didn't come in trains anymore, or, if they did, they stood loaded on the siding, like a freight full of lumber waiting for a powerful engine to shove it to port." Alvine got his ideas like office memos, "stamped and questioned by the higher ups before they reached him." He was like an old stage star who couldn't find a play that was good enough. And he envied Earl his freedom "to roam all over the city, from arty Park Avenue salon to Bowery mission, talk to strangers, do and go as he pleased, pack away enough juicy human material for a dozen Zolas." Powell lets him envy Earl and also lets him fantasize about new material and a new take on life—perhaps young Jonathan, as Earl suggests, is Alvine's son.

Meanwhile, Jonathan is becoming everybody's new experience. The ditzy girls want to take him over. An NYU professor finds him to be a "son image." Alvine could use him—an attractive illegitimate son—to humble his society wife. And Cassie Bender, the larger-than-life gallery owner (perhaps based on Peggy Guggenheim), wants Jonathan to satisfy her sexual cravings. This woman is a hilarious blend of ambition, lust, venality, and New York nerviness. No longer a youngster, she carries on extravagantly at parties, throws herself at men and pursues art deals with gargantuan appetite. Being embraced by Cassie is like getting a "bruising hug" from a statue. And being used by Cassie—as Jonathan is when it turns out that his father had been both his mother's lover and Cassie's, entitling the latter to a share in a legacy—is equally bruising. Jonathan is about to wind up as lackey-partner in the gallery, yet another lost person in the new Village. But he decides to disentangle himself from the crowd that is "free-loading on other people's genius." As the son of a country mouse, he has always looked with awe at the glamour of New York artists and writers; but when he becomes an insider he doesn't like what he has to do. Cassie uses him as a front man and bouncer, and he winds up having to further the careers of the third-rate while the first-rate are thrown into the darkness. As a big party breaks up, so do Jonathan's illusions: "a regular bouncer, he thought, and his name in gold letters on a door meant just that. . . . He wished he were going with the mob to the other party, cardless, thirsty, mannerless, tieless, absolutely free."

Powell's book is yet another protest against conventionality, this time the predictable ways of upper and lower bohemia. Cassie and her crowd want to regulate the art market, force up prices, trade off old lovers, and keep creative people in line. She's offended by the rough and ready, impulsive Hugow, a real artist who just doesn't know how to be "considerate," "mature," and "responsible." He wants to chase new experiences, not new deals. In the end that's what Jonathan himself wants—the adventure of the Spur, a kind of platonic idea of the artistic community. But the problem is that in the late 1950s the Spur is no longer quite a hub of creativity: it's actually a kind of limbo for inert souls, wannabes. Although such people have existed from the start-up bohemian generation of the nineteenth century, in the present tense of the book they are the featured players. Lize and Darcy, the barfly girls, get it right: "anybody with a tube of paint and a board was an artist. But writers were not writers unless decently unpublished or forever muffled by a Foundation placebo. The Word came only through grapevine gossip, never through print. The printed word on any subject was for squares." Cassie's world of mink coats and inflated price tags on mediocre canvasses is one part of the Manhattan pretense; the other is the world of the do-nothings and the disenchanted. Hugow, once attached to the grit and sweat of the real painter's life, ends up turning on art altogether. In a cynical twist, he goes into the demolition business, hoping to make the Metropolitan Museum his first job. This of course is Dawn Powell, putting a curse upon both houses. What she's come up with is a dark comedy of futility, a not-so-innocent romp that shows up every aspect of artistic New York.

Randall Jarrell's academic novel *Pictures from an Institution* is another marker in the history of comic transgression. It's a scathing look at a different segment of bohemia, the left-wing professoriate: in telling a rambling, diffusely focused story about an academic year at Benton College, Jarrell manages to mock and deride just about every piety and convention of a 1950s ultra-liberal institution. Nobody—not the boyish president, not an old-time professor of English—manages to escape Jarrell's savage barbs. A Humbert Humbert-like disdain for American education is the lifeblood of the book. A Nabokovian sense of the ludicrous, a sheer love of folly, is what keeps the narrative going. Jarrell has no gift for narrative drive, but he has a terrific ability to create conflict within his small-college situations; his pictures substitute for storytelling.

Here, one finds the age-old conflict of classic satire—the battle between moderation (possessed by our poet-narrator) and various kinds of established excess. The characters at Benton are like-minded in their trendiness, worship of the faux avant-garde, and isolation from the humanizing message of the humanities. Unlike more conventional academic novels where faculty are tearing each other apart—Mary McCarthy's *The Groves of Academe* is your typical tempest, with a

Joyce scholar and a tenure battle—this one is basically about a lovefest of fools. At Benton, each character brings his or her bounty of extremism or silliness to share with the others. Almost a half century before the triumph of PC on American campuses, Jarrell wrote about people who were giving their all for a culture of intellectual evasion and tyrannical niceness. Jarrell, like Nabokov, knows how to situate these people—both in terms of setting and intellectual climate. The acid description of Charlotte Haze's pseudo-bohemian living room is matched by Jarrell's first sentence: "Half the campus was designed by Bottom the Weaver, half by Ludwig Mies van der Rohe." Gracefulness and accommodation to the human scale are nowhere to be found. A master analyst of surroundings—from a faculty office with a cobbler's bench to a home packed with ill-assorted pieces of folk art to a gallery filled with welding—Jarrell misses nothing and has the right asides to make his descriptions memorable. Of the folk-art living room he comments that Jeremy Bentham's stuffed body would not have been ill-at-ease. Of the sculpture—done by an art class—he remarks that it looked like the students had divided a piece of furniture among themselves and exhibited the pieces. Going after the vacuity and lack of creative instinct behind such externals, Jarrell builds his pictures of the institution. The sculpture teacher, a minor character, is either mired in technical details about welding or apt to engage in windy philosophical discussions that only an "imbecile" would appreciate. This is Jarrell's main tactic—to show his characters engulfed in their petty worlds, or what seems worst, trying to think big. People at Benton leap from the trivial to the grandly inflated, with no time spent on the humanly useful, comfortable, or genuinely imaginative. Jarrell's overarching idea—and the book is a comic novel of ideas—is that a "way of life is a way of escaping from perception as well as of perceiving." His characters are immured in their smug conceptions of life and art.

Beginning with the president of the college, Jarrell takes on nothing less than the limits of the contemporary mind. The head man, a boy wonder who seemed younger than the freshmen, believed what "Reason and Virtue and Tolerance and a Comprehensive Organic Synthesis of Values would have him believe." These comic abstractions amount to nothing much—and the president himself is a kind of phantom— "so well adjusted to his environment that sometimes you could not tell" him from the environment. Lacking any intellectual substance, he depends on a weak solution of Dewey—"Tolerance" and "Synthesis of Values"—and a kind of sentimental populism. When he addresses Benton parents we hear him at the top of his game. He thanked them "for the experience of working with, of learning from, and of growing to . . . love . . . such generous and intelligent, such tolerant and understanding, such—and here he paused quite a long time—such . . . good . . . people." Jarrell's narrator comments that the president's voice not only took you into his confidence, it built a fire and brought you your slippers "and then went into the other room to get into something more comfortable." If you have a taste for comic one-liners about institutional dedication, try this one about Benton's leader: "the really damned not only like hell, they feel loyal to it." Each reader must decide whether Jarrell's sarcasm is overkill; yet no reader should forget that the objects of the attacks are powerful people using language badly for dubious purposes. The president is, above all, a great man in love with the World, not some shuffling, self-effacing thinker and intellectual: the latter type—for Jarrell the true hero in the world of mind—is pushed to the side and "the Vice-Chancellor of the—no, not of the Reich, but of the—School of Agriculture at the University of Wyoming" is the star player in academic America.

If you once allow Jarrell his dyspepsic diagnosis of postwar American academic leadership, you will discover that your judgment is well founded. The narrator can see around the corners of Benton and is capable of a wide-ranging critique of the intellectual class, something quite beyond a mere ridiculing of college administrators. Everyone in the Benton enterprise feels the pressure of Jarrell's mordant wit. From the politically correct ninnies to the above-it-all emigré set to the sardonic novelist-in-residence, the characters all pose for pictures. Jarrell's critical spirit—and a good bit of his spleen—goes everywhere. He is even critical of the critical mind itself, offering a razor-sharp portrait of the satiric novelist Gertrude Johnson, perhaps modeled on Mary McCarthy. The ironies of the book are compounded as Gertrude—who can spot a human flaw at a hundred paces—is examined in the act of looking for material. She says of Benton's president "that Rift's *loaded*," but she herself is one of the richest comic pictures. At Benton as a writer-in-residence for the year, she has a chance to observe a choice group of possible subjects for a novel. Meanwhile, Jarrell's narrator is observing her doing her fieldwork. The results are a very rich blend—and one that reveals the narrator's basic compassion and sense. He has his fun watching Gertrude take shots at Benton folly, but he doesn't let her get away with a thing. At first the book seems concentrated on the silliness of types like Flo Whittaker, a PC

faculty wife who is over the top—even as far back as the early 1950s.
Flo is the type—and she is a type—who has trouble reading "Old
novels": "I get too upset at the status of women in those times. It was
so degrading." She also believes that the "real life was public"—"what
you voted at or gave for or read about in *The Nation*." As a cause
junkie, Flo would say of a primrose, "We musn't blame it for its
color." But no sooner does this begin to wear on the reader's nerves
than Jarrell turns on himself and honestly says, "To someone I am
Flo." Which is to say that he knows folly is part of the human condition, not simply a clownish defect to be found among a select group
of bohemians and intellectuals.

When Jarrell focuses on Gertrude—his most incisive mind—he
shows that outsiders with wit are not immune to the perceptual problems that plague the academic herd. Gertrude—as novelist and social
observer—was "most disappointed" in everything. Jarrell's narrator
pinpoints the out-of-control critical mind: she would have complained
to God that the apple in Paradise wasn't a Winesap but a pulpy Washington Delicious, and that the Ark and the animals were not at all like
what was described in the prospectus. Nothing met her expectations,
least of all humanity, which was "irritating." Her books were "a systematic, detailed, and conclusive condemnation of mankind." She appealed to the original La Rochefoucauld in all of us; she loved Swift
but couldn't understand the Houyhnhnms—those philosophical
horses who couldn't understand human baseness. Firing off quip after
quip, Jarrell becomes a kind of superior Gertrude—hot in pursuit of
the human weakness of someone who specializes in exposing human
weakness. The book itself is about a poet-critic exposing a novelist-
critic who is exposing various critical and creative types. And once
said, it should also be added that Jarrell's narrator directs his spleen
against the Gertrude in himself: against critical acumen gone wrong.
The book is filled with warnings against the very thing he is doing.
Spinoza once said that he "labored carefully not to mock, lament, and
execrate, but to understand." Our narrator says that Gertrude did the
opposite. And at first blush, he himself seems to be evaluating his people in Gertrude's vein—to the reader the narrative voice seems to relish folly, ignorance, and the capacity for self-deception. And that
voice seems to relish someone who is mired in the subject of human
stupidity. Gertrude's primary concern is human awfulness—the herdlike qualities that make us disgusting and predictable. But Jarrell, the
humanist observer, lets her have it: although she can render reality

with exactitude, she is a novelist with no access to human feeling. If a child in one of her stories had drunk furniture polish and if the child's mother had fallen and torn her skirt, Gertrude knew the names of the polish and the garment maker: "But how the child felt as it seized and drank the polish, how the mother felt . . . ." Gertrude's response is Jarrell's ironic comment on moral emptiness posing as critical acumen and originality: "Everybody knows *that*!"

Jarrell's pictures of the academic world also include less-bitter images. As he takes on nothing less than the unreality of the thinking classes circa 1950, he necessarily has to come to grips with the emigré professor bemused by our culture and our ideas of the intellectual life. The European caught in the trendiness of postwar America—Nabokov's subject in *Lolita* and in his academic novel *Pnin*—is also one of Jarrell's favorite subjects. In attempting to understand the institution—despite the mockery and raillery and silliness—Jarrell brings in a wonderfully drawn old couple, Gottfried and Irene Rosenbaum. After all the acid in the book, they provide something that is necessary for true evaluation: gentle reason. Put plainly, their function is to see the extremes of the American intellectual scene from a balanced and seasoned point of view. This comic novel of ideas and manners gets two essentially funny foreign people to look at the absurdities of being American. And Jarrell also continues to be his quirky, non-ideological, incorrect and ever-critical self by beaming the light of criticism on the European critics as well. The fun moves in several directions; the result is a wide-ranging and complex critique of people who are critical. The Rosenbaums are musical—he an experimental composer and teacher at Benton, she a singer who once performed with Chaliapin. They are the polar opposite of Gertrude—outsiders who seemingly accept everything that comes along in their new environment. Polite, gracious (they would shake hands with the cat, Jarrell quips), open-minded, tolerant, they seem to be emblems of the understanding mind that Spinoza wanted to cultivate. And after the tediousness and trendiness of the Benton crowd, they seem to be richly endowed with intelligence and sturdy selfhood. Their one-liners are on the mark. Of Gertrude, Rosenbaum comments: "She is just like everybody else, only more so." Irene says that if Moses had lived among Americans, he would have come back and found them worshiping the Golden Girl. The house—filled with great books and prints and framed letters from artists—was a place of "confusion and richness," but a genuine expression of being rather than a political statement or a theme park.

"The house floated on tea and Rhine wine," Jarrell comments. And we float on their aperçus—most of them delightfully sly ways of warding off Benton-style uniformity. Take Gertrude's Tocquevillian evaluation of American opinion: "Here you truly think—no, it is worse than that, you not only think, you *feel*—that you can find what is beautiful, or right, or true, by asking everybody, and some people will say one thing and some another, and what the most people say, *that* is what is beautiful and right and true. So in the end there is no more true, no more right, no more beautiful, there is only what the most people say." The Rosenbaums' gentle contrarianism, their love of reading their new culture and society in critical ways, their passion for generalization: these things delight their creator. But they don't throw him off his task in the book. They, too, are pictures with something wrong in them; they too are part of the intellectual follies of the college. Reason of their kind has its limits: "In ungracious moments I felt that their minds were traps in which things came to an already-agreed-upon end; and they must have felt that my mind was so open that things streamed through it without coming to any conclusion at all." And then Jarrell's narrator adds that European-style theorizing is not for him: "that it is better to entertain an idea than to take it home to live with you for the rest of your life." This line is a generalization about fearing general ideas—and Jarrell at his best. He no sooner utters it than he has to admit that he is living his present life—not altogether unpleasantly—among the fruits of theory, inventions and other practical breakthroughs that result from theory.

Pictures from an Institution is actually a sustained dramatization of the problem of thinking in America at a time when the world of mind had produced so many splendid and so many stupid things, so many Gottfried Rosenbaums and so many Flo Whittakers. The Jarrell vision—complexly self-questioning, ready to turn against even its most attractive insights—points the way to the 1950s world of intellectuals, those informal philosophers of culture, art, and society who taught a generation how to interrogate its own intelligence.

chapter 6

The Eggheads

Randall Jarrell's novel is a loose, freewheeling book about ideas in action on one campus in the 1950s. Its sharpest criticism is reserved for the ideological, the bullheaded, and the rigid. But it also looks more subtly at the problem of the critical enterprise: What do we have to fear from the well-informed and well-educated who think and teach for a living? Is liberal enlightenment a ticket to what Lionel Trilling would soon label "the right condition of the self"? Jarrell's book kept its readers doubting the opinions of the bohemian class about art, society, education, and the good life. It made Benton something like Swift's Laputa, a kingdom of people living in the mid-air of their fixed ideas. This same job of criticizing critical thinking, of interrogating mind in the postwar period, was the principal occupation of an extraordinary group of essayists in the 1950s. Perhaps at no time in the twentieth century had American literature offered so many superb critics of ideas with so many thoughts that reached a general literate audience. Not systematic thinkers and certainly not impressionistic belle-lettrists, the writers of the fifties—particularly Lionel Trilling, Harold Rosenberg, Clement Greenberg, Dwight Macdonald—seemed to take up the mantle of Edmund Wilson as they defined America's artistic and intellectual achievements. Like Wilson in his palmy days as a critic of American culture, before he withdrew from criticizing the contemporary scene after World War II, these essayists were determined to read our national mind at the same time as they read literature, looked at art, and examined bodies of ideas. Their affinities have less to do with the label New York Intellectual than with their drive to correct and deepen the intellectual life of their times: Rosenberg didn't like Lionel Trilling's famous word *we*—the designation for the maturing generation of people who had been influenced by the Great Depression and Marxism. Along with Greenberg and Macdonald, he was too contentious, crusty, and restless to fit any generalization about a group of thinkers.

But one master theme runs through the work of these essayists of the 1950s—and Trilling put his finger on this idea in *The Opposing Self:* they were all seeking "the right condition of the self" through literature and art. They believed that great creative work was an avenue of freedom; they also believed that the political and social consensus of their time was like the shade of the prison house cast on the developing self. And all of them set out to oppose the relentless impress of conventions and assumptions, trends and pieties, and respectabilities and popular tastes that get in the way of genuine sources of life— authentic art, passion, reflection. They specialized in writing arguments in defense of great books at a time when greatness was under fire from politics and popular culture.

These writers did some of their best work in the age of *Rebel without a Cause*, that movie based on a nonfiction book about the new disaffection of teenagers, those who were too young to care about the causes of the Roosevelt era. As critics of our civilization, Trilling and the others had put in time attacking the old causes—especially the orthodoxies of the left. Trilling's *The Liberal Imagination*—composed in the age of Stalinism and the Popular Front—is a subtly reasoned protest against the excesses of rampant liberalism, the social-political-cultural outlooks that could subvert the original liberal impulse toward freedom. The book rebelled against the organizational mind, the drive toward progress as correctness and uniformity. Greenberg, Rosenberg, and Macdonald had affronted the pieties of the left, including the false kinds of populism that led to a drop in artistic and intellectual standards. But when America drifted into middle-class reaction and Republican dominance in the early 1950s, they had a keen understanding of the new situation. In their own ways, they grasped what the James Dean character was rebelling against—the new mediocrity, emotional deadness, and philistinism of a prosperous people. These critics were—if not quite rebels—opposing selves and revolutionists in the cause of art and autonomy. Their modes of expression were not the rages or sullen negations of the new young: they were mature rebels wise to the limitations of the Old Left, and articulate about their new cause—nothing less than the revivifying of the modern self through the experience of art and literature. The James Dean strain in the generation maintained that drag racing and lashing out were the answers to the lumpish lifelessness of the suburbs; the Trilling and Rosenberg strain said that books and art were potent forms of protest.

The new cause of the intellectuals was a recognition of how complicated art and ideas had become since the simpler age of Marxist ideologues, ivory-tower highbrows, and just plain folks who read the papers. The new American cultural scene had a highly developed and numerous intellectual class, trained after the War at the universities in the liberal arts, bred on modernist literature, accustomed to their magazines like *Partisan Review* and their foreign films, and in possession of their own complacencies and prejudices. The essayists of the 1950s—almost like Victorian sages trying to humanize the opinions of hard-bitten Utilitarians—set themselves the job of enlightening the enlightened: making the serious reading public—those who tackled Joyce and knew something of Camus and Existentialism—aware of its myopia, its extremism, its faulty taste, its herdlike tendencies. The writers who addressed this group used a combination of reason, irony, and confrontation in order to enlarge their readers' minds. They did not humor an audience or patronize it—and they certainly never attempted to confirm readers in their opinions. To be unsettling, to question the customs of the educated classes, to toss out challenges, to be witheringly ironic about clichéd ways of thinking—these intellectuals of the fifties dared to do the kind of things that are rarely done in our own time. To correct and reject and revaluate: these are hardly the enterprises of our own politically correct and multicultural world of books and ideas.

Lionel Trilling deserves to be first among the intellectuals who refused to congratulate fifties people on their tastes and judgments. Working the high end of the American cultural scene, he specialized in calling the best-read people up short, giving them civilized and highly nuanced instruction in how to live the life of the mind. No one alive in America today gives—or dare give—this kind of instruction. But in the mid-1950s Trilling's *The Opposing Self* was an urbane challenge to contemporary taste. The nine essays amount to nine highly complex and subtle affronts to 1950s reductiveness. Addressing his readers as "we," he suavely assumes that they are willing to go along with him on brief journeys of cultural awareness. He also assumes that they wouldn't mind taking a look at their own narrowness. What have "we," as readers and consumers of cultural goods, neglected or diminished? His answer is that we have reduced our own lives by not learning how to grapple with the opposing, often exasperating claims of literature. Not quite a matter of stupidity or ignorance on our part, it is really a kind of cultural and literary denial. We simply have trained ourselves not to recognize certain kinds of significant experience. Trilling assumes the role of our guide through the thorny territory of literature that we can't quite accept or appreciate. And like his intellectual ancestor John Stuart Mill, he warms to the task of showing us what we have missed when we neglect writers who are not our sort or who are established fixtures buried in customary thinking. What we resist and neglect is what we really need. Trilling is the teacher-essayist who refuses to let us wallow in our fierce convictions and cherished biases. He takes hold of nine literary figures and shows how they are guides to building the right condition of the self. His strategy is the paradoxical one of engagement through disengagement: teaching us to appreciate and incorporate a writer's vision by showing us how strange he or she seems, yet how life-availing are the insights. Each writer is read not as "relevant," a bad way of reading and never Trilling's; instead each is read—in a wonderfully moral way—as useful for building a self. *The Opposing Self* gives intellectual weight and subtlety to the self-help genre; it tells you not how to climb the corporate ladder or how to cope with conformity and kids but how to manage your resistances and attractions to books, and how to use those books to overcome your own smugness. It shows, certainly, how the writers dealt with were in a quarrel with their culture; but it also shows how they can instruct us in quarreling with our own culture.

The attitude of the early 1950s that Trilling opposed was not all that different from ours. At the heart of his critical task was enlarging the sensibilities of an audience in love with extreme conditions, a generation of intellectuals—bred on Kafka, Eliot, and Lawrence—that found agony and torment and catastrophe and sexual adventure the must-have qualities of art. Essay after essay in the book takes aim at fashionable desperation, love of disorder and dysfunction, fascination with the abyss, and ecstasy as a way of life. Trilling's goal is to return the reader to a more generous and nuanced conception of experience. American intellectuals felt—and still feel—at home with extreme experience; but the complexity and mystery of ordinary existence—the subject of *Anna Karenina*—was something that the modern mind could not quite bring itself to talk about. Trilling dealt with several figures who open us to the complications of such apparently bland topics as class, pleasure, family life, moral rectitude, political integrity, and the uses of knowledge. In the age of beatniks, Existentialism, and H-Bomb scares such things seemed tepid to "us." But Trilling makes them whetstones to sharpen our awareness. To lose sight of the ordinary—of all that conditions and limits our lives, everything from household arrangements and physical appearances and material possessions in Jane Austen and Tolstoy to political common sense and decency in Orwell—is to dull the edge of avant-gardism, to make significant literary experience so many variations on the ideas of Dostoyevsky or Nietzsche. Literature for Trilling was one unexpected experience after another, a constant unsettling of the mind, a confrontation with opposing parts of our nature.

At a time when adolescents were beginning to be the main act in American life—at once the stars and miscreants of our culture— Trilling celebrated adultness: ideas of maturity, seasoned judgment, balancing and weighing pervade his essays. If any critic was ever uncomfortable with what was coming down the road in America, it was Trilling; and yet his unease is not a form or denial or willful ignorance. He gives full weight to passion and adventurousness, but he wants to educate us about the qualities of life that oppose our impulses. His pieces on Keats, Wordsworth, Orwell, and Jane Austen—even dowdy William Dean Howells—deepen our perceptions and make us aware of something more subtle and permanent than instinct and unconditioned feeling. He depicts Keats not as an alienated Romantic genius exploring the realms of darkness, but as a genial spirit trying to reconcile the joy and pain of life. "The Poet as Hero: Keats in His Letters" is written against a backdrop of 1950s commonplaces—that artists are weird outsiders, that they have no access to the warmth and solidarity of family, that they are childlike and incapable of responsibility, that they are all feeling and no mind. Trilling shows Keats's career—with its devotion to connecting "fine writing" and "fine doing"—as a refutation of these feeble generalizations. And besides the platitudes about creative people circulating at the time, there was also Existentialism and the writers and thinkers that surrounded it: Kafka's idea of not cheating the world of its victory over the self; Camus's *Myth of Sisyphus* and the exhilarated consciousness of defeat; Sartre's *No Exit* and the idea that hell is other people; and of course the bandying about of "angst," "nothingness," "the death of God," and other locutions— used and misused—of Kierkegaard, Nietzsche, and Jean-Paul Sartre himself. Trilling's Keats stands forth as a hero and celebrator of the perdurable self at a time when the self was supposed to be in agony or at bay. Keatsian awareness—as opposed to Existential dread—was about seeing life so intensely that we "burn through" evil and defeat. "Beauty is Truth" is about fortitude, "mature masculinity," the ability

to balance the truth of fact and the truth of affirmation—and then to
endure and live well. And it is this idea of balance that Trilling throws
into high relief—our most intense poet was sane and most gifted in his
ability to reconcile the world of the senses and the intellect, the childish and the mature, "energy and truth, passion and principle." Trilling
made Keats's "Negative Capability"—the ability to live with doubt
and conflict—the benchmark idea in his own book: to take in the complexities of literature without being confused or immobilized, to live
without insistence upon unitary explanations or ideologies, to throw
away the received opinions and get the mixed, ambiguous experience
of literature.

"Wordsworth and the Rabbis" is yet another essay that makes us
transcend our familiar reactions. As readers of Lawrence and Yeats and
Eliot—or in middlebrow moments Ayn Rand's *The Fountain-
head*—we have embraced what Trilling calls the "spiritual prestige" of
force and violent assertion and the "militant suffering" that goes with
it. We're firmly committed to Blake's maxim that the tigers of wrath
are wiser than the horses of instruction. To us Wordsworth has become
gray and dull, a poet of wise passiveness rather than of passionate intensity. Trilling's object is to reconnect us with a poet whom he believes still speaks to our condition. He accomplishes his task by
bringing in an unlikely text, the Hebrew *Pirke Aboth*, a second-
century series of *pensées* about the conduct of life. He uses this wisdom book to illuminate Wordsworth's view of humanity and to shock
us into appreciating a kind of spiritual prestige with which we have
lost touch. One of his key points about the *Pirke* is a teaching of the
sages that we neglect at our peril—they believed in surrender before
the mysteries of the universe. Trilling describes their vision this way:
"a certain insouciant acquiescence in the anomalies of the moral order
of the universe." Wordsworth and the Hebrew wise men were open to
the indefinable and the indefinite, but we are creatures driven by will
and assertiveness and hunger for answers. Our predilections also make
us unaware of what Trilling—employing the phrase of Wordsworth—
calls the "sentiment of being," the sense of life within all creatures,
the elderly, the simple, those who endure rather than those who shine
forth. In plain terms, the non-sexy and unglamorous have no hold
on us.

As a result, we live in a world surfeited with driving will and energy,
and know little of a more comprehensive vision of human joy and
pain. In connecting us with this underrated vision—the philosophical

acceptance of living and dying in a common routine—Trilling turns to the genius in the twentieth century who understood nonmilitancy best—James Joyce, the creator of Leopold Bloom. Bloom's "sentiment of being"—not a matter of intellectual distinction or prestige or extraordinary personal fulfillment—is instead a kind of rabbinic wisdom for Trilling—nonmilitancy, acceptance of "cosmic contradiction," indifference to the idea of evil. Elsewhere in the essay, Trilling has defined the sentiment of being of Wordsworth and the Hebrew wise men—and of ourselves, if we would learn the lesson of opposing the will of our culture. The sentiment is a "condition of the soul" that supports "responsiveness" and "high-heartedness and large heartedness." Trilling's literary essay turns out to be Montaigne-like in its intent: a wide-ranging meditation on the conduct of life that enjoins humility and a healthy distrust of received wisdom; the hidden side of the self—the opposing self—will tell us more about how to live than the glittering side.

In the books Trilling chooses to study, we are shown the dimensions of his master theme: that certain texts embody hard-won experience not easily available elsewhere. The discussions of *Mansfield Park*, of Orwell's *Homage to Catalonia*, of *Anna Karenina*, and of Howells's fiction, of Dickens's *Little Dorrit*, of Flaubert's *Bouvard and Péchuchet* are variations on the theme of opposition announced so brilliantly in the Keats and Wordsworth essays. Jane Austen's novel—perhaps her least-favored work—is chosen in order to drive home two points that fifties people were likely to find impalatable. The first is that liveliness, wit, and sparkling personality—the qualities found in the character of Mary Crawford—may threaten identity, make us engaging characters and players of roles rather than solid selves. The fun of pretending, acting in amateur theatricals, being charming—vivacity and volatility—is under fire, and at first blush this attack makes Jane Austen—and her protagonist Fanny Price—seem like prudes and drags. But what becomes clear in the novel is that Austen is exploring the dangers of our favorite impulses: they lead us not to a world of infinite fulfillment, but to disorder and loss of selfhood. Trilling the literary critic seems to take his cue from Eliot describing the major artist in "Tradition and the Individual Talent": what we need is escape from personality, which is not to say annihilation of personality but rather a healthy distrust of flashiness, show, and irresponsible acting out. A more un-American sentiment would be hard to find. At odds with Hollywood, be-yourself psychologists, and other champions of happiness, it seemed like a prescription for a dour existence. It also seemed to turn against Austen's own love of vitality, her own pursuit of the rightly formed self. The novelist who had pioneered the modern, fully developed personality—the well-shaped self as against the vulgar product of circumstances—suddenly seemed to turn against the whole idea of personality. Principle, custom, and tradition seem to win the day in *Mansfield Park*, making Austen not the precursor of the moderns but a kind of stoic in search of peace and rest. Austen's persona Fanny Price—no scintillating Elizabeth Bennet—wins the day in a book about opposing the expected social triumphs—brilliance, intensity, vivacity, spirit. Trilling's "wholeness of the self" now becomes a matter of rejecting a culture that demands a driving spirit and a judgmental mind. He shows us that moral integrity may oppose liveliness, and true wisdom may oppose wit. And it is this yearning for solidity, character, the well-built self that permeates Austen's novel—and makes Trilling's essay a curious and provoking statement about what we should look for in literature and in our lives. He challenges us to seek the "secret inexpressible hopes" that society cannot yield. In a time of extraordinary progress and hope—a time when people have talked endlessly about the promise of tomorrow and the American Dream—he developed this discomfiting interpretation of happiness. The promise was not to be found in the finely tempered nature or the charming manner or the brilliant mind. The right condition of the self was a spiritual condition, difficult to attain and at odds with many admirable and attractive human qualities. Trilling affronted his audience with the wrong book for the times—which is to say that he fulfilled the critic's highest obligation to unsettle and arouse.

When Trilling turned to George Orwell he went so far as to tell us that genius is not everything, that what a culture needs is figures who are sturdy truth-tellers. Orwell is an English man of letters rather than a wondrous phenomenon—he's willful, cantankerous, and eccentric rather than wildly inspired; and his lack of inspiration makes him a possible model for us rather than an Olympian. *Homage to Catalonia* teaches us less about the Spanish Civil War than it does about a way of being. Another Trilling hero, Orwell embodies a charm that is quite different from the magnetic hold of the moderns: it's an ancient appeal that comes from personal courage, responsibility, orderliness. He opposes "the institutionalized life of intellectuality" and "the sentimental malice of populism"—both of which are still very much with us. Forget the cant about the People and remember sportsmanship and dutifulness and decency. Trilling seems to revel in the Orwellian corrections: say no to absolutes and ignore the inside dope of your group. He is the intellectual without a theory—which is to say the intellectual opposing his own identity. He ends with a cry that is at once exasperated and joyful: "if only life were not so tangible . . . so made up of facts that are at variance with each other." If only we didn't have to think. If only we could turn on an absolute channel and get the right condition of self and society.

Tolstoy is depicted as yet another bearer of unfashionable truths, things pushed to the side, or condescended to by "us." *Anna Karenina* is notable for emphasizing the conditioned nature of human life—all the things that limit our spirit. But unlike the bread-and-butter naturalists who moan, sermonize, and eventually resign us to our fate, Tolstoy is unique in being able to tell us "of pain in terms of life's possible joy." Although—as Trilling phrases it—"the spirit of man is always at the mercy of the actual and trivial," the spirit cannot be reduced to those terms. And this essay on Tolstoy is a protest against the main naturalistic platitude around in the 1950s—that there's not a lot to be done about human pain and misery. It seems to answer the determinism of *By Love Possessed* or *The Man in the Gray Flannel Suit* before the publication of those representative works. The Trilling answer—conveyed through a generalized consideration of Tolstoy's masterpiece—is that we must understand that the mixed character of our lives is neither cause for resignation nor euphoria. Use *Anna Karenina* as your wisdom book: it produces happiness because it renders life intelligible. It does not satisfy because of any theory of life or any attitude or prescription, but instead because of "the energy of animal intelligence that marks Tolstoy as a novelist." Trilling has elsewhere in the essay indicated that the literary critics of his time—often obsessed with language and the text itself—could not quite account for this magic of Tolstoy: it is neither language, nor ideas, nor attitude, nor contemporary relevance. This essay shows Trilling the literary critic risking vagueness, proposing indescribable causations and magical effects. But it also shows him reaching back to the speculative criticism of Dr. Johnson and Hazlitt, trying to make a book a breathing document about our sense of being alive. The essay has no methodology, not even Trilling's characteristic technique of illuminating a work through elaborate comparisons with other works. But it makes Tolstoy an immediate concern for "us" if we want to break out of our narrow perceptions.

Trilling's essay on Howells—perhaps the un-sexiest figure in the American canon—is wonderfully offbeat in its approach. He writes about a careful realist, chronicler of class and money in New England, by bringing in James Joyce, André Gide, and Hannah Arendt. Howells is a master of the conditioned existence—and we are warned that to forget his explorations is to forget, in Gide's words, that "art inhabits temperate regions" and must guard itself against inflation and the consequent devaluation of tragedy. All anguish devalues anguish—and makes bad literature. A literary culture must cherish writers who talk about class and marriage and house-hunting. We are again reminded of Joyce, Bloom, and the life of quotidian fact. Sheer data is crucial to the art of *Ulysses*—without it the book would not exist as a splendid rendering of society. Howells is saluted as a pioneer of sorts, a respecter of such material things, a writer who helped fulfill the destiny of the novel form. In the age of Arendt's *The Origins of Totalitarianism*, readers might well tend to forget that something else counts besides the charisma of evil. We still need the writers like Howells who refuse to let evil be "preponderant over the sense of self."

Trilling lets Howells stand for the artist as defender and chronicler of ordinary social routine. He (or she) is a bulwark against the extremism in modern literary culture, bringing us back to a measured sense of ourselves. But *The Opposing Self* has more visceral and passionate things to say about literature. Three of the essays are involved with violent reaction to our social condition. They turn against what Trilling calls "the social will"—the will to status, the drive to impress our opinions on others, the hunger for social success and fulfillment. Dickens's late novel *Little Dorrit* provides Trilling with an opportunity to write about an artist turning against his own triumphs. The book is about Arthur Clennam, a protagonist who realizes that his life has gone stale and that the cause can be found in the social sins of his own family. Dickens himself at this time had a strong sense that he had reached the summit of life, and that he was henceforth on a downward spiral—the titanic superstar of the novel form had a sense of diminished enthusiasm, tiredness, frustration with family, lack of relish for delightful comedy and fabulous invention. Dickens without gusto is Trilling's theme—which is to say not the familiar Dickens. Taking the place of the relish and energy is a systematic destructiveness: the novel is a comprehensive attack on Victorian life—crooks and gentlemen, the pious and the profligate, the merely respectable and the socially exalted, the exploiting classes and the exploited. Great ladies are in-

dicted for crimes against human decency, but so are ladies' maids. It
is a novel about how the characters play out a drama of making each
other and themselves prisoners. In it we encounter people who are responsible for others' misery—who literally play a wrongful part in
throwing other characters into prison—and at the time torment themselves with guilt, envy, and social pride. To take one's part in the social
life of *Little Dorrit*—to be a gentleman or lady, a moneymaker, a son
and heir, a daughter looking for a husband—is to be caught in a tragic
drama of futility. Insofar as you try to fulfill your social dreams, you
will incarcerate yourself. Trilling presents Dickensian tragedy—a crisis involving the efficacy of human actions—to an American audience
trained to believe in the efficacy of will and the power of determination. He makes us question our professional and business ambitions,
discover neurosis at the bottom of our own drives, doubt our own
instincts. And he makes us feel differently about a novelist who we
have always entrusted with our most idealistic notions of human life.
If Dickens means this, how can we rest easy about reformist ideas and
dreams of progress—even about our sentiments? The essay is a disturbing call to doubt. More intense and explicit about the failure of
the social will than the essay on *Mansfield Park*, it is Trilling's most
powerful blow to modern complacency. As he does in the Jane Austen
and Wordsworth essays, Trilling asks us to turn against all the asser-
tions of our culture and find solace in the totally alien idea of peace
and resignation.

"Flaubert's Last Testament" is opposed to our impulses as modern
people in yet a different way from the other essays. The social will and
drive is not the object of the great French novelist's satire in his famous
last work, *Bouvard and Péchuchet*. This study of two bourgeois who
set out in middle age to remake their lives by becoming cultured is
about books, ideas, and facts—but most of all it is about the limits of
our life in culture. The "thinking person" has accumulated a great deal
of prestige since the eighteenth century—since more and more people
have gained access to general ideas due to the growth of liberal democracy. Splenetic Flaubert—through the interpretation of skeptical Trilling—is made into a student of intellectual follies, buffoonery as
bookishness, thinking as a vain and futile enterprise. The most bookish of novelists is shown turning on a vital part of his own nature and
career—playing the intellectual who cannot stand self-conscious intel-
lectualism. And Trilling—by exploring the depths of Flaubert's negativism—is engaged in his own turning away from the systematic, all-

too-earnest, dead serious life of the mind as it is often lived in his own time. Doctrinal, abstract, tending toward aridity, the enterprise of the Bouvards and Péchuchets of this world is something every genuine thinker must guard against. It denies life, concreteness, the actuality— and ambiguity—of human beings. Trilling himself once mentioned that there were times when he was revolted by the prospect of reading a book. This essay—subtle, self-reflexive, highly cerebral in all its deflation of the intellect—is another discovery of something beyond the familiar territory of progress, assertion, and the fierce pursuit of achievement. It is a celebration of a great artist's crucial last insight: that there is deep affirmation in the denial of cultural ideas; that heroism is self-sacrifice, not questing and aggrandizement. This paradox is a mouthful and a mindful for any generation, but particularly for the 1950s. Back then, popular science and ideas of progress dominated the bourgeois mind. Schools of thought—from Existentialism to positivism—dominated the intellectual class. And Trilling dared to assail that prestigious type called the *thinking person*.

In the slenderest essay in the collection, a piece on Henry James's *The Bostonians*, Trilling strikes off one of his most precise formulations. *The Bostonians* is about the woman question in America—and in a controversial way about how the feminine character and the masculine character collide "in the bitter total war" we know from modern writers like Strindberg and Lawrence, and from life itself. Trilling rates this fairly unpopular novel very highly because it hits a raw nerve: "It is a question of what it means to be a man and what it means to be a woman—about the quality of being which people wish to have." He goes to the heart of the book and to the essential spirit of James's masculine protagonist, Basil Ransom. And what develops in the brief argument is that James offers "the tragic awareness of the intractability of human circumstance." James, like T. S. Eliot and D. H. Lawrence, depicts masculine anxiety, "fear of the loss of manhood," "primitive fear." Trilling presents us with what we cannot face in our commonsensical, progressive daily lives. He offers literature's unsettling version of ourselves.

Dispelling complacency was also the major enterprise of the art critic Clement Greenberg. Another questioner of things established, he worked to provide nuanced understanding of mid-twentieth century avant-garde art. The audience that he addressed—equipped with a grasp of classic modernism, Picasso and the early masters of the century—needed an authoritative critic to show the new paths of the post–World War II period. Greenberg met the need with verve, precision, and style. And like Trilling, he had no intention of humoring an audience or catering to its ingrained resistances. His landmark book of essays, *Art and Culture*, published in 1961, was a record of twenty years of overcoming the preconceptions of viewers and readers. The consumers of modern art were getting smug, becoming used to the conventions of the early twentieth century. For Greenberg, experimentalism was moving into a new phase. He made the avant-garde an issue rather than a branch of chic—something to care passionately about, watch in its trajectory, observe in its processes, and judge. He took American and European figures of the century, a few writers, and the perennial problem of quality and decline in art and made a book that stands as a remarkable record of exercising taste. Like Trilling, he wanted to bring out the ambiguities and subtleties in a work, expose the contradictions in an artist's vision, study the difficulties and demands of a medium, and highlight the puzzling nature of great art. Trilling wanted readers to be aware of the dialectical qualities of a book, the mysterious crosscurrents, and the struggle of opposing instincts that are played out. Greenberg thought that "the art public should continue to be reminded of anything by which it can be puzzled." Paintings that puzzle "are almost always of ultimate consequence." This 1952 pronouncement is Greenberg's master theme as a thinker and critic—he wanted to lead an audience to the great art objects of his time and warn them off the predictable, grasp-at-a-glance works of inferior quality.

Art and Culture is a wonderfully congenial work of criticism—searching in its insights and a pleasure to read. His justly famous "Avant-garde and Kitsch" lays out the terms of a debate that is still raging in our culture: What is the distinction between breakthrough art and literature and the artistic expressions of mass culture? Or does such a distinction exist? Or should we care about it if it does? Greenberg's reflections, produced in 1939, were as relevant to the late 1950s, perhaps more relevant, than they were to the pre-war period. Kitsch—as he predicted—truly became the first universal culture, not a peasant culture flourishing here and there in the West, but a ubiquitous, immediately graspable kind of popular art that everyone was compelled to know about simply by being alive. Avant-garde art shrank as kitsch occupied most of the cultural space on the globe. Kitsch was valued by the many for its true-to-life qualities, its constant reminders of familiar situations and sentiments, and its messages. Avant-garde art was valued by the few for its discontinuities, its detachment from conventional situations and sentiments—and for its plastic and verbal ingenuities rather than for its messages. Greenberg took sides in what now appears to be a totally unfashionable way. He branded kitsch as rearguard, associated it with philistinism—and even, because of its ability to convey content, with totalitarian propaganda. Kitsch is the fascist and communist medium—not to mention the medium of indoctrination in all societies; avant-garde instills a reverence for craft and technique—and most often does not deal in anything as definable as a doctrine. In the middle years of the twentieth century, such distinctions served as a protection against Stalinist realism and Hitlerian cultural swill, and a warning against lies and mental slackness of all kinds; Greenberg made them count in the formation of taste and the condition of the self. To be stuck with kitsch was to be imprisoned by popular taste and deprived of the vital, rare, and original. To be in touch with the avant-garde was to be part of something almost divine.

> The avant-garde poet or artist tries in effect to imitate God by creating something valid solely on its own terms, in the way nature itself is valid, in the way a landscape—not its picture—is aesthetically valid; something *given*, increate, independent of meanings, similars or originals. Content is to be dissolved so completely into form that the work of art or literature cannot be reduced in the whole or in part to anything not itself.

Greenberg states his case in absolute terms, but immediately qualifies what he means by the true artist's mission: it's a devotion to aesthetic values, to the processes of the craft and to the demands of the medium—not to the kitsch demand "to communicate." And Greenberg is keenly aware of the fact that avant-garde art can be as dismally unsuccessful, as out of touch with its materials, as the worst and clumsiest kitsch production. But avant-garde is always absorbing because it insists on its own terms, not the terms of a mass audience.

From our twenty-first century vantage point, Greenberg's essay raises a point about mass art that seems permanently disturbing. Kitsch is a product of industrialism and modernity, of a mature state of society, behind it is a vast expanse of genuine art, literature, and craftsmanship. This tradition is there as a given—to be manhandled, twisted, travestied: take the average junk movie and you will find that it is an attenuated version of some well-crafted work—a brilliant horror story, a witty sexual imbroglio, an epic tale of violence. Greenberg leaves us with the notion that the watered-down qualities of kitsch, its new "twists" and cleverness, are the crucial factors that cloud our judgments and cause us to accept fakery as the real thing. Like a highbrow of his age, he places Steinbeck's novels and Simenon's mysteries in the borderline territory—an error in judgment if you consider the devotion to craft of those writers. But he leads us in the right path when he identifies the mass product with clever concepts, special effects, and plenty of relevance. The kitsch work is a debased version of what Eliot meant by tradition—it is grabbed from the warehouse of the past. As for Eliot's "individual talent," the mass product must take care not to strain an audience untrained in the demands of genuine art. It's a blend of faux tradition and faux originality. It asks nothing from the audience—except money, Greenberg quips. He's totally honest about the power of kitsch—and nothing of a social snob; the easily graspable and predictable and derivative article is the staple of most academic culture, which he labels scathingly as the stuffed shirt front for kitsch. For Greenberg the term mass culture is not some put-down on the taste of the lower economic bracket but rather a comprehensive term to describe the slack, the undemanding, the inauthentic.

Back in 1939 Greenberg was wise to the market-driven, the ideological, the chic, and the trendy—all the substitutes for the craftsmanly; by 1961 he published a book about his long period of reporting on the good and the great, the borderline, the botched, and the spurious. Most of the reporting is from the fifties. The long essay titled "The Plight of Our Culture" first appeared in 1953 and set out to correct simplistic notions of decline in the arts. Greenberg's critical sights are set against T. S. Eliot's social snobbery and sloppy thinking in "Notes Toward a Definition of Culture." While Eliot had been the brilliant pioneer critic who analyzed "deadness of sensibility" in modern society, he had lately turned to crisis mongering rather than true criticism. Greenberg accuses the great man of confusing social and aesthetic questions, with assigning blame to liberal democracy for cultural decline, and with peddling cant and journalistic sensationalism about the end of standards in our time. While conceding that our age has not produced the geniuses of the Renaissance or the great early period of modernism, Greenberg sees the problem not as matter of an end of aristocratic elite culture but as a matter of the nature and fate of leisure in an age of efficiency. Work in the twentieth century is life's fundamental activity, and the leisure that once produced and consumed art and literature is totally separated from work. Contemporary leisure has become an escape and an attempt to recover from work's tedium rather than a space in which people seriously recreate. And Greenberg goes to the root of our troubles with cultural decline by offering a kind of Marxist analysis—what we need is a victory over the relentlessness of efficient work, or put directly, work leavened by play and play leavened by seriousness. He frankly offers this speculation as an attractive prospect, not a total solution; he is not naive enough to see genius on tomorrow's de-alienated horizon, nor is he as retrograde and ahistorical as Eliot with his notion that quality and aristocracy must go together. But Greenberg is visionary, dreaming of a breakdown of absolute categories and pointing out that the enemy of high culture is not "jukeboxes" but despair and submission to marketplace terms. While Eliot yearns for the artistic culture of the past, Greenberg brainstorms about the ingenuity of new creative people.

That brainstorming becomes something definite and brilliantly realized when he discusses the art of his time. He shows how numbers of American artists set new standards, preserved the avant-garde against the odds of commercial culture, the temptation to imitate what was already successful and established. In "'American-Type' Painting"—that awkwardly titled pioneering work of criticism—Greenberg followed the processes of artists who were making American painting of the 1940s and 1950s a great movement within avant-garde history. He also set down a permanently important standard for the artist—truth to the "autonomous laws of the medium." This absolute in his critical writing is like Eliot's absolute devotion to poetic music and phrasing in his essays of the 1920s. Without the total dedication of the creative artist to his medium, there is nothing much but repetition, slackness, haphazard effects. Greenberg—despite his coolness toward Eliot's social views—is America's Eliot in the realm of the plastic arts: a critic who compares techniques, knows his artists inside out as craftsmen, sees them in the long procession of modern art history—and has little to say about their opinions, themes, and subject matter. Art is not a pretext for Greenberg, an excuse to sound off about society and politics. "'American-Type' Painting" is practical criticism of painters and painting as well as a wonderfully generalized reflection on what—given a specific demand of the medium or form—a painter's mission should be.

Greenberg celebrates a tendency he has observed in Pollock, de Kooning, Rothko and others: the drive to purify their painting of expendable conventions. Each continues to "renew the vitality of art" by removing the inessential elements of a painting—the usages of the past such as representationalism and spatial illusion that are not a necessary part of visual expression. The big project of Greenberg's time— observable in the best painters—is "loosening up the relatively delimited illusion of shallow depth that the three master Cubists— Picasso, Braque, Léger—had adhered to since the closing out of Synthetic Cubism." Greenberg observes the individual revolutions of each American artist—the ways the painter retains and breaks out of the traditions of the early part of the twentieth century. Like Eliot, he sees his painters as part of a long process of experimentation—Gorky and Pollock and de Kooning are said to "catch" "some of the uncaught hares that Picasso had started." In true Eliotic spirit he says that "de Kooning's nonfigurative paintings are haunted just as much as his abstract ones are by the disembodied contours of Michelangelo's, Ingres's and even Rubens's nudes." There is a clear sense that de Kooning can't bear to "tear himself away" from certain conventions— notably "sculptural firmness." Greenberg finds that the Dutch-American painter has a need to preserve the past and "forestall the future," if only to reassure an audience that finds Jackson Pollock's dispensing with conventions "incomprehensible." Pollock is Greenberg's hero— "alone in his power to assert a paint-strewn or paint-laden surface as a single synoptic image." Pollock's "all-over" paintings, beginning in 1946, are the bench mark for the avant-garde: the most puzzling and the most detached from modeling, shading, and subject matter. Greenberg described them this way: "filled from edge to edge with evenly spaced motifs that repeat themselves uniformly like the element in a wallpaper pattern, and therefore seemed capable of repeating the picture beyond its frame into infinity." In this way, Pollock broke with the discrete, shaped, enclosed world of the easel painting—but this rupture is only one of several heroic risks that Greenberg highlights. He writes of another revolutionary feature of an American-Type painter, Clyfford Still: the breakdown of value contrast. Like Monet and Turner, Still muffled light and dark—"bunched value intervals together at the light end of the scale." When Turner first did this, his public forgave him because he seemed to be naturalistically depicting the effects of steam, mist, and clouds. But looking elsewhere in the paintings, Greenberg seems happy that Still cannot be forgiven—that he has an "unsettling and estranging originality." The work defies—in a Whitmanesque way—established modern good taste, including Cubism and other experiments with physiognomic and perspective distortion that the public had gotten used to. Greenberg sees Still as "indulging . . . in loose and sweeping gestures, and defying certain conventions (like light and dark) in the same *gauche* way that Whitman defied meter." And he also sees that his colors—often bright and open air-like in their impressionism—manage to be innovative and startling even though they seem to begin with the palette of Greenwich Village art show amateurs. Still forces his colors to do things they never do on the canvasses of wannabes. He risks staleness but achieves "serious and sophisticated art." By this last value judgment, Greenberg means to say that the painter is wise in the ways of his medium—exactly the kind of craftsman, when at the top of his form, who can never be accused of schmeering and dribbling aimlessly. Robert Motherwell is said to have "promising chaos in him," but don't take this chaos for aimlessness: it's a sense of adventure, a wildness, "in which seeming confusion resolves itself into an almost elementary orderliness." That's what American-Type painting at its best is—a new kind of order and control, not the mess that the philistines saw.

Greenberg is one of our greatest sympathetic discriminators. Each of his essays says yes when it finds an advance in the use of the medium, and no when it finds something derivative. And it often says yes and no when discussing the same painter, as is the case with Braque and Léger and Lipchitz or Motherwell and Pollock and de Kooning. Despite his reputation as a champion of the Abstract Expressionists, Greenberg—like Trilling—is wary of using absolutes in regard to groups. In his funny essay condemning Wyndham Lewis's small-minded attack on abstract art, he puts it this way, "One cannot condemn tendencies in art, one can only condemn works of art." This is a very open, anti-ideological, "empirical" way of being a critic—it sees the unsuccessful canvas as the result of concrete decisions; it has reverence for individuals not ideas. It is the kind of criticism that will not let us rest, that finds a "conventional sensibility" behind Rouault's portraits, that sniffs out periods of decadence "when personal gifts are no longer borne up and extended by the circulation of new ideas and new challenges." The last shot at failure has to do with Braque's work in the 1930s. If truth be told, Greenberg thought the period had a great many inferior works, "luxury" articles as opposed to what he called the brilliant expanses of Pollock.

The importance of *Art and Culture* inheres in the critic's relentless pursuit of the genuinely experimental. He looks closely at many painters in order to educate in the discovery of what is permanently new. The essay on Marc Chagall has some Greenbergian observations worth holding on to: the Russian painter's new hectic style—with its indispensable clumsiness—is something to be excited about; roughness in composition—which came from the clash of Eastern European conceptions and the Paris art world—was what made Chagall the real thing. And, as usual with Greenberg, this adventure in style was a matter of revealing the nature of the medium—"the genesis and process of the work of art were what was to be most permanently offered to the spectator's attention." Greenberg's mission—whether showing how Pollock volatilized "paint alone" or how non-easel painting broke down the hierarchies of art history with its "sheer texture," "sheer sensation," and "accumulation of repetitions"—was not a pursuit of novelty for its own sake, for playfulness and irony and upending of convention as a deconstructive sport. On the surface of every one of his essays is an earnest, almost nineteenth century belief in spiritual and emotional value. A painting is not a game or trick—or a set of conventions to be adhered to or ironically sent up—but a work of imagination in the old Coleridgean sense of a fusion of opposing forces that produce an emotional effect. He writes of "intense unities that start from an experience." In writing of Kandinsky, Greenberg describes the "realization of an urgent vision"; in praising Léger and his ability to expose the "rawness and inertness of matter," he sees the artist as conveying human feeling. In the essay on Jacques Lipchitz, Greenberg's curse words are *bombastic* and *declamatory*—words that fit the ideological art of the 1930s as well as a good deal of the conceptual art of the early twenty-first century. The artist's passion for his medium and his fidelity to an inner need—these are the permanently important things to look for in a work.

Greenberg's book—about judging the experimental and separating the genuine from the fake—leads us to another breakthrough critic of the 1950s, Harold Rosenberg. Passionately involved with the art scene, with books, and with the state of American culture after the war, Rosenberg covered some of the same ground as Greenberg. He pulled no punches in evaluating artists, had a reputation as a terror, and liked to roam over long stretches of cultural terrain—contemporary painters' sensibilities, Marxist fallacies left over from the thirties, American illusions about the good life, the follies of intellectuals and philistines. His essays of the 1950s—a series of brilliant general reflections rather than a concentrated body of analytic art or literary criticism—can be found principally in two volumes, *The Tradition of the New* and *Discovering the Present: Three Decades in Art, Culture and Politics*. The first book, published in 1960, is a manifesto for contemporary art, a celebration of "extremist art"—by which he means the Abstract Expressionists, among others—and a denunciation of the "social disciplinarians" of his time—Communists, conservatives, and others who clamored for relevant content in painting and writing. He champions the American tradition of no tradition, the improvisational nature of painting in the 1950s—what he calls our "coonskin doggedness" as against the "Redcoatism" of Europe. The book is an exhilarating ride through an era, but by no means his best criticism. The reader who wants to know Rosenberg at his most scintillating and contentious—at the top of his game of anatomizing modern culture—must read *Discovering the Present*. Pick out the essays from the late 1940s to 1960, and you will have a compact, rich little book about being a critic.

"The Herd of Independent Minds," first published in 1948 in *Commentary*, is Rosenberg's bulldog attack on the intellectual conformity of the era. Without the subtlety and grace of Trilling correcting "us"— and without any sense that he is one of us, an American intellectual of his generation—Rosenberg goes after groupthink and mass cultural formations wherever he finds them. His goal, like Trilling's, is the discovery of the genuine; his approach, unlike Trilling's, is the exposure of the fake. Impolite and even a bit brutal in his treatment of fellow intellectuals whom he does not admit as fellows, Rosenberg goes after Edmund Wilson and Lionel Trilling himself, at the top of the cultural pyramid; he also attacks the middlebrows and the lowbrows at the base. High and middle and lowbrows have embraced what Rosenberg calls *common experience* in the arts, and have had little taste for "the experience of being." Individual perceptions—and the art forms that emerge from them—are considered precious and socially irresponsible. Even *Partisan Review* considered Thomas Mann self-absorbed. But for Rosenberg, the artist's job is "the single human being's effort to arrive at a consciousness of himself" and "his practice of a distinctive method of giving form to his experience." Such an effort "puts the existing mass conception" of the social situation into question.

Genuine art makes most high and low and middlebrows uncomfortable: it rarely succeeds as a commodity, never quite falls into a category. Rosenberg characterizes the real thing in writing and painting as something that cannot be easily shared—its producer is regarded as alienated, which is to say sick and living in an unreal world. But Rosenberg—a latter-day follower of the humanistic Karl Marx—believes that the alienation of the artist is a matter of being alienated from his work and drowned in the commodity and fetish world of capitalism. Estrangement is detachment from craft and loss of "spiritual independence." It's also the false trust of the individual man who knows that mass culture is not about his experience but nevertheless blindly feels that it is about most people's common experience. Rosenberg mocks examples of this self-deceiving game: he exposes the most-intellectuals-felt-thus-and-such game that is really about illusions not ideals.

He justly praises Robert Warshow, the author of *The Immediate Experience* and critic of popular culture in the late forties and early fifties. This young man, according to Rosenberg, understood that mass culture as such—culture meant to be understandable to all—was "the Trojan horse that brings the ready-made into the halls of the original." And at this point, Rosenberg picks up on Warshow's idea of "the mass culture of the educated classes" and has terrific fun with it. First of all, the general experience of the intellectuals—"the experience of Communism," "the thirties"—"sounds familiar . . . but does not communicate with mine." The "faintness" of common experience has to do with the fact that it contains so few of the "anachronisms and cultural fragments" of actuality; Rosenberg says that in the 1930s there were many things in his life that were just as important as the shared politics of the Left: "The Old Testament and the Gospels, Plato, eighteenth-century music, the notion of freedom as taught in the New York City school system, the fantastic residues of the Jewish family. If one expanded and deepened this compendium, one might get to a kind of tiny *Finnegans Wake,* which, incidentally, in contrast to *Memoirs of Hecate County,* I do find very communicative." In taking a slap at Edmund Wilson's novel about the upper middle class and its encounter with the proletariat in the thirties, Rosenberg is lashing out at naturalism generally—the literary style rooted in undeniable fact; he is saying that all kinds of other things—irrelevancies if you will—go into the experience to be found in a great mythic novel like *Finnegans Wake*. Is this fair to Wilson? Of course not. And yet it does arouse, provoke, and challenge. It reminds us of all the unpredictable things in postwar American literature—Saul Bellow's *The Adventures of Augie March*, the noir novels of Jim Thompson and Patricia Highsmith,

Flannery O'Connor's stories, Malamud's tales—that don't march along with contemporary issues. Those literary surprises—what the era does not seem to demand or help explain—constitute the glory of the period. Rosenberg helps us to be ready for such things; he helps us not to become "a prefabricated audience of experience-comrades" who learn what they already know.

"I regard communal 'wholeness' . . . as an unattractive and bad idea," Rosenberg wrote in a 1958 essay titled "Professors of Man Estranged." His war against the "total impress" of culture—primitive or modern, Leftist or Rightist—was his critical mission. Trilling carefully picked through the tyrannies of culture; Rosenberg went after them with a hatchet. One of the best polemics is "The Twilight of the Intellectuals," a demolition job that pulls down the pretensions of anti-intellectuals posing as wise men. The scourge of ideologues who sought to heal and improve us—those "social disciplinarians" he referred to—Rosenberg was also the scourge of self-proclaimed anti-ideologues like the French philosopher Raymond Aron who attacked mind, general ideas, and the work of the critical intellectual. A conservative and glorifier of can-do pragmatism as against a creator of abstractions like Jean-Paul Sartre, Aron believed that "all ideas have turned out so badly" because real progress in society emerges from "the idea of no-ideas." This submission to the powers that are always around—to men of action—is especially distasteful to Rosenberg. He drily comments that it's dishonest to lay the blame at the feet of intellectuals when the men of action are always in the driver's seat. And he comes out fighting as a critical thinker, reminding his readers that ideals and dreams are sustenance. What we have to fear is a kind of intellectual poison, "the ideal of practicality, of a politics and social philosophy stripped of 'myth' and 'ineffectiveness,' of a subordination to 'reality.' . . . This is the drug that has transformed the fighting humanitarianism of Dr. Jekyll into the bureaucratic and 'responsible' Mr. Hyde."

When it comes to being concrete about what is valuable—exemplifying the impractical realm of authentic art—he does an especially fine job in an essay called "Tenth Street: A Geography of Modern Art." This gritty portrait of a time and place—the East Village in the early 1950s—also manages to be an expression of Rosenberg's own idiosyncratic nature. Tenth Street—like some geographical equivalent of Marxian de-alienation—is everything that modern artistic culture hardly ever is. "Devoid of local color"—no quaint Greenwich Village—it is also devoid of the glamour, mystique, and charm that the Village possessed as an imitation of Paris. Tenth Street is bohemia without the trendiness—it is not even picturesque like a downtown slum. Without a category—or an image—it is

> hospitable to anything, except what might denote a norm. Apart from the two pawnshops facing each other on the Third Avenue western corners, everything on Tenth Street is one of a kind; a liquor store with a large "wino" clientele, up a flight of iron steps, a foreign-language-club restaurant; up another flight, a hotel workers' employment agency; in a basement, a poolroom; in another, something stored; in the middle of the block, a metal stamping factory with a "modernistic" pea-green cement and glass-brick front; on the Fourth Avenue Corner, to be sure, an excavation.

This crummy diversity—an urban version of Gerard Manley Hopkins's dappled things in "Pied Beauty"—is exhilarating and strange, in part, because it is threatened: that excavation plainly says that Tenth Street is not an institution but a curious short time in the history of art. It also has an "ethnic openness" and freedom from the "generation-propaganda" that prevails out on the Coast with the Beats. "On Tenth Street the individual prevails against the band. . . ." Rosenberg profiles bohemia in such a way as to make it a locale of the anarchic, a place that strives to resist categories: "The absence from Tenth Street of fixed group identities, whether of nationality, race, class, ideology, or age, is one of the superiorities of this colony and its novelty." Tenth Street has no style of dress, no willed identity, no desire to improve itself; yet it has "the rugged individualism of American pioneering—an impossible contradiction and therefore most likely to fit."

"Tenth Street" was a marker in avant-garde history—and gave Rosenberg a chance to soar and rhapsodize; but the gruff side of his criticism is no less important. In "Literary Form and Social Hallucination," a 1960 piece about literature, he takes on nothing less than the whole "me" tendency of modern writing. With a classicist's devotion to literary form, inner coherence in a work, and balance, he goes after the excesses of life-history confessional writers. Nothing could be more pertinent (and embarrassing) for our literary culture than his attack on the great American idea that everybody is entitled to tell a private tale in public. The victims, whiners, St. Augustines without a City of God in our own time, are better captured by Rosenberg's analysis than they have been by our own critics. His essay rests on a belief in the enduring value of genuine literary form as opposed to faddish subject matter. T. S. Eliot is his master here, a classicist who championed the autonomy of the art object at a time when many intelligent and not-so-intelligent people were demanding that books and paintings be socially relevant. Rosenberg shows that the work of art has something much subtler to offer than in-your-face relevance. "The form, in short, carries its own independent feelings, which play against the feeling aroused by the subject; and the artist, according to Eliot, is most interested in the 'fitness' of these contrasting feelings to each other, so that a 'balance' may be reached." Our trouble, however, is that we are suspicious of such highfalutin effects—we want facts and the emotions that come from them to constitute our literature. In short, we want a literature that isn't really literary at all; we find Eliot's balance and fitness so much reactionary nonsense. Rosenberg puts our philistine doubts this way: "the temptation of art to betrayal of the social conscience is irremediable." We are like the Social Realist dreamers in the Soviet Union, yearning to break out of all constraints and conventions. Our version of the dream—what Rosenberg calls *hallucination*—is a fable about triumphing as ourselves—and this conquest must inevitably include the "opposing fantasy of being deprived, the nightmare of being nobody; in no other literature is there so much suffering from ontological handicaps, the handicap of being an artist or an adolescent or a Jew or a Negro or a wife or a husband or of not having gone to Princeton or of having been changed into a G.I." Norman Mailer's *Advertisements for Myself* is offered as a prime example. Rosenberg comically remarks that the writers of such fables of the bedeviled self use a "minimum of patterning" and are "eruptive." His reply to these champions of raw experience is this: "To honor fact, art must honor itself." For him this means that artistic experiment brings out the finer tones of fact and helps us see beyond the commonplace of sheer information. Art lets us escape the hallucination that raw facts speak for themselves—and it liberates us from the provinciality of stock responses. "Immediacy" was not one of Rosenberg's favorite words; he believed it traps us in illusions and confirms us in the narrowness of the moment.

Roughing up confessional writers like Mailer—and other celebrators of the glories and agonies of Me—is far from being Rosenberg's main enterprise. He is a general critic of what Trilling called the terror of culture and, as such, hammers at any cultural expression that takes on an ideological life. When it comes to defenders of tradition who attack modern industrial society, he is keenly aware that their screeds can be a cover for snobbery and reactionary politics. Reviewing the Marxist scholar Raymond Willliams's landmark study *Culture and Society*, he endorses the critical skepticism that the author brings to bear on conservative "inwardness." Yet, as we have seen, he is no es-pouser of the "mass culture of the educated classes"—which is to say those old leftist ideas that had not disappeared. He finds his critical stance in a cool rejection of polarities—he's no Stalinist sympathizer masking as a progressive, no Republican masking as a cultural conser-vative. He's also no antimodernist, despite his mockery directed at the junk culture. He has little use for English traditionalism, in spite of his respect for Eliot the critic of poetry. The British lack the critical spirit, and he makes a cutting comment on what this entails: "Nor does the British artist or man of letters tend, like Whitman, the Russians, or the vanguard movements of the Continent, to see in the total overthrow of dead form the beginning of creation under conditions of freedom." Rosenberg is one of the great American contrarians—against the tend-encies of his age, finding kinship with the humanist Marx and with the originals in painting and writing. This is a position of no position— and in "The Threat of Culture" he expresses his fears about solidarity with others in the cause of art and progress. Isn't this yet another temptation to be uncritical and part of a herd? And the fear of losing the critical edge can be found everywhere in his writing. No matter what you're thinking about—a book, a painting, a community, an idea—you're in danger of falling into a kind of groupthink. In "Road-side Arcadia"—an essay about America's love of the pastoral myth—he found that we glamorize the American small town while ignoring the fact that in the postwar period it has become an extension of mass culture and the corporate way of life. He says that in such a faux-idyllic setting, the only genuine way to exist is to be an outcast, one of the shack people who live on the fringes of society. This brings us back to the variousness and stubborn resistance to trends of Tenth Street. In looking for a place to locate the critical spirit, Rosenberg has succeeded in finding something out-of-bounds and therefore useful for interrogating our art, our community, and our life-in-culture.

Dwight Macdonald's *Against the American Grain* is about preserving standards in art and in discourse. It overlaps the concerns of Trilling, Greenberg, and Rosenberg, especially as it defends the unsettling and puzzling qualities of first-rate writing. It shares Rosenberg's provoking attacks on herdlike behavior—and his elitism; it's scalding about kitsch in the Greenberg manner; but—it must be said—it lacks the philosophical subtleties of the others' works. Yet it stands as a landmark because of its rapier prose, its good sense, and its rare honesty. Very few books about our cultural situation are quite as biting, witty, idea-infested, and intelligently confrontational. By and large, Macdonald is a negative kind of critic, specializing in—as his two best chapters indicate—"Pretenders" and "Betrayers." But his demolition jobs on bad writing are far from the hatchet jobs of reviews of every age. This man's negative responses are permanently interesting because he identifies the verbal follies and half-baked ideas of modern times. With a solid grasp of the origins of mass culture, he cuts a wide swath, moving from mechanical tendencies in the work of Walter Scott to the prefabricated world of self-help books. He's essentially a reporter about books—and in the age of TV, he's a critic of mass culture who ignores the defining medium. Once said, however, this should not obscure his importance in that he is taking as his focal point what has happened to language itself in his time. With no pretense to objectivity, he writes like the "amateur" journalists that he admires. "English reviewers speak in their own individual voices—the headlong rush of Pritchett, the neat, balanced style of Connolly—and yet are clear and to the point, like good conversationalists." This kind of critic and commentator is quite rare in America: we prefer specialists, writers who have advanced themselves in a field—or pundits who command vast audiences and therefore dare not write in their own voices. Our magazines typically link up likely suspect-reviewer with likely book; the British periodicals—Macdonald explains with enthusiasm—like recklessness in the mix, some selfhood with their expertise. The reviewer "can write simply, informally, personally, sticking his neck out as far as he likes." This is a thumbnail portrait of Macdonald himself in *Against the American Grain*. But the other quality that makes him such a durable critic is his ability—at times almost Johnsonian in its richness of notation and forceful style—to convey the spirit of his subjects. He is a terrific describer who lays out the characteristics of his material with singular vividness. After reading him on James Gould Cozzens, you are not likely to forget that the author of *By Love Possessed* had a style "as Gothic as Harkness Memorial Quadrangle (also as unaesthetic)" or that his observations about life had a "Confucius Say" flavor. A Macdonald essay conveys the vital—or unvital—sense of its subject along with "a slug of pure opinion," as he says of the

Brits. The "pure" in pure opinion is the point. He arrives at his conclusions before consulting the herd of independent minds. This set him apart from many a clever and witty writer of his time—or ours.

Macdonald didn't mind sticking his own neck out by reminding us of the relationship of amateur (in the true sense) to lover: he intended to report on what he valued or what otherwise attracted his attention because it was the occasion for drawing on his personal learning and personal response. He wrote—despite an earlier phase of his career in which he was a Trotskyite—to please himself. And he was even willing to risk a certain amount of sententiousness—the tones of a prep-school teacher with a very smart class. He didn't mind nailing his elitist colors to the mast at a time when popularizations—new versions of the Bible, science for the average guy, Great Books for the suburban household—were first becoming the rage. He boldly mocked these middlebrow cultural goods—finding falseness and fatuity everywhere; he proudly championed the highbrows and avant-gardists—those who wrote and painted for themselves and refused to cater to a mass audience. The late 1950s was the golden age of Culture for the many—culture-vulture TV programs like *Omnibus*, articles on beatniks in the slick magazines, and what Macdonald calls "we-need-this-kind-of-book" thinking. Macdonald had the bad manners to laugh at the results, take them apart, and look at what they say about our civilization. He intended that we should do the same thing with whatever is around and in long supply.

At first look his essays seem hopelessly old-fashioned: he just doesn't get the whole intellectual and artistic drift of the postwar period—the breakdown of borders between high and low art, the irrelevance of High Modernist standards, the end of the Age of Joyce and Yeats. Macdonald's book has the flavor of a last stand against the barbarians—and this makes it somewhat uncool in tone. But his substance is the eternal substance of judgmental criticism—what are the genuine cultural goods? How can you tell the phonies from the real artists? Without critics like him we would be lost. We would be studiously involved with junk and trivia, "marooned in the present"—to borrow a phrase from Mailer's *The Presidential Papers*. We would become self-important, self-absorbed, altogether detached from the long history of artistic craftsmanship and experiment.

chapter 7

WASP, Catholic, Black, Jewish

The mission of the intellectuals—keeping complexity alive—is also what the reader will find in the best writing that tracks the experience of ethnic and racial groups. Chroniclers of group identity in America—John Cheever in *The Housebreaker of Shady Hill*, J. F. Powers in *Morte D'Urban*, James Baldwin in *Notes of a Native Son*, Philip Roth in *Goodbye, Columbus*—asked penetrating questions about what it meant to be an American in the postwar period. What is the right condition of the self? How can the modern American preserve integrity in the midst of the newest kinds of conformity, phoniness, consumerism, not to mention the weight of conventions and prejudices from the past? How can one be a self—autonomous, questioning, growing—and yet hold onto one's cultural heritage? Is one's race and ethnicity a vital part of one's humanity? What wrenching feelings and challenging ideas arise from being black or Jewish or Catholic or WASP? These writers' books are not quite pioneering treatments of color and roots in America, yet their depth of vision makes them invaluable and permanently interesting. They are not feel-good exercises about origins, hymns of praise, or proudly assertive studies of the lives of heroes and victims. They each have a negative charge and couldn't be further from the self-congratulatory strain in our contemporary literature about religion, race, and ethnicity.

Cheever comes at the end of a long line of interrogators of Anglo-Saxon America. From that vantage point, he tells stories about characters facing a crisis in their history. Despite their Dutch Colonial homes and family heirlooms and traditions of gracious living, the WASPs in his tales are an edgy, endangered group who constantly take stock of blessings in order to keep up their courage. J. F. Powers—a groundbreaker in studying his group in the age of Eisenhower—had more to say about the uncomfortable states of being of his Catholic priests—and a broad section of the laity—than anyone to date in our literature. His study of a troubled priest's career is not the stuff of

Going My Way, the hit movie of the 1940s that showed Bing Crosby able to handle the untroubling problems of his parish. James Baldwin's landmark book also does not make us comfortable. No pioneer in exploring what happens to the black man with a good mind and a rich inventory of memories, he nevertheless comes at the point in our history when he can define himself in relationship to a protest tradition and then stake out his own territory. And Roth—not of course the first to explore Jewishness in Gentile America—becomes the most vivid, disturbing, and critically intelligent observer of American Jews in the midst of middle-class prosperity.

Each writer offered a book with a distinctive style, a signature way of looking at social experience. There was nothing quite like these four books in the twentieth century canon. Each had a tone and vision that was original—Cheever elegiac yet comic and lyrical about the Farquarsons and the Bentleys; Powers sly but tragic about his Church; Baldwin scalding yet humane about conventional ideas of race; Roth, loopy yet cutting about the social ideals of Jews.

John Cheever published two books of stories during the 1950s, *The Enormous Radio* (1953) and *The Housebreaker of Shady Hill* (1958). The former has some of his brilliant tales of Manhattan, wildly imaginative stories of people in an exhilarating and eerie city. The enormous radio of the title story—bought by a smug upper middle class couple—broadcasts the dirty secrets of the neighbors in an East Side apartment building. Other stories move strangely and often comically through a lost New York: they are filled with references to the War, to changing one's clothes for dinner, to live-in servants, devoted doormen, and the mandatory cocktail hour. They are also charged with uncanniness; there's always something disturbing intruding on the lives of the well-bred New Yorkers—the pathos of a runaway child on Sutton Place, the antics of a self-pitying doorman, the sounds of that radio. And, be it said, the lives of the poor and struggling. The later book, however, is about a newer America—the suburbia that Cheever himself retreated to and then depicted with the ardor of a poet and the analytic eye of a great social observer. The pleasant "banlieue" of Shady Hill is made to hold the staples of contemporary America. The car culture, the centrality of child rearing and babysitters, the commute, the relentless socializing with one's neighbors, the overbooked mother and tanked-up father, the conflicts within one's class and the scramble to earn (and hold onto) more and more money: Cheever adds freshness and piquancy to them. He also gives them to us Anglo-Saxon style: with the guilt and decorum and family pride and pretentiousness and narrowness of his own heritage. What the stories show is how his group played such a large part in forming our conception of the good life—and the threats to it: Cheever's Shady Hill is in some respects a crucible of our experience. Upper-middle-class WASPs help us read our situation.

The title story is a complex and hilarious tale of social sin and atonement that bridges the gap between Johnny Hake, reared on Sutton Place, and the rest of us. It focuses on a man faced with financial ruin, someone at the mercy of the economy, luck, and his superiors on the job and in the community. Johnny has lost out at a parablendeum company—and an old fox named Gil Buckram has used his stock of amiability and a few gifts of (soiled) cashmeres to trick the younger man and get him out of the firm. Thereafter Johnny is forced to go into business for himself—with no takers. In order to live, he must turn to theft. The tale has lodged within it a variation of the old saw about needing cash, "What should I do, rob a bank?" No, worse than robbing a bank is robbing the neighbors: they, after all, have trusted you, opened their homes, and treated you like a gentleman. Cheever plays with the word *common*, as in "common thief." And Johnny fears nothing more than being outside the uncommon circle of his group; he knows that his desperate—and funny—larcenies have "broken all the unwritten laws that held the community together." But the bitter irony of it all is that classy neighbors like the Warburtons, the victims of Johnny's desperate scheme, are rather vulgar and, if truth be told, victimizers themselves. Listen to Johnny on Carl Warburton: "He is the kind of man that you wouldn't have liked at school" or "The Warburtons are always spending money, and that's what you talk about with them. The floor of their front hall is black-and-white marble from the old Ritz, and their cabanas at Sea Island are being winterized, and they are flying to Davos for ten days, and buying a pair of saddle horses, and building a new wing." Carl's wife says he has to walk through a "terrible slum to get to the station," and she's afraid "he'll be *victimized*." Johnny of course will soon victimize them, but it shall not keep them from having parties "where some old cook has been peeling mushrooms or picking the meat out of crab shells since daybreak." One of Cheever's specialties as a social observer is the devastating, acidic one-liner: "Then Carl came home and told a dirty story to the mixed company, and we went in to dinner." The social sin—and then the resumption of the class ritual.

Johnny, too, is part of the compromise. At the end of the story, he's willing to go back with Gil Buckram, thinking that it's not "the smell of corn bread that calls us back from death," but "the lights and signs of love and friendship." He believes Buckram's lies; he also returns the money he stole from Warburton—the honest and honorable thing to do, but not without a bit of trickery. We see Johnny sneaking over with the stolen cash and lying to a patrolman about why he's out so late. The atonement has become a kind of reinstatement. Johnny is back inside the fold, and he is feeling like a winner rather than like all those "melancholy people who, out of an excess of sympathy for others, miss the thrill of their own essence and drift through life without identity." Now Johnny has an identity all right, but as the story ends, it is ironically damaged. "Where were the trout streams of my youth, and other innocent pleasures?" he cries at one point. In a brilliant lyric outburst he sees fishermen and sandlot ballplayers and old men playing pinochle as stitching "up the big holes in the world that were made by men like me." But these icons of everyday decency don't sound a bit like the Warburtons with their tiles from the Ritz and the community to which Johnny Hake is restored. Without quite knowing what's happened to him, Hake has tasted dread and dangerous knowledge of suffering and hurried back to the old life of compromise—sweet at times, but wholly conditioned by money and class. Here, and in other stories, Cheever is the kind of writer on society that Karl Marx himself admired: not a mouthpiece for the working class with a sermon to deliver, but an original who can use his mastery of detail and his own vision—even his own attraction to the pleasures and compromises of his class—to reveal the terms under which people are forced to live. Johnny is a descendant of those characters from the nineteenth century novel caught in the gears of a venial society; the trouble is, however, that unlike Pip and Julien Sorel, he doesn't move beyond the emotions and social terms of his initial situation. The story begins in an exhilarated tone—with his brave aria about the markers of his class. "I was conceived in the Hotel St. Regis, born in Presbyterian Hospital, raised on Sutton Place, christened and confirmed in St. Bartholomew's, and I drilled with the Knickerbocker Greys, played football and baseball in Central Park, learned to chin myself on the framework of East Side apartment canopies, and met my wife (Christina Lewis) at one of those big cotillions at the Waldorf." For all the brio and brilliance of the tale, it's a bit dismal. Johnny has embraced the compromising aspects of the conditioned life—and what makes this ending forced and sad is that he doesn't know that his good humor is a form of false consciousness. Cheever, nevertheless, has left a trail of unattractive things that his character doesn't quite understand. Johnny is the apologist for the rich neighbors, down to glamorizing and falsifying their tastes. Any reader who has heard about the Warburtons is likely to find something wrong in this picture:

> My neighbors are rich, it is true, but riches in this case mean leisure, and they use their time wisely. They travel around the world, listen to good music, and given a choice of paper books at an airport, will pick Thucydides, and sometimes Aquinas. Urged to build bomb shelters, they plant trees and roses, and their gardens are splendid and bright. Had I looked, the next morning, from my bathroom window into the evil-smelling ruin of some great city, the shock of what I had done might not have been so violent, but the moral bottom had dropped out of my world without changing a mote of sunlight.

The fine taste of the suburban rich is about as dubious a matter as the smelliness of the urban poor. Cheever leaves us to sort out the truth.

"The Country Husband" has the same clever, witty, and subtle way of representing compromise. Francis Weed is another 1950s family man in crisis, more complexly constituted than Johnny Hake, but also destined to wind up where he started. Cheever's resources—bizarre comic invention, close scrutiny of social circumstance, puzzling ironic details—bring Shady Hill into focus. Francis's transgression—his way of violating the terms of the community—is erotic rather than economic: he falls in love with the babysitter Anne Murchison (a girl from the other side of the tracks, no less), and his forbidden love seems to echo an old memory from the war years. At a stuffy dinner party Francis sees that the maid is someone he recognizes from his Army days, a wretched victim who was ritually humiliated and paraded through a small French town because she had been the lover of a Nazi officer. Francis is soon to be in a situation as painful as hers: in high spirits because of his ardor for a young girl, he forgets himself and speaks his mind to a society woman. Mrs. Wrightson, a formidable matron, had been jabbering at the train station about exchanging curtains, and Francis answers her nonsense with a cutting remark. He is soon taken down by his wife who reminds him that their happiness in the community—their congested social life and their daughter's invitations to the club assemblies—is all in the hands of Mrs. Wrightson. And Francis gets an additional dose of humiliation as he faces the fact that he has violated another trust—he's lied, out of sexual jealousy, about the character of Anne Murchison's real boyfriend, and tried to ruin his reputation in the eyes of a prospective employer. In trying to love and live intensely he's made a mess of his existence—so much so that his wife is about to leave. Her speech says more about the dangers of being yourself than any other passage in the story: "You can conceal your dislikes. You don't have to meet everything head on, like a child. Unless you're anxious to be a social leper. It's no accident that we get asked out a great deal! . . . . How would you like to spend your Saturday nights at the movies? How would you like to spend your Sundays raking up dead leaves?" Francis is like other dreamers in the fifties, like those intellectuals described by Lionel Trilling who couldn't appreciate the ordinariness in Tolstoy or William Dean Howells and valued extremes and the unconditioned life of feeling. His wife delivers her short sermon on maturity, a bland and compromised defense of accepting the terms of community. And Cheever brings Francis's passions to a pitch of intensity, only to cut him down to community size at the end of the story. One of Francis's friends had referred in a sentimental way to his conjugal passion: his wife made him feel like Hannibal crossing the Alps. As "The Country Husband" draws to a close, Cheever echoes this corny use of the classical reference by having Francis—back to normal as a result of psychotherapy—muse and yearn and reveal the pathos of his situation as a settled country husband: "Then it is dark; it is a night where kings in golden suits ride elephants over the mountains."

These two showpiece stories—with their mix of humor and ardor—are the best in the volume, but they do not diminish the value of fine, less textured pieces—notably "The Sorrows of Gin" and "O Youth and Beauty!" Both of these stories have a gimmick, but both tell us things about WASP suburban life that are more than the gimmick would suggest. On the surface, "The Sorrows of Gin" is about a little girl who can't stand her father's martini swilling, running from party to party, and brisk disregard for her own ten-year-old world. She solves things by pouring his gin down a sink—and running away from home, at least as far as the train station. During the action of the story she has her eye on him—and we do the easy job of inferring. He is a self-absorbed—and neighbor-absorbed—case; he is overtaxed by his job, overburdened with business travel, and under-endowed with insight into his own household. As he makes himself foolish with his drinking, studied attempts at gentlemanliness and more obvious displays of arrogance, his daughter takes in the pathetic show. But Cheever has more than this in mind as he lets the story turn on a dime—what seemed to be Amy's tale, the story of a child watching the social failings of her parents, becomes a very tricky tale about the father's capacity for self-deception. By the end, Mr. Lawton, to a greater degree than even Francis Weed or Johnny Hake, is immersed in his illusions: the main lie is that he can rescue a little girl from the train station and make her understand that home-sweet-suburban-home is what he values and she has strayed from. In a bravura paragraph—a splendid example of Cheever's lyricism and his satiric ability to trace consciousness—Lawton wakes up to his daughter's terror for a moment, only to sink back into his clichés.

Cash Bentley in "O Youth and Beauty!" is another self-deluded man whose problem is part economic strain, part social impotence due to the loss of his youthful status as a college track star. Cheever depends heavily on the absurd and incredible—making the Shady Hill neighbors ready to enjoy the sad spectacle of a middle-aged man doing the hurdles late at night when parties are about to break up. And Cash—for a time disabled with a broken leg as a result of proving his athletic prowess—is a wonderful distillation of what can happen to you if you're out of the Shady Hill loop. On a resplendent summer night—filled with stars and sounds from the club, and smells from the barbecues—he sits at home watching his wife sew the elastic in children's underpants: "all the unbeautiful facts of life that threaten to crush the breath out of Cash" leave his neighbors untouched. Of course, the reference point that he uses in evaluating himself is the young people. Yet, the sadness comes from the fact that there seems to be little available for the aging in Shady Hill. "He feels as if the figures in the next yard are the specters from some party in that past where all his tastes and desires lie, and from which he has been cruelly removed. He feels like a ghost of the summer evening." Whereas Francis Weed learned how to make peace with the conditioned life, Cash is too far gone in his illusions to resign himself. His long-suffering wife—humiliated by his antics and bedeviled by responsibility and financial worry—fires the starting gun and shoots Cash in mid-air. Accident or mercy killing? It's unclear. But before the end, Cash has been to Christ Church for eleven o'clock services, and we learn from the narrator that "the most he ever felt in church was that he stood outside the realm of God's infinite mercy, and to tell the truth, he no more believed in the Father, the Son, and the Holy Ghost than does my bull terrier." The note of desolation—struck in almost every Cheever story—reminds us that some people can't survive the terms of Shady Hill. Cash is an extremely neurotic case, but then again the entire volume deals with men, especially—and to a lesser extent women—who have been bent out of shape by the demands of their beloved banlieue.

Without being the sledgehammer kind of satirist, Cheever manages to show that a good deal of the pain and suffering of his characters emerges from their group identity. Yes, there is light and lusty love-making, and the smells of nature and "the miraculous physicalness of everything," and the love of family, but these things are damaged by relentless conformity—and the deception and narrowness that goes with it. Francis Weed complains to his wife that they are trapped by all the people around them—deprived of all that is "bawdy and dark" and exciting. Young Clayton in "The Country Husband" thinks Shady Hill has no future—all the partying and drunkenness and club dances leave no room for "big dreams." In another fine story, "The Trouble of Marcie Flint," an endearing young wife comes up against a fairly horrible bunch of locals who don't want a public library because they are afraid it would attract builders and more developments. One obnoxious character of real wealth refers to a middle-middle class de-fender of the library as a "meatball." A nasty old woman gets her wealthy husband to denounce the defender in the papers. Shady Hill—upscale, physically beautiful—fears the "cheeseboxes" that developers would put up; it fears lower-middle-class Maple Dell. And Cheever, a writer of great honesty and integrity, does not mind letting his narra-tor take some swipes at the unloveliness of the cramped homes: "Who would ever come back to the little living room where you couldn't swing a cat around without knocking down the colored photograph of Mount Rainier? Who would ever come back to the chair that bit you in the bum and the obsolete TV set and the bent ashtray with its steel-frame statue of a naked woman doing a scarf dance?" He doesn't mind revealing the narrowness of the upper-middle-class WASP look-ing at the narrowness of the less fortunate.

J. F. Powers's *Morte D'Urban* is a study of a different kind of Ameri-can narrowness—the constricted culture of provincial Catholicism in the 1950s. The Urban of the title is a highly intelligent and progressive priest who belongs to a mediocre order called the Clementines. He has enjoyed a good run as a star preacher traveling out of Chicago, when all of a sudden, near the opening of the novel, he finds himself transferred by his superiors to Duesterhaus, Minnesota. His new assignment is to assist one Father Wilfred in starting a retreat house. A bit of a worldling and lover of the good life rather than a saint or a scholar, Father Urban nevertheless has a quality that any organization needs: he's a man with a desire to put some verve and taste and class and spirit into the bureaucratic working of things. He has a dream of Clementines—and Catholics generally—playing a bigger role in the American scene. A man of moral and intellectual sensitivity, standards, and decency, he casts a cold eye on some of the features of the Church of his time: the McCarthyism of the small-time Catholic press, the preciousness of the Catholic intelligentsia, the relentlessness of clergy who would want a religious component in a children's cartoon program, the hole-in-corner defensiveness and isolationism of priests who should know better.

Powers's talents for storytelling are immense. He may be one of our most neglected tellers of social fables. In this case his story is tragicomic—the misadventures of a man of action and ideals up against the hard collective will of the majority. Urban hits up against every variety of inertia, obtuseness, obstructiveness, groupthink, conventionality, and sheer ill-will imaginable. Powers populates his book with a gallery of rogues, clucks, do-nothings, and know-nothings—yet he does so with a subtlety and dramatic sense that makes scourges of provincialism such as Sinclair Lewis and H. L. Mencken seem heavy-handed. His territory is, to a large extent, Mencken's booboisie; yet he is after more than ridicule. This novel explores the nature of a complex man, and looks at the limited people who oppose him as human beings, not spectacles.

Father Urban—as the title suggests—is a figure of some magnitude who is to be destroyed in the course of the book. He's a dreamer and doer—not the king of Camelot of course—but someone who has a vision of a better Order and a better Church. Pre–Vatican II and not without his own narrowness—about the role of women in the Church, about social activism, about the laity generally—he's nevertheless a superior man of his time trying to do a good job as an all-around priest: preacher, man with outreach and ideas, leader, and model. His story is a beautifully plotted tragicomedy of good works and good ideas gone awry. Cheever's characters are generally compromised by their conditioned existences; Powers's protagonist is broken. In the course of his decline and fall, we get a comprehensive picture of the 1950s American Catholic scene—a swaggering businessman with a taste for religion (but little faith), a pious old lady of wealth who cheats her maid, her pretentious and arty son, assorted prosperous middle-class married people, anti–Communist cranks, canny old farmers, burnt-out priests, sour priests, tricky priests, hopelessly provincial priests. Powers possesses an almost Chaucerian ability to make his social types into real people. Watch Monsignor Renton who thinks any community service destroys the role of a "priest-priest." Or consider the obstructive and cagey bishop with his love of golf (badly played). Or chipper Brother Harold at St. Clements, obsessed with cooking and his electric mixer.

Father Urban's story is an American tale of disillusionment and destruction, but one without the violence and luridness of Algren's *The Man with the Golden Arm* or the bizarre experiences of a Flannery O'Connor story. Urban's fall involves such things as failing to get a parish, being thrown overboard on a fishing trip, being knocked unconscious by a bishop's golf ball—not to mention being hit again by the shoe of a woman who is trying to undress and seduce him. The bourgeois and quotidian and the ridiculous are Powers's chosen fields on which to depict Urban's agonies. Note this description of what Urban envisions as the Order's new headquarters and contrast it with what finally materializes:

> He wanted the handsome room facing the street to be a showplace—mellow prints, illuminated manuscripts, old maps, calf-bound volumes, Persian carpets, easy chairs, and so on—everything in keeping with the oak-paneled walls, the bow window, and the fireplace. He wanted the room to be a rendez-vous where passers-by would always be welcome to drop in and chat, to peruse the latest in worth-while books and periodicals . . . not all on religious subjects and none on narrow, controversial lines . . . But Father Boniface had said no to all this—the idea of such a nook was associated in his mind with Christian Science—and the room was furnished with junk trucked in from the Novitiate: clawfooted tables and chairs, inhumanly high and hard, and large, pious oils (copies of Renaissance masterpieces, executed by a now departed Clementine) in which everybody seemed to be going blind. The room could have been a nuns' parlor at the turn of the century. And lying about in the noble bow window were poisonous pamphlets (*Who, Me? A Here-*

tic?), issues of the *Clementine* (that wholesome monthly devoted to the entire family and therefore of interest to nobody in particular), and a number of unpopular popular histories and biographies from the Millstone Press (a millstone having been the means of St. Clement's death at the hands of the Huguenots).

It's almost as if Powers were adapting Matthew Arnold's ideas about the ugliness and narrowness of the Dissenters in the nineteenth century—"the dissidence of dissent and the Protestantism of the Protestant religion," Arnold called it. Powers's send-up of Catholic contentiousness is a marvel of significant detail, down to the Millstone Press. Later on in the book, he profiles characters whom Arnold would have loved to dissect. Mrs. Bean, wife of a rich man in rural Minnesota, is deep into the issues expressed in a paper called *The Drover*. Once a publication for the farmers, it has turned into a full-time anti–Communist rag (with, according to Urban, "the worst features of the bully and the martyr"). Powers makes its editors the Shrapnel brothers. He also shows us that Father Urban wouldn't accept a free subscription. Mrs. Bean—a ruthless ideologue—is nevertheless humanized by Powers and given a whiff of sexuality ("damned attractive redhead," as Urban muses) that keeps her from being a monster. (Be it also said that Urban doesn't mind tooling around the area in Mrs. Bean's red Barracuda, a fact that puts him in a direct line to Chaucer's Monk.) Another crank is old man Zimmermann, a backwater anti–Communist who spends his time writing letters to the editors of various publications. Urban, the man of the world, is given the rare treat of seeing his scrapbook of clippings. Perhaps Powers is at the top of his satiric game in portraying narrowness when he gives us Father Wilf, a kindly enough superior at St. Clements Hill who nevertheless eats away at anything resembling excellence. Vaguely jealous of Urban's pulpit eloquence, stingy, obsessed with every petty detail of administration, yet completely out of touch with what retreatants might want in the middle of the twentieth century, he rules St. Clements Hill with an unparalleled ineptitude. He needs Urban's superior skills, but can't endure to see them exercised. He too has a vision for the Clementines, and Powers distills it in a description of the refectory at St. Clements Hill—wainscoting varnished like old office furniture, plastic covered tables, green rockers with foam rubber seats, and a tray with a dish of horehound drops. Father Urban—a gifted preacher—is made to spend his time painting and plastering. He's subjected to

Wilf's smallness—everything from watching Wilf remove the Christ Child from the crèche before Christmas morning ("He's not born yet") to being made to play his part in drawing up a hideous brochure for the retreat house.

And when Urban finally escapes and takes the next step downward—a chance to fill in as pastor at St. Monica's in nearby Great Plains—things don't get much better. Although he thrives on parish work, he's not allowed to carry any of his ideas through; when the time comes for a permanent pastor to be named, he's passed over. What remains for him is a scheme to enhance St. Clements by building a golf course for the retreatants. He falls back on his proven ability as a fundraiser among the rich. We return to scenes with Billy Cosgrove, the man who got the Order the lease on its Chicago headquarters. Billy was impressed by Urban's preaching in his "high he-who manner" ("Charles of the Holy Roman Empire, it was he who, you might say, owned and operated Europe but who, in the end, desired only the society of monks"). Fancying himself a new Holy Roman Emperor, Billy goes in for medieval largesse: he loves the idea that the Order will supply him with three cords of wood each year in payment for the huge Chicago rent that he absorbs. He deals with the world in an imperious and crude manner. Part of the drama of the book is watching Urban, a man of fine sensibilities, deal with this vulgarian. The scenes usually involve Billy pushing around some underling, while supposedly trying to do Urban and the Order some good. And this mixing of coarseness and good works is part of the tragic vision of the book—a Church runs on the bullying powers of the Billys of the world; moral delicacy and high-mindedness are likely to be crushed.

Father Urban himself is an especially poignant figure. Born into a fairly poor family, he met one of those legendary inspirers of youth, the superior cleric. Father Placidus—a jovial lover of music and sports—swept the young boy up and took him out of a little town into the great world. Urban's story—in its ludic, agonizing way—is an American version of Stendhal's *The Red and the Black*—the bright young man from the provinces gets a leg up in society by taking Holy Orders, spends his life among dangerous worldlings, and meets his tragic fate. Powers's protagonist has none of Julien Sorel's grandeur, but he does have some of his pride and contempt for the higher-ups. His observations are devastating: Nature—he tells us in his evaluation of Father Provincial Boniface—abhors a vacuum, but the Clementines do not. Or take this one about his assignment to St. Clement's Hill:

"Why had he been cast into the outer darkness, thrown among fools and failures?"

Urban moves us because his plight is devoid of sentimentality and heroics, a matter of awful circumstances—the air that one breathed in the Clementines—and weaknesses of character. Why does a rather talented man wind up accomplishing so little? It is true that he doesn't know Henry Moore from Thomas More—and that he gives sermons sprinkled with commonplaces. But he is several cuts above the provincials who want to argue about putting Christ back in Christmas, the slow-moving priest who dreams of writing the life of St. Adalbert, the rich old woman who watches two TV sets at once. In Powers's world the high heart sinks under the weight of 1950s style Roman Catholicism. The cozy conflicts of *Going My Way*, the heartwarming solidarities of *The Bells of Saint Mary's*—all the staples and stereotypes of clerical life—give way to brute fact: the struggle for power, the inertia of bureaucracy, the mediocrity of corporate life. The comic wrangling of Bing Crosby and Barry Fitzgerald in the former movie are supplanted by the depressing spectacle of Father Wilf trying to dampen the spirits of Urban. The culture of Catholicism is subjected to the scrutiny of a master social critic—someone who has the courage to see the defects of his Church as well as the illusions of his own sympathetic protagonist. When Urban's story reaches its grim end, we cannot help but take stock of the fact that the good priest was complicit in his own downfall. His eagerness to be out in the world—to make a difference—was what invited the good deeds of a Billy Cosgrove. The double darkness of Father Urban's world—the conventionality and false hope—is Powers's devastating view of his time and place.

James Baldwin's *Notes of a Native Son* also has a brilliant negative charge as it takes on the lies and delusions that engulf race relations in America. Baldwin the essayist of the 1950s has a lot in common with the masters of American group experience: he focuses on narrowness of outlook, distortion of purpose, and limitation of possibility. Too subtle and complex an artist to hang back with leftover ideas from the 1930s—infra-human white people beating down blacks, virtuous rage as the only expression of black identity—he offers an analysis of race that had only been surpassed in complexity by Ellison's *Invisible Man*. Baldwin's great moments are contained in this slender volume: although he never attained Ellison's mastery of tone and humor, characterization and general ideas, he had an intellectual and artistic triumph with this group of essays. Aside from a few stories—most notably "Sonny's Blues," his study of a jazzman and addict—Baldwin never matched the balance and humanity of *Notes of a Native Son*. The book offers a view of the American blacks and whites that rises above commonplaces, Manichean scenarios, scripts for disaster, Sunday-school solutions. Like Cheever and Powers, Baldwin knows his group inside and out, relentlessly questions the instincts and motives of his own, and exposes them to critical scrutiny in order to arrive at the truth about all of us. He assumes the role of protagonist-critic, the main actor—the bringer-on of conflicts in the essays—and at the same time the interpreter of the situation. This curious mix is similar to Mailer's blend of story, essay, personal account: it creates and critiques and ironizes. In so doing, it succeeds in conveying a world of complications and ambiguities that are not to be found in his poetic novel of 1953, *Go Tell It on the Mountain*. That good book is far less nuanced and interesting than *Notes*—its rhetorical flights are impressive, its story moving, but its powers of mind do not equal what we get in the essays.

Notes of a Native Son is filled with intelligent anger—not rage at ordinary people but attacks directed at the thought processes of Europeans and Americans in modern times. His purpose is the exposure of various kinds of bad faith and intellectual confusion. He comes fresh to his subject, which is to say that at this point in his career his work is amazingly free of the cant and jargon of the Communists and the Black Separatists. Richard Wright's important protest novel *Native Son* is ironically employed throughout the book—yet this collection of essays turns the race question in a different direction; it is meant as a series of reflections rather than as Wright's fist in the face of America. Baldwin devotes one of his best essays to dismantling the vision of the master's book: *Native Son*, for all its brute power and popularity, is symptomatic of what's wrong with American consciousness. Wright's protagonist Bigger Thomas is at once too monstrous and too limited to convey anything complex about race. A character who commits murder to assert identity is quite far from what Baldwin conceives to be a valid representation of race consciousness. Bigger, a racist nightmare come to life on the page, is displaced by a writer of a different generation who has a subtler, more ironic sense of American blackness. Baldwin's purpose in his book about a native son is to upend Wright's hopelessly superstitious vision—and the equally absurd conclusion that one day there will be no black and white. What actually takes place in the course of the *Notes* is a rewriting of the American black-white story. Baldwin refuses to let it remain a lurid melodrama, a Calvinist myth unpeopled by distinct characters with personalities, likes and dislikes, weaknesses.

At the start of the book there is an understated autobiographical sketch, intended to set the tone of the volume. The writing is frank, unself-serving, without a heavy ideological burden. Baldwin is an interloper in the West, like all descendants of slaves; and he admits to a kind of paralyzing hatred of his own—a resentment of a culture he can never fully be part of, a contempt for his own people because they have not produced a Rembrandt. But once he has acknowledged his own demons, he finds a way of seeing beyond them: he knows that if it were to be sustained, such rage would prevent him from writing. He calls that negative state—which he needs to pass through—"a self-destroying limbo." You're not really anything while you're in it. But Baldwin's intention is to break out of the nowhere position of frustration and hatred into a valid and original writing life. To do this he has to dispense with the reductive traditional attitudes toward blacks. He wittily calls them "For or Against" and can't quite decide which has caused him most pain. The reason is that there is no place to go with the old way of looking at race—it produces bad writing, bland clichés or rabid nonsense, prose that is "too pallid or too harsh." The *Notes* are to be his way of transcending this mountainous body of received opinion. The bracing quality of Baldwin's prose comes from its total honesty and personal directness: we watch him struggle with ideas, reveal himself at his dour and somewhat cynical worst as well as at his humane best. T. S. Eliot's insistence upon emotional authenticity in poetry—the poet confronting what he really has observed, dispensing with all that is secondhand, overheard, fashionable, correct—is one good way to understand Baldwin's stance. In *Notes of a Native Son,* he is not mouthing any doctrine of the time. The essays are fully rendered experiences—self-contained, free-standing, and ready to live as accounts of one person's pain and belief.

The essays are subjective reports about race that attempt to sweep away the old pretenses and obligations of the black writer: Baldwin stubbornly refuses to take responsibility for representing the consciousness of 13 million fellow blacks. But he offers himself and his own perceptions in place of groupthink—it's the "everybody" in "Everybody's Protest Novel" that he is trying to escape. Like Harold Rosenberg, Baldwin is driven wild by the notion of common experience. To read his sentences is to hear a writer who feels as oppressed by popular rhetoric as by the history of his people. What's been said about blacks in America (and oftentimes by blacks)—and said so carelessly and callously—is a terrible part of the damage that has been done. His essays are an attempt to argue down and expose the cliché mongers and mythmakers. Whether he's on his native ground or in Paris or in a small Swiss village, Baldwin listens to the false terms of discourse about race.

Notes of a Native Son has three ways of looking at race that correspond to its three sections: through books and other cultural productions, through urban experience, and through the wider context of European civilization. The first approach—a kind of stylistic-moral criticism—sets the tone of the volume. Baldwin uses Wright's *Native Son* and Harriet Beecher Stowe's *Uncle Tom's Cabin* as touchstones and points of engagement that help him to define a position. Stowe's classic gets rough treatment from Baldwin the literary reformer: like a modernist critic taking on the excesses of the nineteenth century—say Eliot attacking the loose quality of Tennyson's ruminations—Baldwin lets us see the intellectual and moral sloppiness of a so-called great book. After talking about the "self-righteous, virtuous sentimentality," Baldwin moves in several directions. He eviscerates the lurid style and answers those who revere the book because it puts moral outrage above good writing. Stowe—and her descendants in American protest novels like *Gentleman's Agreement*—has no time for nuance or for the "resolutely indefinably, unpredictable" in human nature. Her stereotypical characters and "catalogue of violence" contribute to the history of indignation not to the novel as an art form. The reader is awash in a gothic, Calvinistic world of horror, numbed and confused by the relentlessness of the rhetoric. Baldwin says that the overheated style also produces a certain comforting complacency: the audience comes to feel that as long as such books are produced, everything will be all right. His point, however, is that the writer who is a retailer of violence and victimhood is not really fulfilling the artist's responsibility. There is no representation of the everydayness of injustice and no attempt to plumb the human sources of inhumanity. For all the bloodshed in lurid novels, there is a bloodless quality to the literary experience. Baldwin shows how readers can be trapped in a kitsch version of race relations—derived from clichés, stock types, knee-jerk responses. In striving for a formulation to describe the insipid, good-guy side of the protest novel, Baldwin comes up with the following: "The aim has now become to reduce all Americans to the compulsive, bloodless dimension of a guy named Joe."

"Many Thousands Gone" depicts Wright as a meat-cleaver stylist. His most famous book has established "the Negro in America" as a "social and not a personal or a human problem." Like Stowe, Wright had no time for tracing causes of injustice or the crooked road of human suffering; he went straight to the myths and legends in our national warehouse rather than to history and social dynamics. Darkness and blackness in *Native Son* are not categories to be critically examined; they are buttons to be pressed in a melodrama about a monster and his revenge against monstrous white people. In this critique—and throughout *Notes*—Baldwin argues for a finer understanding of the past, of origins and genesis as the crucial factor in a writer's representation of race. Without personal and communal history suffusing his story, the writer is left with various infantile fantasies. Baldwin, in this work of demystification, is passionately committed to creating an adult, illusionless, yet unembittered version of race in America. The powers of the analytic mind and the open heart are absent from *Native Son*; but in his own *Notes*, Baldwin is determined to let them do battle with simplistic cries of anger and superstitions.

A small essay like the review of the movie *Carmen Jones* has the peculiarly tart flavor and excitement that Baldwin can create when he goes after creative work below Wright's level. *Native Son*—for all its raging—is an important work of art. Baldwin argues that the run of books and pictures about race in his time is well below this level. He's an expert at identifying the trivialization that passes for discourse on race. With his fine eye for kitsch, he goes to work on Hollywood. *Carmen Jones*, an Otto Preminger work, is about black people who—because of the temper of the 1950s, the special brand of proto-political correctness in the movie industry—must be treated as though they were white. The speech of the characters reminds Baldwin of antebellum Negroes imitating their masters. Any force and precision of black speech is "liberalized," which is to say denatured in the interests of niceness and goody-goody tolerance. Baldwin wonders whether blacks will become ciphers in the pictures of the future. That fate has not come to pass, but Baldwin himself should be given credit for a great deal of the matter-of-factness and tough reasoning that have brought us to a more mature and honest representation of race. In saying that Hollywood has the ability to milk the cow and the goat and "peddle the results as ginger ale," Baldwin takes a salutary shot at the cant about race and ethnicity that always threatens to crowd out clear observation.

The more ambitious pieces in the book turn directly to social life and the ideas about race that prevailed up to Baldwin's time. For better or worse, those ideas still have a good deal of life in them. The title essay is a chilling treatment of black estrangement; it combines social, family, and personal history, reporting, and philosophizing to explore the terrible question of being locked in a world of hate and separatism. In the course of some thirty pages, Baldwin manages to expand Wright's theme of rage into something altogether larger and more interesting. Baldwin's father is evoked as the awesome preacher whose "asperity" and relentlessness give depth and context to James Baldwin's own youthful rage. The preacher is a masterfully realized portrait of what racism can do to consciousness: he sermonizes about punishment and sin and wicked whites and deluded blacks and the hellishness of existence. And Baldwin traces the evolution of that grim series of lessons, finding that it has poisoned his own youth, made him into a maniac raging for justice. The young man who imbibed hatred became a case—ready to take on every instance of Jim Crowism he encountered, ready to throw a glass of water at a waitress who says, "We don't serve Negroes here." The essay starts with this negativity and moves to some remarkable affirmations; these latter are not sentimental turn-arounds and I-saw-the-light recognitions but wonderfully realized passages in which we see the narrator discovering the humanity of those around him. His father's death and his own birthday, and the Harlem riots of 1943 and the birth of his youngest sibling came cascading down on him in the same week. At his father's funeral, he loses contact with his monolithic hatred and is flooded by a sense of life's variousness:

> While the preacher talked and I watched the children—years of changing their diapers, scrubbing them, slapping them, taking them to school, and scolding them had the perhaps inevitable result of making me love them, though I am not sure I knew this then—my mind was busy breaking out with a rash of disconnected impressions. Snatches of popular songs, indecent jokes, bits of books I had read, movie sequences, faces, voices, political issues—I thought I was going mad.

The remainder of the essay is about going sane, developing the capacity to accept life without rancor and yet reject complacency. The process—analogous to Lionel Trilling's search for the right condition of the self—is a form of modern soul-making. It recognizes the conditioned nature of existence—that if we are to live well, we must live with the mixed character of our selves and our society. Such living is not the easy road of demonization or denial—the Calvinist hell of Baldwin's father or the blind innocence of the white middle class. It is a matter of seeing that race relations are human relations, and therefore subtle, complex, and not to be settled with riots, slogans, sermons, and denunciations. What he offers instead is a meditation on the narrowness of the American mind at mid-century—his own, his father's, his white contemporaries'. The essay is a classic of intellectual and spiritual development, a work that charts one man's escape from mindless despair to guarded wisdom.

A couple of minor essays—on the Harlem Ghetto and on a trip to Atlanta—round out the section about urban life. The first piece looks at the culture as well as the social conditions of Harlem in the mid-1950s, and in some ways seems more about discourse—newspapers and rhetoric—than material conditions. Baldwin uses his ideas about American distortion to evaluate his hometown publications and their general-outreach writers. The stridency of columnist Lena Horne—"an embittered Eleanor Roosevelt"—and Paul Robeson—"tricked by his own bitterness"—is only part of the problem. The defensiveness, sensationalism, feel-goodism, and just-as-goodism of Harlem publications are a dispiriting spectacle; honesty about the lives of oppressed citizens is pretty much confined to the letters-to-the-editor columns, whereas the bulk of the material is about keeping up with whites—and if truth be told, trying to think like them. "Within the body of the Negro press all the wars and falsehoods, all the decay and dislocation of our society are seen in relief." "Journey to Atlanta" is a piece about a group of black singers who went on a tour with the Progressive Party during Henry Wallace's campaign in the late 1940s. It's a small tale of blacks getting shafted by supposedly progressive whites. Baldwin's sourness—while hardly the best mode for a critique of dishonesty—is part of what makes the essay quite genuine as a response to the maddening compromise of the whole excursion.

The third part of the book contains Baldwin's European reflections: he's in Paris and Switzerland, but wherever he finds himself, he's still a native son, equipped with his American heritage and his skepticism. Totally unromantic and illusionless, he reports on racial attitudes over there and refrains from cant and hot air about feeling liberated among those oh-so-tolerant foreigners. In "A Question of Identity" he senses something careless and indifferent in the Parisian's relationship to Americans: the Parisian does not "exhibit the faintest personal interest, or curiosity, concerning the life, or habits, of any stranger." Such denial—arrogant innocence—is a major theme for Baldwin. *Notes* has been about various conscious and unconscious blocking out of perception; and, as always, Baldwin looks at the other side, the fact that Americans living in Paris are often pretenders and deniers: "This little band of bohemians, as grimly singleminded as any evangelical sect, illustrate, by the very ferocity with which they disavow American attitudes, the inability to believe that time is real." Their vulture-for-culture existence sorts very well with the French politesse and withdrawal from finer intimacy. Together they can chat aimlessly about wine, Racine, and l'amour and forget the real passions and pasts that make them what they are. Nobody has to confront the tough facts of selfhood. And so it is that Baldwin's Paris is one great disconnection. When he is arrested in "Equal in Paris," he spends days agonizing about whether the French authorities will be able to figure out the truth of his innocence, the fact that he "stole" a bed sheet from a hotel by accident.

The dehumanizing experience of being in jail—at the mercy of bureaucratic forces that take no account of what you are—is a crucial piece of foreshadowing that points the reader in the direction of the best essay in *Notes*, "Stranger in the Village." This meditation on race in Europe and America is about being cut off from one's fellow men and struggling to find a connection. It's Baldwin at his most paradoxical and subtle—looking for light in the dark regions of ancient superstition. It's as if he has gone to the bottom of the pit where confusion and ignorance originate. The abyss in this case was a remote Swiss village where Baldwin had holed up one winter to write. Once there he found that blacks were regarded as exotic spectacles—children made sport of the "Neger," found him a hilarious and wondrous phenomenon with hair that could be fashioned into a winter coat and skin color that might rub off. Adults would bid the time of day and drink in the same bistros, but they too regarded him as something infra-human. And Baldwin's smile and amiable demeanor—what he refers to as his American Negro habit of wanting people to like him—does nothing to break down the barrier. A presence such as his offers infernal awesomeness or comic entertainment. The essay takes this perception and expands it into an argument about Western civilization—about the

blackness of the Christian hell, the devilish gargoyles on Chartres Cathedral that say one thing to white people and another thing to blacks.
"I doubt that the villagers think of the devil when they face a cathedral
because they have never been identified with the devil." Baldwin's
point is worked out with great skill: it's about European innocence
and our own American innocence. Europeans have not had a long and
tortured relationship with blacks on their native shores—and yet they
somehow know about blackness and have made it into a controlling
metaphor; they, after all, invented white supremacy. We Americans
have a different kind of innocence: our repression and denial, our
"shrillness and brutality" are lurid in everyday life—race is not the
anxious joke that it is in a remote Swiss village; it is a serious occasion
for drawing boundaries—and using every violent means to do so.

Although Baldwin uses Europe to gauge America, he never falls
into the trap of imagining that Europeans think the way we do. Their
innocent and abstract ideas about race are not ours: you'll hear the
word "Neger" in the small village, but it will not be the racial slur that
it would be on the streets of New York. But once said, we must also
recognize that Baldwin's intention has been to let us hear the brutal
chiming of the word on both sides of the Atlantic—different in intent
when used by the children in Switzerland, but at the same time arising
from some deep white instinct that may express itself with malevolent
intent in America. Baldwin's intercontinental survey wears well after
all these years: a study in detachment and connection, it makes the
reader aware of the fact that distant lives are a direct commentary on
our lives.

Philip Roth's *Goodbye, Columbus*, a 1959 collection of stories, is a
landmark in American Jewish writing. Like Baldwin's *Notes*, it's a
complicated vision of what it means to be a minority in America.
There is rage and love, and self-criticism and criticism of one's own as
well as questioning of the environment. Unlike Baldwin's book, it
does not have to confront appalling injustice and inhumanity in the
1950s. It deals with veiled anti-Semitism, not the raw racism that Baldwin explores. It is the most complex exploration to date in our literature of what it means to be a modern Jewish-American. Bellow's
Augie March is about the sadness and struggling of the Depression;
The Magic Barrel is about age-old Jewish burdens in a new land. But
Roth's book is about new collisions and conflicts—with Gentile
America, with prosperity, with conformity. This isn't to say that Roth
drops the old themes of suffering and deprivation. What he gives is a

series of scenes that embody the experience of Jews in the speeded-up society of postwar America. Neil Klugman, the protagonist of the title novella, sits waiting for his girlfriend Brenda in St. Patrick's Cathedral (hardly a spot for a Malamud character). Admitting his carnality and acquisitiveness, he asks God where he should look for "the prize," the way to meet Him. Roth gives God's answer: "Which prize do you think, *schmuck*? Gold dinnerware, sporting-goods trees, nectarines, garbage disposals, bumpless noses, Patimkin Sink, Bonwit Teller—" The joke—with its blasphemy, silliness, and irony—is at Neil's expense: it's about a young man looking for bliss who meets the conditioned life of the prosperous Jewish-American middle class. Roth's first book stands as a penetrating critique of that class. Venturesome, playful, but always pointed, it looks at the main aspirations and anxieties after the War: the yearning for peace and harmony, the desire to fit into the American scene, the doubts about the new good life in suburbia, the cautionary attitudes and echoes of the old neighborhood, the fear of losing Jewish identity.

The title story is about the hilarious and painful results of throwing the meek and the powerful together. Neil Klugman, a studious boy from Newark, meets Brenda Patimkin, a "Radcliffe smarty" from Short Hills. Class, money, style of life, ideas of decorum separate these members of the same tribe. What's at stake is neediness facing self-possession, lower-middle-class meagerness looking at the big earners and spenders. But the result is not just another social study of local America, John O'Hara for and about Jews. Roth uses all his comic resources and his poignancy to explore the mentalities of bourgeois life. He goes to a great deal of trouble to show that Neil and Brenda come out of the same heritage, yet are utterly different. No matter that Brenda's prosperous home has a shut-off room filled with all their old furniture from their Newark days of struggle. Those days are over. No matter that Neil has a big libido, an ironic line, and a cool view of the nouveau rich. He has one Brooks Brothers shirt and a job as a librarian. Roth skillfully tells a same-but-different story about two families, two status groups, two different styles of Jewishness; in some ways the little novella is a comic disaster story about Jewish differences. Dinnertime at the house of Neil's Aunt Gladys is a wonderful distillation of lower-middle-class Jewish life, circa 1950: the woman of the house frazzled with preparing five different meals, the others eating in shifts. Neil, a kid who studied philosophy, tries to bring a little logic to the situation: "Suppose tonight we all eat together." Aunt Gladys's riposte: "I should jump up and down twenty times? What am I, a work-horse?" When Neil observes the Patimkin dinner table, he's watching a different version of the same thing: the disorder, the jagged conversation, the warnings and naggings and corrections—but there's the "colored maid" Carlota serving and Mrs. Patimkin presiding at table, watching out for the proprieties. There's also that famous line directed by Mr. Patimkin ("tall, strong, ungrammatical, and a ferocious eater") at Neil: "eats like a bird." The line is a key to the story. Neil does not have the appetite, the will, the drive to be a Patimkin; his sex drive is not matched by the energy that propelled Ben Patimkin to the suburbs. Neil says dinner was "a pleasure, except that eating among those Brobdingnags, I felt for quite a while as though four inches had been clipped from my shoulders, three inches from my height, and for good measure, someone had removed my ribs and my chest had settled meekly in towards my back." The bird phrase is picked up again when Neil goes to Mr. Patimkin's sink business in Newark: the young man sees what it takes to join the richer branch of his own tribe. He bursts into a Kafkaesque rhapsody of self-laceration as he imagines Mr. Patimkin watching him botch a routine job of loading sinks. There is a good deal of irony here and lots of superiority as well: Neil is the pathetic creature, but he still expects to win. The complication is that smartness cannot match money and power:

> "Okay, boy, you want to marry my daughter, let's see what you can do." Well, he would see: in a moment that floor would be a shattered mosaic, a crunchy path of enamel. "Klugman, what kind of worker are you? You work like you eat!" "That's right, that's right, I'm a sparrow, let me go." "Don't you even know how to load and unload?" "Mr. Patimkin, even breathing gives me trouble, sleep tires me out, let me go, let me go. . . ."

When questioned by Mr. Patimkin, Neil knows what the word *gonif* means, how a bit of the gonif is necessary for business success; but he is completely devoid of the right business stuff. Ben Patimkin gives the orders and likens himself to the Rockefellers; Neil comes from people like Aunt Gladys, those who seem happy enough being slaves. And Neil doesn't realize that his lust for Brenda is part of a gigantic confusion about life: he imagines that passion comes without consequences, without the conditioned life that includes the patterns on the sterling-silver dinner service—and the "light classical" musical tastes of Brenda's brother Ron. Neil mocks plastic surgeons without considering the deep desire that Americans have for physical beauty. He finds Ron's corny homecoming record about Ohio State and the memories of days in Columbus a ludicrous commentary on American naivete—when in fact he's the one who doesn't know that sentimentality and self-protectiveness go together well. Neil imagines that Brenda stands out from the rest of her group of Jewish princesses. The suburban women "compared suntans, supermarkets, and vacations. . . . Their fates had collapsed them into one. Only Brenda shone. Money and comfort would not erase her singleness—they hadn't yet, or had they?" In fact they had—and Brenda would choose the conditioned life over Neil's charm.

The story is a 1950s fable, but one with a great deal of staying power and a solid place in American fiction. Neil—like Jay Gatsby with Daisy—believes that there is some extraordinary connection between himself and a woman from a different social world. The truth is that danger and the wrong circumstances could sever the erotic bond, and that the woman of superior position would disappear into her world of money and security. Neil—with that one Brooks shirt tossed on the bed of the Patimkin's guestroom (and what more poignant connection could be established between him and the prodigal Jay Gatsby with his stupendous collection of shirts!)—never understood the power of the world he had entered. Imagining himself clever and special and witty—part Pip in *Great Expectations,* part Gatsby, part the beggar-joker of Jewish folklore (as in Freud's *Jokes and Their Relationship to the Unconscious)* who has the put-down lines for the vulgar rich—Neil never imagined that he would be put down. He's dealing with people whose sinks are found in the restrooms at Lamont Library at Harvard. And he should have realized that the differences were not just comic and vulgar features of the social system; they carried meaning. Mr. Patimkin's question about the meaning of *gonif* is no less important than Mrs. Patimkin's questions about religion. In a wonderful scene, Mrs. Patimkin cross-examines Neil about whether he's Orthodox, Conservative, or Reformed. And he doesn't quite know! He has desperately tried to convince her that he's not an infidel, even tried to make a reference to Martin Buber. Mrs. Patimkin's riposte should have told Neil all he needed to know about being a smart guy among his betters: "Is he reformed?" The brute facts are what undo Neil the dreamer.

Neil's pursuit of Brenda has all the pathos of the little black boy at the Newark public library who loves the beautiful Tahitian women in a Gauguin art book. "Ain't that the fuckin' *life*?" the young boy exclaims as he looks at a picture of "a young brown-skinned maid" drying her hair. Neil saw Short Hills "in my mind's eye, at dusk, rose-colored, like a Gauguin stream." His outsider status—along with his taste for the good life—also ironically connects him with Ben Patimkin's brother Leo, the schlemiel of the family who talks about his sexual yearnings and his low rent in Queens. Leo is an uncensored Willy Loman going on, after more than a few drinks at a wedding, about bad luck, the bad New England territory, and the one or two good things in life. Neil brushes up against this nightmarish version of the wimpy minor player in the story of Jewish-American success. Ben Patimkin's greeting to the poor brother could just as well be given to Neil the librarian, "Well, how you doing, *starke*?"

The title story sets the tone for a book that delivers a series of critical punches: Roth attacks the illusions, screw-ups, let-downs of American Jews in the 1940s and 1950s. Each story looks at a different facet of American Jewishness and offers a sharp, ironic recognition about people caught between an older world of tradition and tragedy, and a newer world of promise and fantasy.

"The Conversion of the Jews" is a story about payback time in a narrow environment of Orthodoxy: here the wise-guy character wins in a battle with a powerful group of elders. Young Ozzie Freedman, the troublesome kid in a Hebrew school run by a martinet rabbi, dares to challenge the theological order by asking his teacher the most provoking of all questions about Jewish belief: if God is all powerful, can't he make a virgin pregnant without intercourse? Or, put plainly, is a sustaining of Orthodoxy more important than the truth? Roth's career—and certainly this book—rests on the question. What do you seek, the predictable answer or the mysterious possibility? *Goodbye, Columbus,* turns this question over and over, looking at the various complications of discovering the true, the real, and the genuine. In Ozzie's case, the results of the inquiry are side-splitting and outré. You practically have to kill yourself, Roth's tale seems to say, in order to get people to open their minds. Ozzie has to climb up on a roof and threaten to jump if the rabbi and others won't admit the possibility of the Virgin Birth. With complacency vanquished and buffo riding high—with a colossal Jewish joke being told to his own—Roth has Rabbi Binder on his knees like a Gentile, affirming the central Christian mystery. Ozzie, a little boy who has been cuffed for his impudence earlier in the story, also gets a chance to assert his own humane doctrine: that nobody should be hit because of God. The rogue-rebel nonconformist wins the day. The conditioned life that won out in the title story is defeated—at least for an evening—by a trickster who refuses to submit. The buoyant, clever side of Jewishness wins out as the plodding, conventional side winds up "converted." Sententious Rabbi Binder, unlike Mrs. Patimkin, didn't win this battle of wits.

But this is the only story in the volume that represents the Jew liberated from American life and Jewish law. Elsewhere there is more irony than exhilaration: the characters kick back a great deal of their happiness to the community, shoulder heavy moral responsibilities, or face their own limitations. "Defender of the Faith," the finest of the shorter pieces, is about obligations and allegiances. The protagonist Sergeant Nathan Marx is arguably the most complex character in the book. In conflict because of his Jewish identity—Am I a by-the-book Sergeant or a compassionate Jew?—Marx goes through a period of ethical questioning during the final months of World War II. Roth always loves to study a questioner—be it an intelligent one like Neil, a narrow one like Mrs. Patimkin, a brazen one like Ozzie. Here he deepens the analysis of the questioners by making their questions more complicated. Roth's questions in "Defender of the Faith" are quite difficult. Sergeant Marx is called upon to judge a challenge posed by an Ozzie-like young recruit. What's more important in the Army—rules or humane living? Cheeky Sheldon Grossbart comes up against war-weary Sergeant Marx. He wants concessions for the Jewish personnel—and Marx must ask himself a number of crucial questions: Am I too grudging? Am I an officious sergeant rather than a responsible man? Have I forgotten the meaning of understanding—of tolerance and mercy? Marx's patience is tested as Sheldon pushes the envelope, but at the same time his moral sense is sharpened. He looks back to his family past, transcends the hardened life of the barracks, identifies with certain cultural habits and customs about which Grossbart reminds him. Is it not true that in the exercise of authority we may compromise our humanity? Are professional obligations an excuse to negate human claims? For a time, Marx is in danger of losing his head because of the claims of his heart; the complexity of his situation threatens to make him forget the paramount consideration: that truth and honesty and decency rate above the lies and tricks and equivocations that Grossbart uses to defend his faith. Marx's faith is ultimately a hard-won belief in being straight with yourself and others; his decisive moral moment in the story won't win the sympathy of the reader looking for a caring and sharing protagonist. It's a hard judgment—surprising and difficult to arrive at, but a decision that refuses the illusions about group solidarity. Grossbart and Marx may both be Jewish, but this does not mean they share the same faith. Roth's story is meant to be a challenge to the warm-and-fuzzy school of writing about ethnic experience: he cannot let the solidarities, the problems, the buzzwords, and the guilt trips laid on by the Grossbarts affect the workings of the critical mind and informed heart.

"Epstein," a loser's tale, is about a middle-aged man—a schlemiel like Leo Patimkin—who envies his young nephew's sexual life, sets out on his own little adulterous adventure with a sexy widow and meets with comic disaster. He gets an irritation in his groin, a hysterical response from his dowdy wife, and a heart attack. On top of being ostracized by his wife and daughter, the poor man has to endure the daughter's folk singer boyfriend who strums his guitar and sings, "I've been down so long / It seems like up to me." Roth seems to be saying that group life can't do any more damage than this. But in "Eli the Fanatic" a highly intelligent and sensitive Jewish lawyer suffers a worse fate at the hands of his fellow Jews. Living in an upscale New Jersey suburb dominated by Gentiles, Eli is given the task of looking into the activities and lifestyle of a group of Orthodox Jews who have a new school in the neighborhood. The assimilated Jewish citizens of the community would like Eli to bring these greenhorns into line with white-bread America. The main issue is appearances: the long black coats and shtetl-style hats in the land of tweed sports jackets. Eli—a man with a history of emotional problems—winds up sympathizing with the greenies—and, to the horror of his neighbors, trying on their identity by parading around in the shtetl outfit. Roth embraces Eli's decision—but has the honesty to indicate that the man winds up being sedated and carted off by the mental health professionals. This Jewish Cuckoo's Nest is a slender but effective fable about what happened to people who went against the American grain in the 1950s. And Roth has shown that his middle-class Jews are part of that grain, giving grief to those who are out-of-step. This hard and clear critique of group life has not endeared Roth to many readers, but it has made him one of the best skeptical intellectuals writing fiction in America. Judgmental above all else, he has looked at American Jews and helped us see many aspects of our national life. The illusions of his people fit most of us.

chapter 8

Naturalism Reinvented

Goodbye, Columbus, used the 1950s suburbs as the locale for a satiric look at American Jews. Yet while the emphasis of the book fell on manners and morals in the promised land of Short Hills and environs, there was also room for the older world of Newark, memories of the Bronx, and portraits of people connected with a more traditional way of life. Neil still lives in the old neighborhood. He goes off for erotic adventures among his well-to-do co-religionists, but is essentially rooted in his library job in the city and his home life with people like Aunt Gladys who have only the vaguest notion of what suburbia is like. Roth is not the master chronicler of 1950s suburbia—its promises, limits, and desperations. And John Cheever, as we have seen, had his eye on a group rather than a locale—the WASPs who migrated from Manhattan after World War II. Their story, to be sure, is conditioned by Shady Hill, but it has deep roots in an older America. They had the protection of being upper middle class—often, admittedly, not a thing to stake your life on, but also a protection against the rawness and newness of suburbia. Their fate is the fate of a privileged class and an esteemed ethnic group, not of people consigned to tract houses, tacky commercialism, and mass culture. For the stories of the average and below-average strugglers faced with the limits and desperations of suburbia, we should look to John Updike and Richard Yates. They emerged a year apart and produced mordant accounts of the newer communities that were springing up around the country. Morris Dickstein nicely refers to their books as "the classic novel of middle class disappointment in the late Eisenhower years, when the social confidence of the fifties was breaking up, when John F. Kennedy was building his presidential campaign on a sense of national malaise, on the contrast between Republican stagnation and his own well-projected vigor."

Updike set his novel *Rabbit, Run,* in 1959 (with *Some Like It Hot* playing at a local theater); Yates set *Revolutionary Road* in 1955. They both had savage things to say about the period and the setting—about mindlessness, the junk culture, the rise of psychobabble, the pressures and conformities that drained the joy out of many young lives. They both dealt in human catastrophes—and why the suburbs were bound to spawn dismal things when they held out such bright prospects. They both exposed their suburban people to brutal analysis, leaving no room whatsoever for comforting resolutions. All the talk in the world—all the religious counsel or mature understanding or discussion about getting a new start—cannot heal the relationships, the two horrible marriages, that Updike and Yates depict in the era of Mouseketeers and popular Freudianism. And while Updike's Rabbit Angstrom and his bewildered wife, Janice, are lower-middle class—and Frank Wheeler and his desperate wife, April, are educated and have social airs—the picture of desperation is similar: the gaping maw of the TV set, the squabbling, the dashed hopes, the recollections of something that was once better. Both Updike and Yates bring tremendous intelligence to the task of representing America in a muddled emotional and social state: so anxious to believe in the future and so unable to take the next step toward a better life; so stalled and hemmed in by circumstances that seem as dreary as those in a naturalistic novel. Rabbit Angstrom has a job demonstrating a gadget called MagiPeel; he's a father of a small boy and his pregnant wife drinks old-fashioneds while watching kiddie programs on television. Frank Wheeler fantasizes about being a writer but works for a business-machine company; he has two daughters and his wife is a frustrated actress who would like to start a new life in Europe. These books do not offer any of the comforts of the standard best seller about struggle: no better tomorrow, no better house and better understanding of oneself, as in *The Man in the Gray Flannel Suit*. The characters—if not caught in the old web of destiny that Dreiser wove in *Sister Carrie*—are caught in a massive confusion of desires and expectations. It's not the old grinding poverty and dog-eat-dog world of people who are crushed by gears of capitalist society. It is a reinvented naturalism, subtler and more mysterious in the ways that it depicts failure. It is a style and a mode for a different country, one in which people's despair emerges from a seemingly innocent-looking social setting.

Rabbit (Harry) Angstrom lives in Mount Judge, Pennsylvania, a suburb of Brewer, the state's fifth largest city. As everyone who is aware of Updike's forty-year run of fame and fortune knows, Rabbit—his signature character, a man whose life will be spun out in three more novels—is the young married man who was a great high-school basketball star a few years before the action of the book. His life of speed, grace, and precision has been exchanged for the stultifying dullness and mediocrity of the absurd job, the bad marriage, and all the slovenliness that goes with letting life happen. After a quick game with some local kids on his way home from work—a reminder of how he once did something first rate on the court—he returns home to Janice, the Mouseketeers on TV, and the prospect of another evening in his badly managed prison house. "An order-loving man," he lives in a terrific mess—with Janice tripping over the TV wires and forgetting about their boy, with nothing to hear but Jimmie Dodd on the Mickey Mouse Club giving advice about knowing thyself. "Now what does this mean, boys and girls? It means, be what you are. Don't try to be Sally or Johnny or Fred next door; be yourself. God doesn't want a tree to be a waterfall, or a flower to be a stone. God gives to each one of us a special talent." Updike is a master of dramatic irony who loves to create his ironies from the messages that culture sends us: TV self-help—certainly one of the main features of modern culture, is here made into a grim, but central, fact of Rabbit's life. The basketball star was not meant to be a demonstrator of MagiPeel, the sexual adventurer was not meant to sit around with his complaining pregnant wife and listen to the advice of his in-laws. Updike is wonderfully sardonic in showing that the truth of one's being may be heard from the most unlikely source—that the law of development for Rabbit is all mixed up with sports and media. A child of his age, he is in touch with its messages—all of which is to say that he is also allowed to be colossally selfish, hurried and heedless, and mean and hard as he pursues the real me. Rabbit's authentic self is lecherous, unfaithful, unkind, caddish, self-absorbed—yet also unsettled, curious, vaguely ambitious, dissatisfied, and yearning for something that he calls the light. His agility, his sexual need and prowess, his impatience with sloppiness are what that light amounts to.

After the horrible opening scene with Janice, Rabbit runs out on her and takes his fabulous night ride south, a desperate escape to the light of the Gulf of Mexico—which turns out to be no further than West Virginia. One of the most memorable rides in postwar American literature—a frantic escape, a tour of the road with the radio broadcasting its songs and its commercials (and its ironies)—the pages of running are a stylistic triumph: pleasure, exhilaration, hope, fantasy, glances at happy people all over, diner food that's better than in

Brewer, good songs playing, some news. Updike, unlike Kerouac, doesn't dig the pop American scene, and Rabbit doesn't rhapsodize like Sal Paradise; and despite his critical acumen, he doesn't make the capital out of it that Nabokov does in *Lolita*. Humbert's 1950s America is so thick in texture, so rich in suggestion, that it constitutes the art of the novel. Every bit of the junk culture is meant to do its work. With Updike, the night ride is less focused and high-powered—it runs many things past us so that we get the spectacle and the buzz—and the blur—of popular culture. His general intention seems to be to confuse us—as Rabbit is confused. "No Other Arms, No Other Lips"—for pretty obvious reasons—is the first song he hears. Then it's " 'Stagger Lee,' a commercial for Rayco Plastic Seat Covers, 'If I Didn't Care' by Connie Francis . . . ." Of course, Rabbit doesn't care, but his lack of regard for his wife is a part of a big confusion about what he wants. Updike uses this particular passage to hammer home the idea of not quite knowing what's happening or where you're going. The radio says that the Dalai Lama is lost. Rabbit drives on an unmarked stretch of road, hearing things like "Yanks over Braves in Miami, somebody tied with somebody in St. Petersburg" and "New Formula Barbasol Presto-Lather, whose daily cleansing tends to prevent skin blemishes and emulsifies something." The half-heard radio messages and the drive to nowhere seem to distill his confusion. "The farther he drives the more he feels some great confused system, Baltimore now instead of Philadelphia, reaching for him."

When he winds up back in Mt. Judge, he faces the conflicts and confusions that he tried to run out on: the desire for order, decency, and family life but the strong pull of his own wild sexuality; the call of maturity—sounded by a conscientious Episcopal priest who wants him to go home—versus the attractions of a part-time local prostitute with whom he has a fling. Rabbit, like Roth's Neil Klugman and many another 1950s hero, has a dream of the unconditioned life. The grace and achievement of his basketball days make him fantasize about other kinds of grace and release. But Updike puts him in an essentially deterministic world where his only way of escaping is by humiliating and betraying poor Janice. The freer and more unconstrained he becomes, the lousier he looks as a human being.

The Reverend Eccles—a golf player and good husband—tries to get Rabbit to play the middle-class respectable game as a way into reconnecting with wife and child. Updike holds Eccles up to a certain amount of ridicule, turning him into a prosperous, Buick-driving fellow who preaches drivel about growing up and facing responsibility. Whereas the Mouseketeers talk about being yourself, Eccles wants Rabbit to stop being a moral vagrant. He wants to deglamorize visions of the light that Rabbit has, make him realize that we're here to serve God, not be God. But such advice is not for Rabbit—or for Updike either. In a fabulous, explosive scene, he has Eccles consult the local Lutheran pastor Kruppenbach on the problem of Rabbit and his misdeeds. Updike's writing grabs the reader by the throat as it denounces the nice nosiness and temporizing of the new-style man of God. The fiery preacher will have nothing of Eccles's Episcopal, genteel suburban spirituality, a religion that Dickstein calls "altogether enlightened and reasonable but spiritually null." Kruppenbach wants the ministry to be a place of intensity—else it's nothing but decency and busyness and hypocrisy.

Anyone who has listened to Rabbit's shots directed at everyday life in Mount Judge has heard something similar: that light, grace, and precision—those things from his basketball days—are worth more than temporizing and niceness, a patched-up relationship and a compromised life. Dickstein connects Rabbit's intensity with the "violent sainthood" of Mailer's White Negro and with the Beats. He makes him seem like a gifted wild man and outsider trying to forge an original destiny. The trouble with this is that Rabbit is a brilliantly drawn character, a sign of the times, but hardly an arresting rebel or a poetic naysayer or an inspired maniac. He's assuredly a "fifties recoil from maturity," but he's also something of a victim and loser and a maker of messes who claims he loves order. Dickstein was better off calling him "a middling sensual male." That label allows us to see clearly what the whole problem of the book is: the situation of a limited type yearning to be a higher type. And all the anger and sex and remembrance of basketball games past will never make Rabbit Angstrom a Sal Paradise or a Dean Moriarty—or for that matter a big-time man of taste and transgressor like Humbert Humbert. Despite the talk of something he sees behind the world of appearances, Rabbit doesn't have the equipment to play in the league with the breakthrough spirits of the fifties—with Ginsberg when he's crazy-as-a-daisy. Now this by no mean makes him a minor achievement as a literary character; it simply sets him apart from characters with bigger spirits.

Richard Yates's Frank Wheeler in *Revolutionary Road* is cut out of the same bolt of cloth as Rabbit Angstrom—a frustrated man, a wannabe,

a bourgeois soul who yearns to try on a larger destiny. Yates's protagonist went to Columbia, spent time in postwar Greenwich Village, and
knows how to discourse cynically on the politics and mass culture of
the Eisenhower era. But his story has no wider expanses than Rabbit's—and it contains the catastrophic element that Updike prepared
for his suburban screw-up. Rabbit's behavior finally drives Janice to
the brink of madness—drunk and in despair, she panics and accidentally drowns their newborn. Frank's pretentiousness and inadequacy
and failure to take his wife out of the dismal suburb result in her death
during an abortion. The two books have a great deal in common in
their vision of suburban torment—the boredom and tackiness and oh-
so-cheerful illusions that lead to oversized expectations that lead to
disaster. Rabbit, of course, knows how to run, and this in itself makes
his destiny more hopeful than Frank's. And he has three books ahead
of him in which to claim a better destiny. But his situation in *Rabbit,
Run,* is a grim testament to what was available for many young men in
the fifties.

Frank is better at talking than running, and best at posing and pretending. Instead of berating his wife, he drowns her in his cool, ironic
talk about "the culture." Frank's stock-in-trade has always been a
pseudo-intellectual knowingness—and April was enchanted from the
start. Since they are a higher class than the Angstroms, their articulate-
ness—with shibboleths like "individualism," "identity," and "finding
yourself"—is a large part of their problem. They talk themselves into
disaster. Marrying young and moving up to Connecticut from the Village, they find themselves trapped in the pastel-and-plastic world of a
community that has none of the beauty of the country and none of
the stimulation of the city. April has pretensions to being an actress
and enjoys nothing more than finding and playing a romantic role;
Frank thinks of himself as an "intense, nicotine-stained, Jean-Paul
Sartre sort of man" and delights in skewering Senator Joseph McCarthy, sneering at suburban togetherness, and exposing sentimental attitudes about child rearing. What has happened is that the Wheelers are
marooned in suburbia with their particular limitations—and that the
place itself makes them more inert and garrulous, lonelier and more
self-deluding than they might be if they were challenged and disciplined by a big city. In the suburbs, they have the excuse to whine and
complain, and be cynical and intellectually snobbish and ultimately
self-destructive. April has a local theater group where she can make a
pathetic spectacle of herself; Frank has the captive audience of Shep

Campbell and his wife, neighbors who are a cut above the people who live in the housing development called Revolutionary Road. And when they aren't intoxicated by their own egos and their own cleverness, they have each other to blame for the emptiness of their lives. Yates makes a world of entrapment and desperation—a stage in Rabbit's life—into a horrible cul-de-sac.

But when Frank and April try, like Rabbit, to escape their fate, they fail tragically. The second section of the novel is about a fantastic scheme to start a new life in a European city. Frank and April take a break from their squabbling and declaiming and plan an anti-Revolutionary Road escape, complete with wonderful possibilities for Frank the writer. One trouble with the whole idea is that Frank isn't made of the material that April dreams of: he's not really a rebel or writer or free spirit. He's an attractive hot-air artist who's probably better suited to bitching and moaning about suburbia than striking out for a bolder destiny. When it comes time to run, he takes cover in his routine job and pretends that he's getting somewhere. April, emotionally unstable like Updike's Janice, sinks into despair and psychosis. Not the little wife of the fifties who wants a nice protective husband, April is the embodiment of mad rebellion; she's depicted characteristically as poised for flight—the adventuress with no adventure in sight. Yates's avowed master is the Flaubert of *Madame Bovary*, and what we get in the portrait of the Wheelers is a restaging and reconception of Emma's downfall. Frank and April prepare the decline and disaster together, meticulously sealing their fate.

Yates's supporting characters enrich the tragic vision of the book, but also provide comic, ironic relief. Unlike Updike, Yates knows how to make the reader laugh at the absurd and pathetic people who are signs of the times. Frank and April deal with Mrs. Givens, a genteel and prissy realtor who is catty about the lower-middle-class neighbors and their rude, Kool-Aid-drinking children. She is Yates's glance at the lower rung of the Cheever world, a pretentious poor soul who has a mentally disturbed son and a love of gracious living and fine furniture. Yates makes her unintentionally funny as she tries to be polite and well-bred. And he turns to a kind of brutal irony when he makes her son a truth-telling nut job who will stop at nothing to embarrass his mother and expose people for what they are. John Givens is a disturbed and dysfunctional man who has a taste for Frank's kind of cynicism about America and "the culture." At first look, one could mistake him for an astute critic of Revolutionary Road's sterility; he

enjoys the Wheelers' brand of negativism and attitudinizing—and especially wants them to follow their fantasy of escape to Europe. When
they don't go through with their plans, he heaps scorn on them. Morris Dickstein sees Givens as a bearer of truth and a breakthrough rebel
who faces the sad death of passion in the Wheelers' lives. But the truth
is that the poor fellow is an image of rage and destructiveness, not Ken
Kesey's delight-maker McMurphy from *One Flew over the Cuckoo's
Nest*, but a gruesome loudmouth. Yates lets us see that John is the psy-
chotic to Frank's neurotic: he takes the anger and resentment over the
edge and shows what suburbia can do when it does its worst. Mrs.
Givens's limitations, the nurturing of a pathetic phony, have made John
what he is. But John is not sentimentalized or romanticized. In some
ways he represents what the literary 1950s did so well. He is a brilliantly conceived character who makes us wonder about the depths of
human suffering, the complexity of what's wrong with our good life.

When you see the *Revolutionary Road* configuration—the sane
lying and posing versus the mad truth-telling, the pretense alternating
with the lashing out—you wonder what will repair the spiritual damage. Paris and Rome? Well, Frank Wheeler—and he can be quite a
frank man—freely admits that he would probably wind up sitting
around all day in an egg-stained bathrobe, waiting for April to get
home from her job at an embassy. These people bring us to the end of
the suburban story, the part where you can neither dream about your
American escape from the city nor fantasize about an escape into yet
another dream.

Yates's book is one of the great works of fiction that succeeds in
informing the old mode of naturalism with a brilliant command of
personalities in the new America: Frank and April and the others are
not holdovers from the days of Dreiser, born under an unlucky star;
they are full of promise, well-educated, and eager—and yet they are
marked for destruction. *Revolutionary Road* has received its share of
critical praise, but are American readers actually ready to see themselves in these fierce terms?

Afterword

Your favorite book of the period isn't one of the books of our lives? I can only say that my study of the landscape is not meant as an all-inclusive or exclusive view of what is valuable. The literature I have dealt with is not a fine club with distinguished members but a community of books that talk to us over the years. There are numbers of splendid writers and books from the postwar period not included here—Carson McCullers's *The Member of the Wedding*, Alfred Kazin's *A Walker in the City*, Mary McCarthy's *Memories of a Catholic Girlhood* (as well as her novels *A Charmed Life* and *The Groves of Academe*), Truman Capote's *The Grass Harp* and *Other Voices, Other Rooms*, Paul Bowles's *The Sheltering Sky*, Gore Vidal's *The City and the Pillar*, Jean Stafford's *The Mountain Lion*, William Styron's *Lie down in Darkness*, Robert Lowell's *Life Studies*, Leslie Fiedler's *An End to Innocence*, Roethke's *Words for the Wind*. But I think in one way or another, the urgency and appeal of these works has somewhat dimmed over time—making Capote's work of this period (in Morris Dickstein's words) "watery, vague, and self-pitying," McCarthy's autobiography and fiction wonderful social history, Bowles's work latter-day D. H. Lawrence, Vidal's narrative of gay life schematic and thin, Styron's book a haunting story—but not the equal of his much-later novel *Sophie's Choice*. Kazin's autobiography is brilliantly written, evocative of a lost New York, but ultimately about cultural conflicts and enthusiasms, and an idea of the self that have—regrettably—failed to take hold with the younger generations. Carson McCullers's work is almost unbearably poignant, but seems to represent adolescent experience of long ago, the turmoil without the rebellion and the youth culture. Jean Stafford's doom-filled novel of adolescence is the finest novel mentioned, but it also lacks the atmosphere that young people have been immersed in for the last half century; superbly written as it is, it has the tempi of an older America. Leslie

Fiedler is a powerful critic, but his 1950s work often has a topical flavor (try explaining the furor over Alger Hiss to anyone under thirty,
and probably a good deal older); what will endure is his work on pop
culture from the 1960s. Roethke's lyrics—"My Papa's Waltz," "I
Knew a Woman"—are of classical quality, but they are not insistent
presences in our day. As for Robert Lowell, his brilliance as a confessional poet and public poet is undeniable: passing on his 1959 book
was the toughest call of this volume (in some respects, he's a "Rough
Customer" like Mailer); but in the end, I found his poems clouded by
grandeur, closed-in, perhaps somewhat inaccessible for a new generation. Every major work does not read our condition. Nevertheless,
these works are parts of our heritage and deserve great respect and
new readers. Yet, they do not seem to be essential for the new century;
and they were not those American works that gave modernism its second wind after the war. In any event, the fact that some important and
well-loved works have gone unconsidered further attests to the richness of the 1950s.

The books considered, what I call the books of our lives, continue
to shape our minds and educate our feelings. They once broke through
conventions, and they still break through our image- and issue- and
personality-saturated world with their unique voices. No one sounds
like Salinger or Bellow or O'Connor or Ellison or Trilling or Roth or
Cheever. Without them we would have huge gaps in the cultural story
of the present. Where did the youth culture come from? Why do people argue over pop and high culture? How do race and ethnicity play
a part in the artist's work? Why do some crime stories seem to be all
plot whereas others seem to have mysterious power? Is confessional
writing about anything but the self? Our books provide the original
contexts from which these questions emerged. Without them we are
lost in the present, wandering among ideas and styles that seem to
come from nowhere. The books not only mirror our condition, but
they correct it: they are moral gauges that show us what's wrong with
our lives, how we are often ridiculous, guarded and limited, and too
full of ourselves. Harold Rosenberg's phrase hits it perfectly: we must
fear our desire to "triumph as ourselves." Every writer considered has
dramatized that fear in his or her book.

A true classic makes you a bit nervous because it judges—rather
than congratulates—you. In his essay "What Is a Classic?," a nine-
teenth-century warhorse of criticism, Charles Augustin Sainte-Beuve

makes the point that imitation of great works is sterile and tedious. We must be ourselves—and yet we must be something else as well.

> To that let us add what is more difficult, elevation, an aim, if possible, toward an exalted goal; and while speaking our own language, and submitting to the conditions of the times in which we live, whence we derive our strength and our defects, let us ask from time to time, our brows lifted toward the heights and our eyes fixed on the group of honored immortals: what would they say of us?

The grandeur of this seems at first inappropriate to our own books, works of our age that have not withstood the test of more than fifty years. Some of our books—the noir novels, Algren's novel—seem a bit rough-and-ready for the realms of greatness. But our own proximity to the works and Sainte-Beuve's rhetoric—and grandiosity—should not make us ignore his central point: the classic work reads our lives generation after generation.

But how do you know that a book is one of these books? What are the marks of the newer classics, the common denominators that let us see a pattern? The books of our lives have unmistakable styles: their authors use social observation or rhapsody or irony or critical inquiry as if they had just discovered the resources of age-old modes. Sainte-Beuve said a classic has its "own peculiar style . . . a style new without neologism, new and old, easily contemporary with all time." Our books—no matter how their authors may deploy slang, period language, or the language of a class or group—are never disconnected from the world of the early twenty-first century. Holden Caulfield has recently provided John Simon with a pungent insight into Alfred Lunt and Lynn Fontanne, the acting couple who lit up the New York stage in the 1940s and 1950s. "They were very good, but I didn't like them very much. They were different, though, I'll say that. They didn't act like people and they didn't act like actors. It's hard to explain." The cadences here—not to mention the irony—haven't dated a day. The drive of the sentences in Mailer and Kerouac—say what you will about their ideas of the good life—is exhilarating, genuine, taken from no one. The sly irony of Nabokov or Jarrell or Powell is nothing like the sledgehammer of most satire. It is also mixed with a curious warmth that most satirists lack. The noir novels are dependent on disturbing tones rather than on their screwy and intricate plots. Baldwin's blend of argument and revelation adds something unique and important to

American discourse about race in the age of *Brown v. Board of Education*. Our books are "easily contemporary" with the present and the foreseeable future—leaving "all time" aside. Their diction and rhythms are never lost in the past—in phony dialects, arch humor, jargon, or other language with a sell-by date. Their characters speak modern American English, and their authors stir up that language in their own ways. It's hard to foresee a time when their sentences will not be negotiable.

All of the books of our lives are confrontational in the best sense of the word. They use ideas and emotions to challenge us; they are thought-infested and obsessed with their views of the world without being ideological. Morris Dickstein is certainly correct in *Leopards in the Temple* when he writes that "postwar culture looks more edgy and unsettling than we once imagined" and that it was "a creative reaction against the official values of the period." Unlike the standard best sellers of the time, the books that I consider seem to be in a quarrel with the accepted values of their time and place. Maturity, stability, the status quo, the orderly life, the resignations and accommodations and material aspirations of the middle classes after the war were punctured and pilloried and overcome in novels and stories that sought ecstatic transcendence or dark interiority. The intellectuals, located in a different sphere of American life, were confrontational according to the needs and occasions of their situation: smugness, clichés about alienation and unlimited freedom, bohemian and academic platitudes were the stale air they breathed and tried to dispel. But each of our books was true to its inner light and not driven by a program, a political stance, a movement. The most that could be said about political influences is that numbers of writers—Trilling, Rosenberg, Greenberg, Ellison, Bellow—had lived through the Marxist period of the 1930s, caught a whiff of the orthodoxy, and turned to other things. Their politics was a kind of irritable, questioning, ironic liberalism. They wanted to put their readers in touch with parts of experience that were blocked by conventionality and doctrine.

All of these books seem detached from official alliances, seem too heterodox for the 1930s or the 1960s or the 1990s. If read out of their season, they could certainly prove "unsettling"; they were unsettling enough in their own time. Now, the fact that these books are not fueled by *isms* does not mean that they are not didactic. They have their worldviews and personal takes and peeves; they champion ideas of the self and visions of society, but they are not doctrinaire. Some of their

authors—including Salinger, Baldwin, Kerouac—lost their way in
later years and became fairly predictable, victims artistically speaking
of politics or belief systems. All of them did work in the 1950s that
still seems confrontational while being something much more enduring than hard-core polemic. Although I am not convinced that the de-
constructionist term *indeterminacy* does all that much to describe our
attraction to the classic works discussed in this book, I can agree with
Frank Kermode that certain works draw out a plurality of responses
from us generation after generation—and on the downside, some
books inhibit a plurality of responses, come to mean one thing only,
and therefore lose their excitement. We keep our classics alive because
there is so much in them that puts our minds to work. In "Why Read
the Classics?" Italo Calvino says that certain works have power because there is no equivalent for them: "the more we think we know
them through hearsay, the more original, unexpected, and innovative
we find them when we actually read them."

The 1950s was streaked with so many colorations and contradictions that it was a good time for writers who thrived on ambiguity and
unpredictability: it was wired with Cold War tensions but not as
driven by crises as wartime or the Great Depression era or the 1960s.
The era of course had its smugness and conformity and provinciality,
but the media had not as yet set a program for the nation. There was
still room for writers to attempt that—and writers' opinions, rather
than those of focus groups, counted for something. There was not
much substance behind all the talk about the conformity and the lack
of character of the Silent Generation. Or as Max Frankel of the *New
York Times* said to Dan Wakefield, such talk was "dumb and inaccu-
rate." Trilling said that no cultural situation is ever really good, but
there was undoubtedly something good about a time when so many
works of superb quality could be written and published and recognized. Marion Magid, an editor at *Commentary* interviewed by Wakefield for *New York in the 50s*, generalizes about the period in a way
that sorts well with what I have been saying. "It was the last time it
was possible to have a 'personal' life. There was a sense of discovery
then, but later everything became so codified. Now relationships are
mapped, there are pre-established attitudes. There's a sense that everything's been ransacked—every secret, ethnic and sexual. There's no
more privacy. You meet and everyone exchanges credentials. We had
more room to live the inner life." The same could be said for the
books. They were not codified; each was a handmade production,

driven by inner need not by the marketplace or the intellectual fashion of the time. Dwight Macdonald got it right when he mocked the we-need-books-like-this call for ideological correctness.

What we do need are books that have "the reverent openness before life" celebrated in F. R. Leavis's now neglected study *The Great Tradition*. The great teacher at Cambridge University literally invented the modern study of English literature, the reading of books for their intellectual-moral-aesthetic value rather than for historical or philological interest. He has been unjustly accused of laying down the law in his most famous book, when in fact what he did was establish criteria for the adult reader of prose. He dismissed mere scene painting, chronicling, and entertainment from his tradition; he pointed out that moral seriousness, aesthetic originality, and intellectual substance do not go their separate ways in first-rate works. He wrote about what he called the "current" classics—works that were "alive in their time and alive *to* it." Such literature is "sensitive to the stresses of the changing spiritual climate." I think that even the wildest, most kinetic works I consider—*On the Road, Howl*—come close to fitting Leavis's standards. They are not derivative, factitious performances propelled by the mere desire to amuse and display talent. They have the seriousness of intent, formal originality, and openness before life that separate the classic from the clever work.

In our own time, the books I consider satisfy a desire for exploration of ethical, social, and aesthetic questions. Postmodern irony and deferral of meaning and all-too-knowing withdrawal from ideals have not worked out for most readers. Citizens who read are looking for something more definite—not pat answers, but vital images and useful arguments. Terry Eagleton has recently pronounced the whole postmodern bag of tricks—death of the author, Derrida's skepticism, infinite play of signifiers, the attack on the normative—old hat. He wants a return to Marxism and a belief in changing the world. In some ways, the whole postmodern literary enterprise seems like a weak branch on the modernist tree—it's there with its sparse leaves, but it has not counted for much because of its flimflamming with questions of identity and principle.

My book has been an attempt to study what is inside certain works that have helped to alter the consciousness of America over two generations. These books are definite records of the modern mind in the very act of changing its attitudes and discarding old contents. They are also about commitment to ideals, ideas, passions—or about the danger (to use the words of Flannery O'Connor's trickster) of believing in nothing. No, they have not altered prices on the commodities markets or made war or peace or put a stop to white-collar crime, but they have been one of our ways of figuring out where we stand, what we are, and perhaps where we are going. They are moral without being moralistic, open before life and possibility without being ironically detached. They point to *Schindler's List* not to *Natural Born Killers*. They are about tragedy and hope, illusions and recognitions, our faultiness and inhumanity, and glimpses of something better than what has been.

From the tabloids to the seminar rooms, where would we be without the beautiful, wrenching ambiguities of *Lolita*, the collision of love and transgression, and the allure and cheapness of pop taste? The best and most subtle thinking about race in America owes an enormous debt to Ellison's championing of pluralism, Baldwin's denouncing of hate. The randomness and "banality of evil" theme—so alive in the age of terrorism and Osama bin Laden—has found classic expression in the noir novels. The suburbs—the crucible of so many of our class attitudes and ideas of happiness—have received microscopic scrutiny in Cheever, Yates, and Updike. I. A. Richards, a now all-but-forgotten critic of the 1920s and 1930s, once said that a book is "a machine to think with." The rather off-putting image should not obscure the truth of his observation. These books are not language games but powerful generators.

Acknowledgments

This book owes a great deal to the consideration, intelligence, and good will of the people in my life. Thanks go to friends and colleagues at Pace University, particularly to Walter Srebnick and Walter Raubicheck. Their encouragement and unwavering support were always there. Steven Goldleaf also helped me over the years with his knowledge of the contemporary American literary scene. Michael Roberts, Acting Dean of Dyson College, understood what I was trying to accomplish. Stephen Donadio, editor of *New England Review,* gave me a chance to try out my ideas. My research assistant Victoria Johnson was a model of efficiency and patience. Dominick DeFalco did some valuable research in the earlier phase of the project. Eileen Gatti of the Henry Birnbaum Library deserves special thanks. My editor, Evander Lomke, was incisive, unfailingly dedicated, and deeply involved with my subject. My friends—including Janet Groth, Foster Hirsch, Burt Besen, James Tetreault, Anne Whitehouse, and Stanford Pritchard—helped a great deal with wonderful conversation about great books. My sister, Val Castronovo, did large and small things that really added up.

Index

INVISIBLE MAN
BY RALPH ELLISON
LOLITA
VLADIMIR NABOKOV
HOWL
AND OTHER POEMS
ALLEN GINSBERG
Introduction by
William Carlos Williams
THE END OF IDEOLOGY
on the exhaustion of political ideas in the fifties
DANIEL BELL
the CATCHER in the RYE
a novel by J. D. SALINGER
Bernard Malamud
The Magic Barrel
FLANNERY O'CONNOR
A Good Man Is Hard to Find
THE POCKET POETS SERIES